Racial and Ethnic Identity: Psychological Development and Creative Expression

Racial and Ethnic Identity: Psychological Development and Creative Expression

*Edited by Herbert W. Harris, Howard C. Blue,
& Ezra E.H. Griffith*

Routledge   NEW YORK and LONDON

Published in 1995 by

Routledge
29 West 35th Street
New York, NY 10001-2299

Published in Great Britain by

Routledge
11 New Fetter Lane
London EC4P 4EE

Copyright © 1995 by Routledge, Inc.

Printed in the United States of America on acid-free paper.

Library of Congress Cataloging-in-Publication Data

Racial and ethnic identity : psychological development and creative
 expression / edited and with an introduction by Ezra E.H. Griffith,
 Howard C. Blue, Herbert W. Harris.
      p.   cm.
  Includes bibliographical references and index.
  ISBN 0-415-90867-1 (Hb) : ISBN
0-415-90868-X (Pb) :
    1. Ethnicitiy.   2. Identity (Psychology).   3. Ethnopsychology.
  4. Afro-Americans—Race identity.   I. Griffith, Ezra E. H., 1942—
  II. Blue, Howard C.   III. Harris, Herbert W.
GN495.6.R33   1994
155.8—dc20   94-25603
                                     CIP

British Library Cataloging-in-Publication Data also available.

Contents

Preface

The chapters contained in this book emerged from a conference held at Yale University on the subject of racial and ethnic identity. This conference was organized with the aim of stimulating thought and discussion of what we feel is a central issue in contemporary life. Race and ethnicity comprise only a single aspect of the identity of the individual. However, the importance of these components in shaping the development of the individual and determining the interactions of that individual with society cannot be overestimated. As mental health professionals, we are inclined to attach great significance to factors that impact upon the psychology of the individual. However, the concept of identity manifests itself not only at the level of the individual but, perhaps of far greater consequence, at the level of societies and interactions between groups. When broadly conceived, the concept of identity has applications that extend well beyond the psychological dimension of the individual or group. In particular, one speaks of the expression of an identity through creative works, beliefs, ideologies, and political interactions. When viewed in this extended sense, racial and ethnic identity must be understood as an important determinant of the creative process and social dynamics, as well as individual psychology. It was with these broad categories in mind that our organization of the conference and this book was undertaken.

Although our ambition was to provide a uniquely multidisciplinary treatment of the subject of racial and ethnic identity, the limitations of time and space precluded a fully comprehensive analysis. In selecting topics, our hope was to survey the major fields for which the understanding of issues of identity are of critical importance. We included psychology, with an emphasis on a developmental perspective that includes adolescence and adulthood. Aspects of the creative process that included film and the visual arts were discussed in some detail. The impact of racial and ethnic identity on the political process at both national and international levels was covered. Lastly, the importance of racial and ethnic identity in the expression of religious belief and ritual was discussed. It is clear that this list omits a number of topics for which identity is a central issue. We most acutely regret that a more complete discussion of expression of identity in literature was not possible. In addition, there is a very important and fascinating history behind the legal definitions of race and ethnicity dating back to colonial times that has great influence on modern society. While not fully addressed, these issues are briefly reviewed in the introduction. Another limitation imposed by practical constraints involves the inclusiveness of our examination of race and ethnicity. The material presented in this book is largely drawn from the experiences of African-Americans and Hispanics. Our belief is that, although this focus is, perhaps, a narrow one, the concepts explored in this book readily generalize to the experience and expression of other racial and ethnic identities.

Given these limitations, we feel that this book is a significant contribution that provides a unique examination of issues of identity as they impact on a wide range of human activity. Our hope is that the cross-disciplinary approach to these issues will stimulate further research and discussion. We would be especially gratified if, through our efforts at placing identity at the center of a multidisciplinary dialogue, we facilitate further examination of this important topic.

Herbert W. Harris
Howard C. Blue
Ezra E.H. Griffith
New Haven, May 1994

Dedication

Dedicated to my parents William and Juanita, whose unwavering support carried me through many difficult years; to Sarah and Campbell, who brought immeasurable joy into every aspect of my life; and especially to Alice, who must create her own identity in the new world that tomorrow brings.

H.W.H.

Dedicated in memory of Daisy Lee Monroe Blue whose generous love and wisdom continue to lighten my path.

H.C.B.

To Brigitte, whose eyes are my support.

E.E.H.G.

Acknowledgments

We wish to acknowledge the American Psychiatric Association for their generous support that made possible the conference on which this book is based. We would also like to thank Edna Aklin, Robert Cole, Sandra Hotchkiss, Gerald Jaynes, Sheila Meyers, and Thomas Rèyes for their indispensable assistance in the planning and organization of the conference. Finally, we would like to thank Carole Smarth and the members of the Yale Chapter of the Student National Medical Association for their involvement in this enterprise.

Introduction: A Conceptual Overview of Race, Ethnicity, and Identity

Herbert W. Harris

Introduction

The central theme of this book is identity. This very abstract word refers simply to an individual's sense of uniqueness, of knowing who one is, and who one is not. The development of a stable sense of identity is one of the central processes of childhood and adolescence. Maintaining the integrity of one's identity is an ongoing struggle throughout adulthood. Identity has been a subject of interest for many years. Terms such as "identity crisis" have been in use for decades, and are now an indispensable part of our everyday vocabularies. One aspect of personal identity that has received increasing attention in recent years is the role played by race and ethnicity in the definition of the self. Our society has always been characterized by great racial and ethnic diversity. The tensions created by this diversity pose major challenges to the individual who must affirm his or her unique identity within the plurality of society. For members of minority groups, these challenges begin early. Consider the Hispanic child who discovers that the language of his parents is not understood by his classmates. Or consider the Black child who cannot avoid getting the message from television, books, and magazines that all successful, powerful, or beautiful people are white. As we become adults in a society that devalues our minority status, we continue to experience forces which tend to make us question who we are and which push us to embrace attitudes and ideas that are alien to us. These forces are compounded by the rapidly changing demographics that separate us from our roots and take away those certitudes of identity that once were passed from generation to generation.

It is therefore not surprising that in recent years, ethnocultural identity has been a prominent theme in numerous articles, books, and films. Indeed, the multidisciplinary nature of the topic is best evidenced by the wide range of recent publications devoted to this theme. For example, *Lure and Loathing: Essays on Race, Identity, and the Ambivalence of Assimilation* (Earley, 1993) contains a series of essays inspired by the concept of "double-consciousness" developed by W.E.B. Du Bois (see below). These essays are contributed by scholars in fields as diverse as law, theology, literature, and the social sciences. They provide a multidimensional overview of the experience of identity at the level of race. In the book *The Color Complex* (Russell *et al.*, 1992), the authors directly address the difficult subject of color-based prejudices that exist within the African-American community. They explore this divisive and often painful issue that raises major questions about the nature of the African-American identity. Philosopher Naomi Zack, in *Race and Mixed Race,* has recently presented a provocative philosophical and historical examination of the concept of race as it is defined and used in America (Zack, 1993). Her analysis calls into question the validity of the categories that traditionally define race. From these examples, it can be seen that the topic of racial and ethnic identity transcends traditional categories, and has become a major topic in psychology, literature, theology, philosophy, and many other disciplines.

Many previous generations of scholars and thinkers have struggled with the problem of racial and ethnic identity. W.E.B. Du Bois took up the problem in his most famous work, *The Souls of Black Folk* (Du Bois, 1903). His often-quoted statement of the problem includes the following:

> The Negro is a sort of seventh son, born with a veil, and gifted with second-sight in this American world,—a world which yields him no true self-consciousness, but only lets him see himself through the revelation of the other world. It is a peculiar sensation, this double-consciousness, this sense of always looking at one's self through the eyes of others, of measuring one's soul by the tape of a world that looks on in amused contempt and pity. One ever feels his twoness,— an American, a Negro; two souls, two thoughts, two unreconciled strivings; two warring ideals in one dark body, whose dogged strength alone keeps it from being torn asunder. The history of the American Negro is the history of this strife,—this longing to attain self-conscious manhood, to merge his double self into a better and truer self. In this merging he wishes neither of his older selves to be lost. He would not Africanize America, for America has too much to teach the world and Africa. He would not bleach his Negro soul in a flood

of White Americanism, for he knows that Negro blood has a message for the world. He simply wishes to make it possible for a man to be both a Negro and an American, without being cursed and spit upon by his fellows, without having the doors of Opportunity closed roughly in his face.

These words summarize what Du Bois felt to be the central dilemma of African-Americans. They describe the search for a truer self (an identity) in a society that has little tolerance for diversity. The "double-consciousness," "the twoness," "the unreconciled strivings," and "warring ideals" are familiar to us all. The problem of finding that truer self is one shared by members of all minority groups, and Du Bois's words apply to all peoples who have experienced alienation and disenfranchisement within our society.

Our intention in organizing this book was to bring together scholars who had explored various aspects of racial and ethnic identity development. Initially, our planning was shaped by our experience as psychiatrists working with populations of disadvantaged, primarily Black and Hispanic patients. Psychiatrists have long known that stability of identity plays a major role in determining the vulnerability of individuals to the burdens of their illnesses. Perhaps of even greater significance is the extent to which negative or conflicted identities internalized from a prejudiced society could be a source of psychological compromise. We sought to include contributions from experimental psychologists as well as clinicians who have made a study of the psychology of identity. However, in keeping with the multidisciplinary nature of the topic, we have also included extensive discussion of historical and social aspects of racial and ethnic identity. Lastly, the creative expression of identity-related themes has been included.

Psychology of Racial and Ethnic Identity

Psychologists have long been aware of the highly complex process of identity formation and of the critical role played by race and ethnicity in this process. An extensive literature exists, dating back to the 1930s, on the development of racial identity. Studies of identity in children arose from consideration of the unique dilemmas faced by children of minority groups as they mature in our society. These studies, typified by the work of Mamie and Kenneth Clark in the late 1930s and 1940s, initiated decades of research and scholarship, and had a major impact on generations of clinicians and theorists. The Clarks focused their investigations on the color preferences of three-to-seven-year-old children. The children were asked to color a picture the same color as themselves or to color a child they wanted for a playmate. The initial findings of the Clarks showed that Black children generally are able to correctly identify themselves as Black, although the investigators believed that a tendency to show White orientation (the preference for White-associated things) was present (Clark and Clark, 1939). In subsequent research, the Clarks employed a doll preference paradigm, in which the children select either a White or a Black doll in response to questions such as: Give me the doll that is a nice doll. Give me the doll that looks bad. Give me the doll that is a nice color. Give me the doll that looks like you. From these studies, the Clarks conclude that, although the children appropriately self-identified, they had a distinct preference for White skin and a negative attitude toward their own skin color (Clark and Clark, 1947).

The work of the Clarks had a profound influence not only in the field of psychology, but also at many levels of society. For example, their work was cited by the U.S. Supreme Court in its *Brown v. the Board of Education* decision. However, a controversial theme that pervaded the writings of the Clarks and many other scholars who followed them is the so-called "thesis of Black self-hatred." Much of the early work on the psychology of racial identity was grounded in the assumption that out-group orientation, as measured by the doll preference and other paradigms, was interpretable in terms of psychopathology. The self-hatred thesis held that identification with one's own racial or ethnic group was normative and that the preferences expressed by Black children reflected the damaging effects of societal racism. As the influence of the Clarks expanded, their results were generalized to adults and to the collective Negro experience. At this level, out-group identification, self-hatred, and psychopathology were conceptually merged and interpreted in the historical context of slavery, segregation, and the cultural disenfranchisement of the Negro in America. At this time other influential scholars took up the thesis of self-hatred, and applied it to a wide range of cultural phenomena. In particular, social scientists such as Franklin Frazier (Frazier, 1968) and Gunnar Myrdal (Myrdal, 1944) embraced the self-hatred thesis and applied it to their accounts of the social forces that shaped the Negro consciousness. An underlying assumption in much of this writing was that slavery and segregation left the African-American with no genuine cultural identity other than the cultural stereotypes of the majority society. Under this interpretation, the out-group preferences expressed by Black children were a predictable consequence of the plight of Blacks in America.

However, the self-hatred thesis rapidly lost its influence during the 1960s, when the social changes coinciding with the Civil Rights Movement culminated in the development of a more assertive Black identity. During this time, the conceptual foundation for an Afrocentric cultural view was developed. As this view gained force, a rich African-American identity was "rediscovered" that was no less valuable, original, and complex than that of the majority culture. It could no longer be assumed that Blacks either lacked a positive identity or aspired to adopt the identity of the majority society. Within the context of these social changes, the self-hatred thesis was replaced in psychological discourse by a more balanced perspective, in which group identification could be discussed in value-neutral terms. Psychologists subjected the work of the Clarks to a rigorous critique from which a number of important new interpretive frameworks emerged. In particular, several authors have attacked the work of the Clarks and others on methodological grounds, questioning the validity of associations assumed to exist between group orientation and other aspects of personal identity. For example, psychologist William E. Cross Jr. has conducted an extensive review of the literature on the psychology of racial identity, and has found evidence that group and individual identity comprise functionally distinct domains within the individual (Cross, 1991). Cross has developed a multistage model of identity development that analyses the psychological process of coming to terms with one's racial identity (Cross, 1978). This process is broken down into several stages that the individual must traverse as the issue of race is incorporated into the structure of the self. The model put forward by Cross includes a stage during which individuals may express out-group preferences. However, this is only one of several stages through which the individual proceeds as racial identity is incorporated into the self.

In addition to the theoretical contributions made by authors such as Cross, many empirical studies of identity development have been undertaken since the work of the Clarks. Empirical studies have shown that out-group preferences are not universal among Black children, and that very complex dynamics are involved in the development of group identity. The work of psychologist Margaret Beale Spencer has made significant advances in our understanding of developmental aspects of racial and ethnic identity. In particular, her work has focused on cognitive development as an important determinant in preference behavior (Spencer, 1984; Spencer, 1987). In addition, another focus has been the identification of factors that contribute to the resilience of minority children, which strengthens their sense of identity (Spencer, 1985).

Since the work of the Clarks more than fifty years ago, major advances in the empirical study of identity development and the theoretical foundations of identity psychology have been made. The most significant advance has been a movement away from the thesis of self-hatred, which underlay much of the design and interpretation of early identity research. Along with this very important conceptual shift has come a major emphasis on psychological factors associated with strength and integrity of identity. This has largely replaced the "psycho-pathological" interpretations of the past. However, the topic of identity is far from resolved. A recent series of articles has revisited the debate over whether own-group or out-group preference should be viewed as healthy, valuable, or normative (Penn *et al.*, 1993; Helms, 1993; Sellars, 1993; Taylor, 1993; Parham, 1993; Kambon and Hopkins, 1993; Phillips *et al.*, 1993). This lively exchange indicates that within the field of psychology, many issues of identity remain to be resolved.

As these developments have taken place within the literature of experimental psychology, racial identity-related issues have also assumed a growing importance in clinical psychology and psychiatry. Among many clinicians to write on the subject of racial and ethnic identity was Freud. Freud wrote of his often conflictual identity as a Jew in an address to the B'nai B'rith Society in 1926:

> What bound me to Jewry was (I am ashamed to admit) neither faith nor national pride, for I have always been an unbeliever and was brought up without any religion though not without respect for what are called the "ethical" standards of human civilization. Whenever I felt an inclination to national enthusiasm I strove to suppress it as being harmful and wrong, alarmed by the warning examples of the peoples among whom we Jews live. But plenty of other things remained over to make the attraction of Jews and Jewry irresistible—many obscure emotional forces, which were the more powerful the less they could be expressed in words, as well as a clear consciousness of inner identity, the safe privacy of a common mental construction. (Freud, 1926)

The most influential author of the psychoanalytic school to take up the issue of identity is Erik Erikson. His observations of identity development in adolescence (Erikson, 1968) have been a major contribution to our understanding of identity development. It was noted by Erikson that adult identity develops as a result of a long period of exploration that takes place during adolescence. Individuals go through a well-characterized set of stages leading to the adult. A *diffuse* status is said to exist when a person has made no commitment to an identity, nor has he or she engaged in significant exploration of possible identities. A *foreclosed* status occurs when an individual has made a commitment to an identity without having made attempts at exploration. Such an identity is usually derived from parental values and uncritically accepted norms. A person actively engaged in exploration without having settled on a stable identity is said to be in *moratorium*. Finally, the development of a firm sense of identity is termed *achieved identity*. These transitional stages are compatible with the stepwise process of assimilation of race and ethnicity into an integrated self, as described by psychologists such as Cross. Erikson himself made many observations on the subject of racial identity (see Erikson, 1968, chap. 8). More recently, the conceptual framework developed by Erikson has been applied to issues of identity development in minority adolescents by a number of authors (see Rotheram-Borus, 1989; Aries and Moorehead, 1989; Phinney and Alipuria, 1990; Phinney, 1989).

Historical and Social Aspects of Racial and Ethnic Identity

Although psychologists have made tremendous contributions to the study of racial and ethnic identity, it is not exclusively their domain. In reviewing the literature, one becomes aware of the contributions of multiple disciplines to the understanding of this subject. Themes of identity and identity-related concepts have great importance in the humanities, social sciences, politics, and the law. The definitions and meanings of race and ethnicity are, to a surprising degree, determined by the historical forces that shape society.

During the colonial period in America, definitions of race were inextricably tied to the institution of slavery. American society became an increasingly complex meshwork, in which slaves, "free persons of color," and persons of mixed race each required a special status within the order of the slavery-based economy. Instances have been described in which free Blacks became successful landowners who themselves owned slaves (Johnson and Roark, 1984). Although extremely rare, such paradoxical situations constantly forced society to redefine the identity and status of the Black in America. During the early years of slavery, the definition of race varied from state to state. In states such as South Carolina and Louisiana, substantial populations of persons of mixed race existed, dating back to colonial times. Consequently, fairly liberal interpretations of racial definitions were practiced. In 1850 in South Carolina, a continuum existed encompassing slaves, a free elite, and those "passing" as White. However, during the 1850s Southern Whites who feared the erosion of their status enacted increasingly stringent legal definitions of race that identified as Negro a person having any African heritage whatsoever (Davis, 1991). The statutes and policies of this time continued into the Reconstruction period and became collectively known as the "One Drop Rule" which, in essence, defines a person having "one drop" of African blood as colored. This definition became fundamental to the policies of segregation in the South.

The definition of race has been an issue that has been tested repeatedly in the courts. In general, the courts have upheld the spirit of the "one drop" principal. In the *Plessy v. Ferguson* decision of 1896, the plaintiff argued that, since he was one-eighth Negro and appeared essentially White, he was entitled to ride in "White-only" seats on trains (Davis, 1991). The Supreme Court held that a person with any Black ancestry was by definition Negro. State courts have held variants of this concept, although attempts to define race in quantitative terms have been set forth in various statutes. For example, in Louisiana, the "One Drop Rule" was officially in effect until 1970. At that time, a statute was adopted defining as Black any person having more than one-thirty-second Black ancestry. This came in response to a lawsuit filed by an individual claiming to have only one-two-hundred-fifty-sixth Black ancestry (Davis, 1991). In 1983, a case was brought before the Louisiana court in which the plaintiff asked the court to change the racial status of her deceased parents. She and her siblings had always considered themselves White, although her parents were classified as "colored" (Trillin, 1986). The court held that the racial identification of an individual cannot affect the legal classification of his or her parents, stating

> We do not believe that an individual may change the racial designation of another person, whether his parent or anyone else. That appellants might describe themselves as white does not prove error in a document that designates their parents as colored. This anomaly shows the subjective nature of racial perceptions but does not give appellants a cause of action to alter it.

These policies contrasted sharply with definitions of race in other postcolonial countries. In Brazil, for example, an elaborate caste system has existed. This caste system is one in which there is a social hierarchy based partly on skin color that was established during the early years of the slave trade and which persists into the present (Deglar, 1986). A similar social organization was the case in Haiti after the revolution ending slavery in 1791 (Davis, 1991). In Latin-American countries where Indian and Spanish heritage is also represented, even more elaborate classification schemas have developed. Terms such as *Mestizo, Castizo, Mulatto,* and *Morsico* have had extremely precise definitions and usage. For example, the term *lobo* is applied to an individual whose ancestry includes half-Indian, one-thirty-second African, and the remainder (seventeen-thirty-seconds) White (Davis, 1991). In such societies, the question of racial and ethnic identity is greatly complicated. The historical forces that led to the development of the dichotomous system in the United States, rather than the multitiered systems that exist in other countries, is a subject of great interest. Much speculation has been directed toward the question of why so rigid a principle as the "One Drop Rule" should have emerged uniquely in the United States. Many scholars have come to regard this historical fact as reflecting the high degree of interracial tension and intolerance that has characterized race relations in the United States. However, there is comparatively little empirical study of the impact of the two kinds of social organization on the psychology of the individual. In particular, it would be of interest to know whether racial and ethnic identity achieve as high a level of saliency for individuals living in societies in which racial tensions are dispersed across multiple castes. Alternatively, might a caste-based society tend to generate a higher level of race consciousness among its members than a dichotomous society?

Despite the rigidity of the "One Drop Rule," a high degree of upward mobility was experienced by some Blacks in American society that created new and sometimes conflictual identity roles. During the years that followed the Civil War, small groups of affluent Black families settled in large cities such as New Orleans, Charleston, Washington, and Boston, where they formed a cultural elite. While they possessed material wealth and education that separated them from the majority of Blacks in America, they were clearly not accepted into the mainstream. Individuals within these societies constantly felt a pressure to escape one's roots and become a part of the dominant culture. The effects of this pressure are evidenced by the well-known tendency in these society to favor those having light complexions. Among these "Blue-Veined" societies, complexion became obsession, to the extent that social standing and privilege were essentially a function of lightness on skin (Gatewood, 1990). This elitist society flourished during the latter part of the nineteenth century and the early part of the twentieth century. While the members of this society have been often criticized for merely wanting to be White, it produced many of the major Black leaders and intellectuals of this century. The disruption of this society has been attributed to demographic pressure causing large-scale movements of Blacks from the rural South to the cities, and to the emergence of the Harlem Renaissance culture which began a movement away from Eurocentric values that continues into the present. However, despite these major social changes, the obsession with skin color, hair, and ultimately identity are at least as prevalent in America today as at any time in the past (Russell *et al.,* 1992).

Creative Expression of Racial and Ethnic Identity

In addition to the social and psychological forces that shape racial and ethnic identity in society, another arena in which struggles of identity take place is in the creative domain. Throughout history, a major component of creative energy, whether in literature, drama, or the visual arts, has come from what could be characterized as the struggle to discover one's identity. Therefore, a major portion of this book is devoted to an examination of the expression of issues of identity through creative acts. Many examples of the expression of identity-related themes can be found in literature. Literary expression of identity can take place at two levels. At one level, one sees the emergence of a distinct body of writing that expresses the experiences of a group. African-American and Hispanic writers have established an identity within the dominant culture that captures the shared experiences of these groups. At another level, one can consider the expression of struggles of identity that take place for the characters of fiction. For example, the "Tragic Mulatto" and the theme of "passing" were major literary devices for the portrayal of conflicted identities.

In early works of fiction, the portrayal of identities made extensive use of mulatto characters to express various forms of identity struggles. For abolitionist writers, the mulatto character often had heroic qualities, while other writers used such characters to propagate the worst of racist stereotypes (Berzon, 1978). During the decades that followed the Reconstruction, more complex characters developed through the writings of authors such as Charles Chesnutt and Francis E. W. Harper. These characters were developed with a much higher level of sophistication, giving rise to the literary theme of the tragic mulatto. With the Harlem Renaissance, new themes emerged in the literature of identity. James Weldon Johnson's novel *Autobiography of an Ex-Colored Man* takes up the complex theme of passing in a highly sophisticated and multidimensional way. The protagonist, a White-appearing mulatto, moves between the two worlds of White and Black, and must find an identity. At the end of the novel, he makes a home for himself and his children in the White world, concluding:

> It is difficult for me to analyze my feelings concerning my present position in the world. Sometimes it seems to me that I have never really been a Negro, that I have only been a privileged spectator of their inner life; at other times I feel that I have been a coward, a deserter, and I am possessed by a strange longing for my mother's people.... My love for my children makes me glad that I am what I am and keeps me from desiring to be otherwise; and yet, when I sometimes open a little box in which I still keep my fast yellowing manuscripts, the only tangible remnants of a vanished dream, a dead ambition, a sacrificed talent, I cannot repress the thought that, after all, I have chosen the lesser part, that I have sold my birthright for a mess of pottage. (Johnson, 1944)

The experience of a kind of "nonidentity," of losing one's self in American society, was uniquely depicted in Ralph Ellison's remarkable creation, *Invisible Man*. At the end of his journey toward self-awareness, Ellison's hero concludes:

> I am an invisible man.... That invisibility to which I refer occurs because of a peculiar disposition of the eyes of those with whom I come in contact. A matter of the construction of their *inner* eyes, those eyes with which they look through their physical eyes upon reality. I am not complaining, nor am I protesting either. It is sometimes advantageous to be unseen, although it is most often rather wearing on the nerves. Then too, you're constantly being bumped against by those of poor vision. Or again, you often doubt if you really exist. You wonder whether you aren't simply a phantom of other people's minds. Say, a figure in a nightmare which the sleeper tries with all his strength to destroy. (Ellison, 1947)

Overview

The material presented in this book covers three broad categories that include: first, developmental aspects of identity formation in children and adults; second, interactions between individuals and society; and third, creative process. Psychological issues of identity development are presented by Margaret Beale Spencer, who has done pioneering work on identity processes in children and adolescents. However, there is much evidence that racial and ethnic identity is in a constant state of development and reworking in the adult. William Cross has proposed models of racial identity that incorporate this dynamism and are readily applicable to the psychological experiences of adults. The complexity of identity formation is further compounded in individuals of biracial origins. The identity experiences of biracial individuals provide important insights into the relationship between racial identity, self concept, and personal identity. Elaine Pinderhughes presents a discussion of the unfolding and resolution of racial identity conflicts in such persons. Child psychiatrist Ian Canino describes a novel community program based in a New York public school that utilizes a community art museum as a training site. This program employs a model that emphasizes creative expression as a means of coping with stress, enhancing ethnic empowerment, and strengthening self-esteem. The use of artistic expression as a therapeutic modality provides an important link between psychological aspects of identity development and subsequent presentations dealing with creative expressions of identity.

The second major topic concerns the interaction between individuals and society. It is recognized that a major determinant of personal identity is derived from social norms. Ethnocultural identity involves concepts that depend heavily on the society in which it is defined. Sociologist Paul Gilroy provides a comparative discussion of racial identity in countries other than the United States. The topic of transracial adoption as an interaction between conflicting social ideals is presented in the chapter by Dr. Ezra E. H. Griffith. Political process has become an important modality for the expression of racial and ethnic identity. Political commitments and affiliations are often a vital extension of an individual's sense of self in our society. How such commitments result in the development of a political power base is explored by political scientist Angelo Falcón.

A third major topic covered by the book deals with creative expressions of racial and ethnic identity. The chapters treating this theme explore some of the ways that individuals express their racial and ethnic identity, and the influence of racial and ethnic heritage on the creative process is examined. We have broadly interpreted the concept of creative expression to include film, fine arts, politics, and religion. While recognizing that this is by no means an exhaustive list, we feel that these represent some of the most vital and dynamic modalities for creative expression of identity in contemporary society. Hazel Carby will show how recent films depict struggles and crises of ethno-cultural identity. Lawrence Kasdan's *Grand Canyon* provides an example of how Black male identities are constructed in film. Art historian Barbara Hudson will discuss how artists of color have evolved symbols and images that are clearly distinct from those of traditional Western art, and how this new language can express an identity apart from the dominant culture. Lastly, religious affiliation has long been a source of division, and therefore of self-identification for peoples of color in the United States. The evolution of beliefs and rituals has become one of the most powerful expressions of racial identity in our society. The historical emergence of religious ritual and creed will be traced and interpreted in the context of other social changes by theologian C. Eric Lincoln.

References

Aries, E. and Moorehead K., 1989. "The Importance of Ethnicity in the Development of Identity of Black Adolescents." *Psychological Reports,* 65: 75–82.

Berzon, J. R. 1978. *Neither Black Nor White: The Mulatto Character in American Fiction.* New York: New York University Press.

Clark, K. B. and Clark, M. P. 1939. "The Development of Consiousness of Self and the Emergence of Racial Identification in Negro Pre-school Children." *Journal of Social Psychology,* 10: 591–599.

Clark, K. B. and Clark, M. P., 1947. "Emotional Factors in Racial Identification and Preference in Negro Pre-school Children." *Journal of Negro Education,* 19: 341–350.

Cross, W. E., 1978. "The Thomas and Cross Models on Psychological Nigrescence: A Literature Review." *Journal of Black Psychology,* 4(1), 13–31.

Cross, W. E., 1991. *Shades of Black: Diversity in African-American Identity.* Philadelphia: Temple University Press.

Davis, F. J., 1991. *Who is Black?* University Park: Pennsylvania State University Press.

Degler, C. N., 1986. *Neither White Nor Black: Slavery and Race Relations in Brazil and the United States.* Madison: University of Wisconsin Press.

Du Bois, W. E. B., 1903. *The Souls of Black Folk.* New York: Vintage Books.

Early, G., ed., 1993. *Lure and Loathing; Essays on Race, Identity, and the Ambivalence of Assimilation.* New York: Allen Lane.

Ellison, R., 1947. *Invisible Man.* New York: Vintage Books.

14 / Herbert W. Harris

Erikson, E., 1968. *Identity, Youth and Crisis.* New York: W. W. Norton.

Frazier, G. F., 1968. *On Race Relations.* Chicago: University of Chicago.

Freud, S., 1926. "Address to the B'nai B'rith Society," in *Collected Papers,* ed. Strachey, J. New York: Basic Books.

Gatewood, W. B., 1990. *Aristocrats of Color: The Black Elite, 1880–1920.* Indianapolis: Indiana University Press.

Helms, J. E., 1993. "More Psychologists Discover the Wheel: A Reaction to Views by Penn et al. on Ethnic Preference." *Journal of Black Psychology,* 19(3): 322–326.

Johnson, J. W., 1944. *The Autobiography of an Ex-Colored Man.* New York: Knopf.

Johnson, M. P. and Roark, J. L., 1984. *Black Masters: A Free Family of Color in the Old South.* New York: W. W. Norton.

Kambon, K. K. K. and Hopkins, R., 1993. "An African-centered Analysis of Penn et al.'s Critique of the Own-race Preference Assumption Underlying Africentric Models of Personality." *Journal of Black Psychology,* 19: 342–349.

Myrdal, G., 1944. *An American Dilemma.* New York: Harper & Brothers.

Parham, T. A., 1993. "Own-group Preferences as a Function of Self-affirmation: A Reaction to Penn et al." *Journal of Black Psychology,* 19: 336–341.

Penn, M. L., Gaines, S. O., and Phillips, L., 1993. "On the Desirability of Own-group Preference." *Journal of Black Psychology,* 19: 303–321.

Phillps, L., Penn, M. L., and Gaines, S. O., 1993. "A Hermeneutic Rejoinder to Ourselves and Our Critics." *Journal of Black Psychology,* 19: 350–357.

Phinney, J., 1989. "Stages of Ethnic Identity in Minority Group Adolescents." *Journal of Early Adolescence,* 9: 34–49.

Phinney, J. S., and Alipuria, L. L., 1990. "Ethnic Identity in College Students from Four Ethnic Groups." *Journal of Adolescence,* 13, 171–183.

Rotheram-Borus, M. J., 1989. "Ethnic Differences in Adolescent's Identity Status and Associated Behavior Problems." *Journal of Adolescence,* 12: 361–374.

Russell, K., Wilson, M., and Hall, R., 1992. *The Color Complex.* New York: Harcourt Brace Jovanovich.

Sellars, R. M., 1993. "A Call to Arms for Researchers Studying Racial Identity." *Journal of Black Psychology,* 19: 327–332.

Spencer, M. B., 1984. *Resilance and Vulnerability: Black Children's Evolving Self and Society.* Washington, DC: Congressional Black Caucus Foundation Research Conference.

Spencer, M. B., ed., 1985. *Beginnings: Social and Affective Development of Black Children.* New York: Erlbaum.

Spencer, M. B., 1987. *Black Children's Ethnic Identity Formation: Risk and Resilance of Castelike Minorities in Children's Ethnic Socialization,* pp. 103–116. Eds. Phinney, J. S., Rotheram M. J. Newbury Park: Sage Publications.

Taylor, J., 1993. "Reaction to Penn et al's 'On the Desirability of Own-group Preference.'" *Journal of Black Psychology,* 19: 333–335.

Trillin, C., 1986. "American Chronicles: Black or White." *New Yorker,* April: 62–78.

Zack, N., 1993. *Race and Mixed Race.* Philadelphia: Temple University Press.

1

Roots and Routes: Black Identity as an Outernational Project

Paul Gilroy

A few hours after I closed at the Apollo I was on an Air France jet headed for the Ivory Coast by way of Paris. It was the first time I'd ever been to Africa. When I got there and got off the plane, I felt I was on land I should have been on much earlier. The Africans were full of pride and dignity, and they were very warm too. It was hard to believe that they knew my music. It wasn't in their language, and most of them probably didn't have much extra money to spend on records and things. We were there for only two days, but I was overwhelmed by the spirit of the place. I think it made me understand some things about my roots as well. Later on I found out a lot of my roots were in China, a lot in Mexico, some in Germany.

James Brown

I looked out over miles and miles of jungle as we flew until we dropped down to land and the blunt heat of Africa hit us. Outside on the tarmac I could hear the drums going and the songs of welcome starting up. When I got to the door I saw crowds stretched out all round, musicians and dancers, local politicians in their traditional African clothes in a small group at the bottom of the steps. . . . We stood, all of us, blinking in the sun at the celebrations our arrival had triggered. All around us were black faces, and I felt for the first time the spiritual relaxation that any Afro-American feels on reaching Africa. I didn't feel like I'd come home when I arrived in Lagos, but I knew I'd arrived somewhere important and that Africa mattered to me, and would always matter.

Nina Simone

This paper situates a discussion of racial and ethnic identity within a concern with the globalization of cultures. In particular, it will examine some elements of the Black cultures that have originated in the United States, and consider the effects of their transnational dissemination on the making and reproduction of Black identities in other parts of the world. It is not primarily about making comparisons between the formation of cultural identities in the U.S. and the similar, though different, patterns to be found in other places. Instead, it looks at the impact of transnational and intercultural factors on Black identities wherever they appear.

My interest in what can be called the global circuitry of Black cultures and the identities they support, nurture, and protect has grown out of a need to comprehend the syncretic dynamics of Black culture-making and use in the distinctive habitus provided by Britain. There, American and Caribbean elements have been changed and adapted to the task of building new and quite distinct Black identities in the years following the Second World War. Recently the Caribbean influences that dominated the cultural lives of the Black communities have given way to a sustained and profound engagement with African-American forms and styles. My concern with the impact of intercultural relationships on identity formation also arises from a dissatisfaction with the way that the problem of identity has recently emerged at the core of Black sociopolitical concerns. I want to suggest that this "identity politics," which, as June Jordan has pointed out, is more concerned with who we are rather than what we can do for each other, expresses a mode of individuation that is central to the mechanics of racial domination, rather than a means to overcome it.[1]

The internal differentiation of Black communities in the overdeveloped countries along economic and other lines is partly masked and inadequately answered by new theories of identity. These essentialist perspectives deny that the growing order of intracommunal differences visible around money and class, gender and sexuality, status and authority are anything other than minor appendages to the grand inscription of racial particularity. The more that Blacks differ from each other, the more identity politics tells us that these differences do not count. In Britain, the slow emergence of articulate Black Conservatives provides a potent symbol of the degree to which the Black community can differ from itself. The implosive obsession with racial identity conjures away material, ideological, and sexual differences, but they live on stubbornly under the very signs of their attempted erasure. In these circumstances, the idea that there is a fixed, invariant, and essential Black identity that can be held constant while supposedly superficial differences like money, power, and sex proliferate is a defeat. It is also a symptom of confusion and inertia, in that it colludes in the privatization of Black culture, and sunders it from its historic association with social change. In its strongest form, this type of essentialism represents the wholesale substitution of therapy for political agency. At best, antiracism becomes a substitute for politics rather than its precondition. The appeal to identity has become little more than an alibi for racial narcissism and a licence for ethnic absolutism. This means that a critical discussion of the concept becomes an important part of restoring a sense of active agency to Black political cultures.

These historical contingencies aside, this inquiry into identity poses a number of complex political and cultural questions. Apart from the metatheoretical issues involved in understanding concepts like culture and identity, there are a number of other, supremely difficult problems that emerge once we enter the contested space in which different "local" conceptions of Black particularity flow into one another and may even begin to compete for popular attention in the secret public spheres that characterize the social institutions of racially subaltern peoples. Occupying this space means that we get referred to the limits of cultural forms and styles—their stubborn borders, frontiers, and thresholds—both internal and external. It also means that we have to comprehend the changing patterns of Black cultural production and use at national, subnational, and supranational levels, as well as in the fragile connections which social and cultural movements have established between these levels: the "strange attractors" that mark the nodal points where identities emerge, endure, and disappear. Communicative technologies, from print to digital pulses, make particular modes of subjectivity and identity possible. They help these outernational and intercultural linkages to constitute blocs—nonnational communities of sentiment and interpretation—that sometimes also aspire to be communities of rights and citizenship. They have by no means always been vehicles for Black dissent or disaffiliation from the agenda of modernity that is premised on the institutional integrity of the nation-state. Theories of Black identity in the modern world have been regularly implicated in the struggle to stretch and amend modernity so that it could accommodate the hopes of slaves and their descendants, postcolonial peoples and other marginalized groups.

Modernity and Identity in the Black Idiom

Even when bounded by the distinctive logic of diaspora relationships that I shall explore below, a global approach to the issue of racial and ethnic identities directs attention towards the question of culture's variations and mutability. Most importantly, a global perspective also makes absolutely untenable the fashionable notion of identity as a consequence of the simple repetition of racialized or ethnic culture. This simple observation on the junction of culture and identity underscores the fact that we must learn to work with the concept of culture in new ways that are capable of somehow operating against its own inner character, which was defined long ago by the notions of rootedness, stasis, and fixity that are intrinsic to its original meanings in the fields of crop management and animal husbandry.[2]

It is also necessary to accept that, in approaching the relationship of culture and identity, we are also being drawn onto the profane terrain of politics. Even where the rhetoric of Black social movements has exhibited an antipolitical character, I want to suggest that there is no innocent idea of purified prepolitical or apolitical identity to which we can appeal as a means to hold the imperatives of politics at bay. Indeed, the history of Blacks in the Western hemisphere can be used to show how the understanding of identity has itself been reconfigured at various times in the service of the inescapably political desires to be free, to be a citizen, and to be oneself which have shaped successive phases in the movements towards racial emancipation, liberation, and autonomy. This means that our discussions of Black identity cannot, then, be easily disentangled from these movements and their changing tactics. Indeed, the concepts, "Negro," "coloured," "Black," and "African" identity have already been tailored to these movements' changing sense of the requirements of politics. To put it another way, the identities which interest us do not exist prior to political action in the broadest sense, and remain outside it and its means of representation. They play multiple roles, but are more likely to be the product of racialized politics than its essential precondition.

Perhaps we need special clarity about the concept of identity today in order to know who is being emancipated by the movements for racial justice, not only because these movements have largely ceased to move, but also because the authority invested in Enlightenment discourses on rights, individualism, and equality, on which those movements continue to rely, has been cast in doubt. Certainly the emergence of Black voices that accentuate the language of racial authenticity in contradictory ways—gay as well as straight, from the "underclass" as well as from the academy, from Europe and America as well as from Africa—have thrown the idea of a fixed and unitary racial identity into a crisis. The challenge and the opportunity this provides is the chance to produce a theory of racial identity which is neither lazily essentialist nor prematurely pluralist.

Asserting the political character of identity formation and reproduction is also a way of emphasizing that writing about identity *in general* is impossibly difficult, if not fundamentally misguided. Identity acquired a special significance in modern Black political culture because of the need to refuse and escape the identities into which we were both coerced and seduced during a history of terror which language has inadequate resources to communicate. The tension between chosen identities and given identities appears in a very stark form in the history of the Black Atlantic diaspora, where the obligation to engage in self-discovery has always involved an act of refusal, and the conventional understanding of what it means to be an individual has been either imposed on its subordinated Others, or premised on their exclusion.

The countercultures of modernity which began to be produced from the irreducibly modern and transnational structures of the Atlantic trade in African slaves have created and employed several quite different notions of identity which reflect this history. Racialized concepts of self and community have been shaped according to an understanding of the dialectics of sameness and otherness produced in the unequal encounter between two multiplicities: Enlightenment Europe and enslaved Africa. Rereading the political culture of Blacks in modernity with hybridity and creolization in mind, and sifting its history for theories of identity, generates a discomforting sense of the embeddedness of Western Blacks in the metaphysical assumptions and conceptual schemes that derive from the forms of political and cultural nationalism produced by Kant and Herder, the notions of authenticity, citizenship, and masculinity that follow in Rousseau's wake and the characteristic language of inwardness that begins with Descartes's identification of radical doubt as the path to epistemological certainty and ontological security.[3]

Successive generations of Black intellectuals have used these tools— both reluctantly and unself-consciously, with joy and with bitterness— to leave behind the zone of sullen silence to which they were consigned by slavery and colonialism, and to initiate a powerful political language of agency, personhood, self, and sameness that was congruent with demands for racial emancipation, citizenship, and autonomy.

The complex formation of identities, and the vernacular theories of racialized selves and racial communities that interpret and influence them, are processes which bridge the brittle boundaries erected between reified disciplines, particularly sociology, philosophy, and politics, and required the crossing of boundaries between national traditions of thought. It is worth trying to specify, even in simplified form, some of the different stages in the development of the racial politics of identity. This is possible and valuable not because they have followed each other in a neat linear or evolutionary sequence from the most simple to the most complex, but because they still coexist as competing alternatives in the political space we inhabit today.

The first approach to self and sameness should be familiar because it currently dominates the Black political movement in Britain as well as here in the U.S. It projects a whole and overintegrated idea of self that I call an absolute or "cleansed" identity. This highly compressed and cheerfully essentialized understanding of identity is the favored subject of all forms of ethnic absolutism, even those that do not rely on phenotype as a marker. I want to suggest that, even when decked out in ethnic garb or the cheerful colours of Afrocentrism, this way of looking at identity is recognizably Cartesian in its dualism and its immodest confidence in the potency of consciousness. This assignment of priority to the emphatically disembodied operations of the mind becomes especially problematic when this essentialism seeks to enlist the symbolism of the racial body. Its practical reliance on renaming, uniforms, and rituals is an important symptom of this problem in its deepest structures. They provide the emblems of sameness that the racial body cannot yield satisfactorily.

The sovereign self, enthroned by this approach to identity, endorses the idea that its inner workings are knowable, stable, and predictable if the correct procedures are followed. This way of understanding identity should be recognizable not just because of its inability to accept the implications of the unconscious in shaping its methods and priorities, but above all because of its elision of gendered particularity into disembodied universalism. Following the pattern of its European antecedents closely, the favored, ideal image here is a heroic, masculine, and patriarchal identity that has been rather arbitrarily selected from its myriad competitors and privileged as the best vehicle for the integrity of the race as a whole. This patriarchal and sometimes authoritarian power presides over ethnic traditions that are imperiled by modernity. Its nonnegotiable authority is offered to the world and celebrated as the only legitimate form of Black identity. Transparency, stability, and wholeness are its most important attributes. It is supposed to be absolutely different from the White powers that dominate it, and yet its topography of self, community, and ethnic identity reiterates their distinctive logic in an act of mimesis that the ever-present rhetoric of disaffection from the White world cannot disguise:

> Before specifically defining our present period of crisis and our response to it, we must contemplate our identity, the self-image that we carry in our brain computers. For all that we can imagine doing and all that we will do or fail to do is a result of that picture of "self."[4]

In my view, this model inflates and exaggerates the coherence of both self and identity. Its reliance on a language of inwardness that is recognizably heir to early-modern European philosophical discourse does not of course, invalidate it, but would surely embarrass the purity-seeking racial fundamentalism that promotes it so effectively today through the invocation and invention of the African cultures to which it is dedicated. This model of identity renders the mechanisms of identification invisible, because identification (a double event which encompasses belonging and referring) presupposes a degree of difference which has to be recognized and negotiated. From this standpoint, a race just cannot differ from itself. There is sameness only, and it is a sameness ruthlessly fortified against both doubt and democracy by myths of origin which, even where they are embellished with the proper name Africa, turn away from that continent's contemporary ecological and economic catastrophes, preferring instead to contemplate the imagined community made possible by an acute overinvestment in the notion of anteriority.

The second, rather less popular, model of identity I want to identify is similarly stamped with these European origins, though its indebtedness to them is more antagonistic, its loyalty more negative. There is necessarily some ambivalence here. This way of looking at identity is premised on a relational idea of self. Selfhood is figured through the desire for respect and recognition,[5] and confirmed through their bestowal. It approximates something of Hegel's account of the development of self-consciousness in the allegory of combat between master and slave, but this model of identity contradicts the former version by inverting the self-certain, Cartesian logic which is still so appealing to ethnic absolutists of all phenotypical hues. The slave's ontological anxieties cannot be resolved in the *cogito*, because the slave knows that her cognitive capacities are the confirmation of her nonbeing—her social death—rather than her being. The elemental struggle between two consciousnesses proceeds along similar lines to those discussed by Hegel. But where the Hegelian slave enters bondage by opting for repression rather than death, thereby initiating the dialectic of dependency and recognition that yields power over the master, the Black idiom differs by asserting an active preference for death rather than accommodation to the continued unfreedoms on which modernity and plantation society both depend. In the present setting, what matters more than the desire to die is the shift from a subject-centred idea of identity to a view of identity as the product of intersubjective relations. The integral subject that emerges from the first model is shown to have some leaky boundaries. Its consciousness is unreliable. Its dreams of mastery require active acknowledgment from the subordinated. If Hegel's allegory seems too unself-consciously Eurocentric a way of summing up this variation, a vernacular counternarrative can be readily constructed from the famous story of Frederick Douglass's encounter with Covey the slave-breaker, to whom he was despatched for breaking by his master Thomas Auld. The spirit of this relational understanding of identity is captured by the Martineaquean Edouard Glissant in a discussion of the dynamics of social and cultural creolization: "This is what I call cultural identity. An identity on its guard, in which the relationship with the Other shapes the self without fixing it under an oppressive force."[6]

W.E.B. Du Bois is the architect of a third approach to theorizing identity that appeared in the nontraditional tradition of African diaspora social thought. He retained aspects of the relational, Hegelian self, particularly in his insistence that a racially stratified world yielded the descendants of slaves "no true self-consciousness" but his view of the problem of identity was deeply colored by academic interests apart from neo-Hegelianism. His interests in psychology and sociology developed while studying at Fisk, Harvard, and Berlin, locations that can be used to triangulate the space that defines Black experiences of modernity. Du Bois admits and explores the internal differentiation of the modern Black subject, and expresses this through the celebrated idea of double-consciousness that reconstructed the relationship between inside and outside in the process that produces identity. This doubling is inconsistently projected, sometimes as a hermeneutic privilege and at other times as an ontological disability. Yet Du Bois's powerful formulations contain, not just an idea of an asymmetrical self, generated from an internal dialogue, but their author's acknowledgments of his own meandering journeys towards the coherent racial identity that he actively made and remade. The journeys he took after choosing "the realm of Mind"[7] for his favored territory led him southwards and then across the Atlantic from west to east in the opposite direction to the crossings that his slave forebears had made. His child-hood in Great Barrington, his reinvention of himself amidst the racially affirmative mood of Fisk in the era of the Jubilee Singers, and the strange spiritual ceremony he performed in Berlin on the occasion of his twenty-fifth birthday in 1893, all emerge from his autobiographical writings as important punctuation marks in a narrative of being and becoming. His understanding of identity is also important because it was shaped decisively by experiences that took place outside the bor-ders of the United States. His view of Black identity allowed for the possibility of nonidentity, and accentuated the restless, provisional, and multiple character of subjectivity. Du Bois's elitism and his democratic aspirations coexisted and combined with a tender love for the rural, Southern Black folk whose substantive differences from himself were explored most notably in the chapter "Of The Meaning of Progress" in *The Souls of Black Folk*.

Du Bois brought a naive yet potent psychology into the sociopolitical theories of identity that preoccupied the Black movement at a time when its certainties had been queried by the increasing internal differen-tiation of Black communities, north and south, by an intense debate over the role of Black intellectuals and the relationship of pedagogy to liberation, and by the possibility of linking African-American political struggles with the global politics of the color line in the era of imperial and colonial domination. His image of two warring souls contained within the same dark body is also significant for our discussion, because it is an important point at which the issue of nationality entered into discussions of Black identity. Du Bois named those two warring souls in national(ist) terms: "Negro" and "American."

Du Bois's doubling of the self was not always valorized as "second-sight." Sometimes it was reduced to the idea of splitting. His work can thus be used as a doorway into those recognizably "postmodern" approaches to the concept of identity that accentuate its fragmentary character. These approaches defy easy summarization. They often see self and subjectivity as an effect of the linguistic and discursive struc-tures into which they are inserted, and argue that secreted inside the discourses on identity is the impossible desire to master the self by making it knowable. They question the equation of consciousness and mind, and deny the unity and stability of identity. In the Black idiom, these arguments were most fully elaborated in the later, European work of Richard Wright. Immersed in anticolonial political action in the intellectual milieu of postwar Paris, and removed from the paro-chial disciplinary influences of Black America, Wright forsook his economistic Marxism in favor of a historical psychology derived from Nietzsche and Freud. He drew heavily on the former source to produce an image of the racial self as performatively constituted in the special dramaturgy of colonial and postcolonial settings that, for him, included the experience of the Southern United States. He placed this theme at the centre of his final published work of fiction, *The Long Dream,* and elaborated on it theoretically in the essay "On the Psychological Reactions of Oppressed People":

> Am I saying that Asians, Africans and Coloured people in general are good actors? No. I'm not speaking of the theater. I'm saying that their life situation evokes in them an almost unconscious tendency to hide their deepest reactions from those who they fear would penalise them if they suspected what they really felt.[8]

The racial self is constituted in these performances. Behind it, barely in control of its scripts and gestures, is a fragmented humanity that exceeds the limits of merely racial subjectivity and can only be narrated with the benefit of hindsight. This realization is what propels the nihilistic antisocial actions of Wright's more murderous protagonists.

It bears repetition that these four conceptions of identity: the integral, clean or absolute self; the relational or intersubjective self; the plural self, double or split; and the fragmentary, unintegrated self are not arranged in an evolutionary sequence. All, to some degree, involve the mutation and hybridization of ideas, theories, and philosophies. All register in different ways the impact of European systems of thought and their internalization by Black thinkers, who have sought to possess them so that they could be left behind or democratized. Though these views of identity emerged at different historical moments in the Black journey through modernity, they still represent different options, and provide different ways of resolving the politics of identity in the present. Each specifies distinct political choices and tactics. Each is articulated to different cultural and and philosophical concerns. They encounter one another in the decentered diaspora of the Black Atlantic world, where flows of information and expressive culture have enabled new modes of identification to take shape.

Routes and Culture

Blacks in Europe or the United States may identify with the struggle in South Africa and selectively borrow elements of Africa's cultures in order to make sense of their own experiences of being in a world structured by White supremacy. Their mode of connection to Africa and its anticolonial struggles has been qualitatively changed now that Africa is accessible via the television rather than the book and the picture postcard. Similarly, Caribbean peoples make African-American cultural forms their own, and the contemporary appeal of dance-hall reggae and its syncretic combination with rhythm and blues are but the latest phase in an ongoing process that goes back through the recombinant forms of hip-hop at least to Louis Jordan's experiments with the "new calypso bebop" in the late 1940s.

Music dominates popular culture. It is central to this consideration of cultural identity because of its global reach, and because it is repeatedly identified as a special area of expressive culture that mysteriously embodies the inner essence of racial particularity. Its sublime, antirepresentational qualities supplement the power of dissident Black cultures. It supplies an ineffable antilanguage that provides ironic compensation for the exclusion of slaves and their descendants from literacy. It is also in music that the most intense legacy of the African past is concentrated, and though the significance of that legacy is open to dispute, the link itself is impossible to refute. It is important, then, that the area of cultural production which is most evidently identified with racial authenticity and Black particularity is also the most mutable and adaptive of forms. Since it emerged into the domain of mass culture through the travels of the Jubilee Singers in the late nineteenth century, the music has changed restlessly, seeking new aesthetic, moral, and technical potency. Indeed, its capacity to change is built into its dialogic rules and ideas of tradition. Conservatives—Black and White—will seek to arrest the creative power of its forward momentum in the misplaced quest to keep it pure and untainted. But Black music is organized through hybrid forms that supply evidence for a view of mutation and adaptation as sources of strength and pleasure. Hip-hop supplies the most obvious example of this, but its borrowing of Jamaican sound-system culture was only one element in a complex interface between Caribbean musics and jazz and rhythm and blues.

Black popular culture does not determine the formation of social and cultural identities in any mechanistic way, but it supplies a variety of symbolic, linguistic, textual, gestural, and, above all, musical resources that are used by people to shape their identities, truths, and models of community. That culture has struggled over a long period of time with its transmutation into the closed form of the commodity. It is used in dynamic ways that liberate it from the logic of commodification and supplement the original creative input of its producers with further contributions. Our DJs mix your beats and change them into something you may not have anticipated. Our instrumentalists perform your "standards" and make them resonate with different histories of our Blackness. This expressive culture is now a global phenomenon which, even when annexed by the corporate cultural industries, still hosts important conversations between constituencies that are closely linked, even if they are widely separated in space and time. It provides analysts with a means to explore the unequal exchanges that characterize the interactive, dialogical relationships between Black populations across the globe. The communicative networks I have described are constituted by the flows between locations rather than by some simple combination of the fixed points they connect. People, capital, technology and information, artifacts, commodities, and ideas have been circulated by different means and at different speeds across the Black Atlantic world in several directions. It is no longer a simple, expressive, and unidirectional diaspora with an identifiable and reversible pattern of dispersal as its starting point. Its nonlinear dynamics have created multiple, looped lines of intimacy capable of conducting the heat of political affinity as well as the possibility of common identity. Yet the concept of diaspora, with its special logic of sameness and differentiation, provides a fundamental theoretical means to grasp the contemporary politics of identity and identification and the self-similar fractal logic that Leroi Jones/Amiri Baraka first named "a changing same" in his rich discussion of African-American music and its relationship to both selfhood and community.[9]

Black Masculinity and the Negation of Diaspora

Diaspora is a useful concept because it specifies the pluralization and nonidentity of the Black identities without celebrating either prematurely. It raises the possibility of sameness, but it is a sameness that cannot be taken for granted. Identity must be demonstrated in relation to the alternative possibility of differentiation, because the diaspora logic enforces a sense of temporality and spatiality that underscores the fact that we are not what we were. The Black peoples of the Americas and the Caribbean may share what Ralph Ellison once called "an identity of passions," but our cultures are irreducibly diverse. The concept of diaspora invites the theorist to think sameness and differentiation at the same time without privileging either term. That is, to consider the differentiation within sameness and the sameness within differentiation. It is here that the definitions of African-American particularity, which so often supply the framework for discussions of Black identity by default, begin to unravel. This happens for several reasons. Specific micropolitical patterns in the process of identity construction do not translate well from one vernacular code to another. Racism may take different forms, and affect the development of identities that answer it in widely different ways. In several European countries, including Britain, it is the experience of migration rather than the presence of the living memory of slavery that provides the centripetal effects that force people together. Where neofascist groups are an everyday hazard, and governments keep the possibility of "reimmigration" and "repatriation" alive as policy solutions to the problems they see embodied in a Black presence that is incompatible with exalted standards of national culture, racial and minority ethnic identities will not take the same shape that they do in situations where the legitimacy of a Black presence is not in itself contested, even though it is allocated a subordinate role. The comparatively small scale and heterocultural character of Britain's non-White populations create another dynamic, in which the idea of "Blackness" has sometimes been politically rather than phenotypically defined, and where the stereotypical view of Caribbean people as indolent, brutish, and unmotivated contrasts strongly with their reputation in the United States. Though its significance varies from country to country, the memory of fascisms is an important factor in the politics of race in Europe. It has important consequences for Black politics because antiracism is not always the same as antifascism.

Though several generations of Black thinkers have tried to connect African-American movements towards racial justice and human rights with other struggles towards freedom from colonial domination and against White supremacy, these outernational links have been intermittent and hard to sustain. The Afrocentric movement common to both Britain and the United States offers a rather too simple version of this connection in its simple denial of substantive differences between Africans here and Africans there. But this argument has been carried over into the contested institutions of Black popular culture. I want to suggest that this global tension between discrepant local definitions of Black identity remains an important issue, and to illustrate that argument with an obvious example: the cluster of monumental myths and symbols that envelops the historical memory of Malcolm X. The social memory of the America's Black movements of the 1960s has an altogether different significance in Britain from that which it enjoys here. Its creative appropriation, especially as an element of youth culture, marks Black Britain's sharp turn away from the Caribbean as its major source of inspiration. Black political culture in Europe now looks to African-American history for guidance, pleasure, and raw material for its own distinct definitions of Blackness. The appeal of the heroic figure of Malcolm X has been central to this development. It expresses not just the collapse of the Black churches' spiritual authority, but a yearning for forms of redemptive and visionary leadership that have never been a feature of Black political culture in Britain. I see it as the latest triumph of outernational and intercultural political forms that make their local equivalents (in our case) still bolted to the decaying chassis of a nineteenth-century nation-state, look tame, redundant, and outmoded by comparison. The crucial role that reading Malcolm's autobiography has played in disseminating his narrative of self-creation and transformation is one reason why this focused longing is unlikely to be completely recuperated into an empty, depthless anti-politics centred on Malcolm's style.

The recovery of Malcolm X is perhaps better understood as a limited symbolic restoration of the forms of Black manhood that White supremacy denies. This is a highly contradictory process in which an unusual and potent mixture of due reverence and psychosexual identification needs to be explained rather than concealed. Why should the image of Malcolm as a Messiah bringing redemption and retribution be so potent and so obvious a symbol of what we lack? It is worth remembering that the resurgence of interest in Malcolm guarantees absolutely nothing about the progressive character or radical direction of Black politics in the future. Part of Malcolm's appeal is the openness of his narrative. This allows him to appear in myriad guises: as a dutiful member of the Nation of Islam, as a prototype for Minister Farrakhan, as an orthodox Sunni Muslim, or as a fledgling revolutionary socialist. We must try to make sense of the apparently limitless postmodern plasticity of Malcolm, because it has been implicated in dissolving the difference that diaspora makes. It is especially troubling that his most enduring and powerful incarnation seems to be as a patriarchal sign in the family romance that Black political history has become. The play of intraracial differences is firmly arrested by the law of the father that makes the racial community into a family, and places the image of Malcolm in command of it. This is especially important when we consider the difference between reading Malcolm's autobiography and seeing Spike Lee's film of Malcolm's life. These different cultural forms impact upon the politics of identity in quite different ways. Malcolm's own story of transformation and redemptive change, like the capacity to remake and mold his memory into a variety of contradictory but equally valid shapes, undermines the impossibility of seeing racial identity in mechanistically essentialist terms. However, this is not the direction of Spike Lee's film and its Americocentric version of Black political culture in which the Stars and Stripes can be readily transmuted into the X that ends Malcolm's name. Between the parentheses supplied to either end of the film by the invocations of Marcus Garvey and Nelson Mandela, we have only a narrative of Malcolm's emergent masculinity. Lee offers this as the antidote to the wrongs displayed before the film starts in the violence directed at the damaged, passive body of Rodney King. The subnational, national, and supranational geographies of identity are are held together by the force of masculinity alone. The brutal assault on Rodney King symbolizes a denied manhood that is eventually cured, if not undone, by the type of man that Malcolm represents. In one of the film's most powerful scenes, the coordinated action of a whole community against the brutality of Harlem police is trivially interpreted as a reified expression of Malcolm's personal power.

The need to love Malcolm can also be interpreted as a desire to set the historical memory of Black struggles loose in a world where memory and historicity have been subordinated to a relentless contemporaneity. As far as Britain is concerned, the power of his image has created an important opportunity to find new sets of racial tactics in circumstances where both Black nationalism and the economistic leftism against which it was so often defined have nothing more to offer. This is because, no less than Du Bois and Wright, Malcolm's understanding of self, community, race, and identity was transformed by experiences outside the U.S. which made him see the racial codes and structures that formed him as but one powerful system among many similar structures in the web of White supremacy. Even when distorted by the Oedipal preoccupations of Spike Lee, Malcolm's importance resides in his global stature and the globalized vision of Black politics that grew through and from his travels. Our discussions of racial and ethnic identities can parallel this change of scale if we aspire not just to comparative study of identity formation and reproduction, but to an approach in which we appreciate how extensively Black identities everywhere have been shaped under the impact of hemispheric and global relations. The various flows from which we construct our cultural identities require more than the old Newtonian analogies of force and power if we are to understand them adequately. The contemporary study of these identities requires careful attention to the politics of influence and adaptation. Malcolm's enduring importance as history and as myth confirms that these inferential powers have not respected the borders of the modern nation-state.

Notes

1. Jordan, June. "Report From The Bahamas," in *On Call*. Boston: South End Press, 1985, p. 49.
2. Williams, Raymond. *Keywords A Vocabulary of Culture and Society*. London: Fontana, 1988, p. 87.
3. Taylor, Charles. *Sources of The Self: The Making of Modern Identity,* esp. part two, "Inwardness." Cambridge: Cambridge University Press, 1989.
4. Cress Welsing, Frances. *The Isis Papers: The Keys To The Colors*. Chicago: Third World Press, 1991, p. 284.
5. Taylor, Charles. *Multiculturalism and "The Politics of Recognition."* Princeton: Princeton University Press, 1992.
6. Glissant, Edouard. *Caribbean Discourse,* trans. J. Michael Dash, Charlottesville: University of Virginia Press, 1989, p. 169.
7. Du Bois, W.E.B. *Against Racism. Unpublished Essays, Papers, Addresses 1887–1962,* (ed). Herbert Aptheker, Amherst: University of Massachussets Press, 1985, p. 29.
8. Wright, Richard. "On The Psychological Reactions of Oppressed People," in *White Man Listen!* Garden City: Anchor, 1964, p. 17.
9. Jones, Leroi. "The Changing Same (R&B and New Black Music)," in *Black Music*. New York: Quill, 1967.

2

Identity as Coping: Adolescent African-American Males' Adaptive Responses to High-Risk Environments

Margaret Beale Spencer, Michael Cunningham, and Dena Phillips Swanson

This chapter examines issues of identity formation for economically vulnerable African-American youth. We examine the developmental processes which undergird and support coping strategies. Given the limited theoretical and empirical research available on the development of minority youth, the goal is daunting at best. Our research is intended to contribute to the filling of the theoretical and empirical gaps. This chapter is organized, first, to offer an improved understanding of normal development under challenging conditions; second, to describe the results of some of our research; and third, to offer policy recommendations based on an interpretation of our findings.

Adolescence is a potentially difficult period for any youth. It is a period when a normative "identity crisis" is experienced that involves the exploration of many new roles in preparation for adulthood (Erikson, 1968). But the difficulty of this developmental period is exacerbated when the adolescent is African-American and male. As a minority group member, difficulties may be encountered that compromise positive outcomes because of prejudice, discrimination, or barriers to full opportunity for personal growth (Gibbs, Huang *et al.,* 1989; Erikson, 1959). In general, the life experiences of minority adolescents in the United States are complicated by issues not faced by majority youth. Political, cultural, economic, and social forces interact in complex ways with particular developmental concerns of adolescence such as identity and self-image, increased autonomy, relations with peers, school achievement, and career goals (Spencer and Dornbush, 1990).

Many researchers have shown that the process of maturation is universal and occurs with minor variations across racial and cultural groups, but acknowledge that individuals are subject to wide ethnic variations in their behavioral manifestations, their symbolic meanings, and their societal responses (Phinney and Rotheram, 1987). African-American youth are socialized in a Europeanized context which is heavily infused with stereotypes, and infrequently perceive their status in American society, independent of social economic status, as one of endless opportunities (Spencer, Dobbs, and Swanson, 1988). Adolescents, like all individuals, develop and adapt through interactions that occur within particular environmental settings (Bronfenbrenner, 1989). By adolescence, minority youth are well aware of the values of the majority culture and its standards of performance, achievement, and beauty. As an undeniable aspect of normal cognitive maturation, they are also aware that unchanging biases, structural constraints, and chronically experienced stress contribute to what Chestang (1972) describes as an ever-present and psychologically hostile environment. Such environments require coping strategies and adaptive responses at each point in the life course.

In contrast to younger children, adolescents evaluate their personal opportunities for attaining valued goals (Spencer and Dornbush, 1990). The life goals of young people and the developmental stages these pursuits represent are quite different from those expected of adults. Thus, from a contextually sensitive perspective that recognizes transactional effects, it is critical to examine African-American adolescent males from a broader theoretical framework. Such a framework necessarily considers both their unique and structural experiences which intersect with developmental status, ethnic group membership, and gender (for instance, perceptions of African-American men in America).

Background

McCandless and Evans (1973) describe "identity process" as an integration of "selves or identifications" with perceptions of future development. Future-oriented perceptions include awareness of group membership and the expectations, privileges, restraints, and social responsibilities that accompany that membership (p. 390). Minority group males must synthesize multiple identifications. In addition to race and ethnicity, additional physiological factors specific to maleness and social factors associated with traditional male role expectations require integration. It is critical to note that gender-specific physiological factors are shared with all males irrespective of ethnicity and social class.

In industrialized societies, women live longer than men, but apparently experience more physical and psychological illness (Wingard, 1987, p. 2). However, not only do women ultimately outlive men, but they have lower death rates at nearly every age and for most causes. Similarly, and of equal importance, deaths due to accidents are also prevalent throughout young adulthood for males generally, since adolescent risk-taking appears very much a part of the male rite of passage. A report by the Secretary's Task Force on Black and Minority Health (1986) indicates that the physiological factors of gender and age—being male and young—are the most important risk indices for death and injury.

The gender differences have been explained in several ways. Some have suggested that the differences reflect better reporting of behavior differences (for instance, perception of symptoms and what is considered ill health). Both variations in willingness to talk about illness and illness behavior itself (that is, willingness to respond to being ill) have been proposed as explanations. As indicated, it has been suggested that the accidental death differences reflect greater risk-taking behavior exhibited by males generally.

In addition to these social risk factors, biological risk factors also exist. Ample evidence suggests that males and females differ in biological factors such as blood pressure, cholesterol levels, glucose intolerance, and, of course, hormones (Wingard, 1987, p. 23). Still unknown is why these differences occur. For example, are these differences genetically determined, either directly or indirectly through the effects of hormonal differences? Or are these differences between the sexes determined by behavioral differences (for instance, dietary variations)?

Findings suggest behavioral as well as physical differences between males and females. Several explanations have been proposed: 1) that men engage in behaviors more damaging to health; 2) that women are biologically "more fit" than men; and 3) that sex differences in morbidity rates actually reflect sex differences in various illness behaviors (Wingard, 1987). Whatever the reasons for these differences, social or biological, these sex-linked effects are exacerbated by ethnicity and race.

Traditionally associated with being a man in American culture is the sex-role expectation of being an economic provider. Along with this expectation, Latino, Native American, and African-American youth must integrate the reality of racism and its effects on their ability to carry out the expected traditional sex roles that accompany biological maleness.

This combination of biological, behavioral, and societal factors is complex, and may constitute an at-risk context for minority males. The situation has implications for identity processes; also implicated are associated adaptive responses (for instance, strategies and coping mechanisms) employed for maintaining some semblance of psychological equilibrium and integrity. Investigating changes in self-esteem during periods of developmental transition represents an important strategy for examining individual methods of coping with role strains and, thus, for planning effective interventions.

Review of Research

Many researchers have examined dimensions of identity development (for example, sex-role orientation and self-esteem) of young boys (under ten) and of adult men (over eighteen). However, available research that demonstrates the complexities of these psychological domains during adolescence is sparse. Empirical work on sex-role development suggests that related identity processes begin in childhood and continue into adult life. However, adolescence is the most crucial period for developing one's identity. During this period, any unresolved conflict from earlier years needs to be resolved as a foundation for the establishment of a psychologically healthy adult life.

Adolescent Identity Formation

The issue of an interactive ethnic influence on identity and competence processes during adolescence is understudied and frequently misunderstood. During the formation of an identity, growing children must, at every step, derive a vitalizing sense of reality from the awareness that their individual way of mastering experiences is a successful variant of the way other people around them master experience and recognize such mastery (Erikson, 1980). As part of the process, and especially given social cognitive skills, children are frequently confused by empty praise and condescending encouragement. At times youth may have to accept artificial bolstering of their self-esteem in lieu of something better. But Erikson (1980) refers to identity formation processes as the adolescent's efforts to accrue ego identity gains from real strengths that accompany wholehearted and consistent recognition of genuine accomplishment. Of equal importance is the belief that demonstrated accomplishments have meaning and value within their own culture. If the peer culture of African-American adolescent males believes that the environment tries to deprive them too radically of all forms of expression, they may resist with astonishing strength. According to Erikson (1968), the development of identity is a process involving personal reflection and observation of oneself in relation to others. Similarly, writings by early symbolic interactionists were the first to integrate notions of role-taking in self-development. Cooley's (1902) "looking glass self" is defined as the process in which children define themselves by taking the perspectives of important others and then reflecting on the self from these perspectives. Mead's (1934) "generalized other" contributes to a sense of self. More recently, Spencer and Markstrom-Adams (1990) examine the affects of acculturation on identity formation among racial and ethnic minority children. However, further theorizing about identity formation using the process of personal reflection and observation of oneself in relation to others, at least for African-American adolescents, has not been forthcoming.

Sex-Role Development

A major task of early adolescents is to develop an identity that integrates accelerating physical growth, impending reproductive maturity, and qualitatively advanced levels of thought and emotion. All occur within a social context. In examining the research on sex-role acquisition, most major theories suggest the important role of parents as models, identification objects, or role reinforces (Freud, 1949; A. Freud, 1936; Kagan, 1958; Mishel, 1966; Kohlberg, 1966). Research also indicates that fathers have an important part in the development of sex roles in boys and girls alike (Staples, 1978; Rubin, 1981; Millham and Smith, 1981). Social learning theory suggests that the father serves as a role model and teacher for the son and as the first safe male in the life of the daughter. African-American fathers have additional pressures (for instance, racism, discrimination, negative stereotypes, and joblessness) that exacerbate the pressures of fatherhood. Fatherhood is accompanied by specific and clear sex-role expectations for instrumentality which affords economic stability for the family unit.

But with underemployment and unemployment rates continuing to rise for African-American men, the psychological stresses associated with expectations for instrumentality increasingly add to the pressures of everyday life. Also compromised, potentially, is the basic viability of Black male-female relationships and, thus, marital stability and the family's economic security.

Perceptions of men and expectations about the male role may vary for some African-American boys. The increased numbers of African-American children living in female-headed households necessitate greater involvement by other significant adults (for instance, uncles, coaches, male teachers, grandfathers) who form affective bonds with boys and serve as models (Hare and Castenell, 1985). Accordingly, since the experiences of African-American adult males entail outside barriers, other adult males represent an important resource as models for youth (Rubin, 1974). Thus, particularly African-American male teachers, coaches, neighbors, businessmen, and others have important dual roles. They serve as models in their personal careers as well as active mentors in fulfilling their social responsibility for a community's youth.

Parents and significant others are not the only influences on adolescent psychosocial development. The context in which adolescents grow and develop also has an affect. Ladner's (1972) work with African-American female adolescents delineates several important factors that influence sex-role development: family, income, education, kin, and peer relations. These factors have implications for motivation, role enactment and role modeling, identity processes, and socialization. Ladner's research on sex-role development suggests that the ideals of adulthood (strength, independence, and self-reliance) are less sex-role differentiated among poor African-American adolescents than their Anglo, middle-class counterparts. From her study of sex-role development as a coping response to the circumstance of being a member of a permanent out-group, she posits that race functions more like sex and less like ethnicity in this respect. The insight may be applied across social classes, and has important implications for issues concerning African-American male adolescents' sex-role development.

African-American Adolescent Male Expression of Masculinity

It appears critical to examine African-American males in their own context. The ways in which these youths express themselves is often misinterpreted (for instance, the style of dress, forms of verbal communication, and physical demeanor). The persona that African-American adolescent males project may be threatening to people who do not examine it in context and fail to link it to normal adolescent developmental tasks (for instance, identity pursuits). Cazenave (1984) examined the effects of race, social economic status (SES), and age on masculine role perceptions. Findings indicated that age was an important factor in determining male role identity, while SES was a major determinant of the degree and nature of male involvement in familial roles. The data exemplify the importance of studying masculine roles within a framework that takes into account the relative social location of American men. Furthermore, research by Rubin (1981) suggests that general community norms and values are influential in developing attitudes concerning the perceived male role.

Biller's (1968) more traditional work examines African-American males in comparison to their White counterparts. He explored the relationship of father absence and sociocultural background to masculine development of lower-class African-American and White boys. The results suggest that underlying sex-role orientation is more influenced by father availability and family background than are more manifest aspects of masculinity. The findings underscore the importance of significant others as father figures in the socialization of African-American boys.

Other research by Staples (1978) examines the special status of African-American men in contemporary society. Considering some of the common stereotypes of African-American men from a historical perspective, he offers alternative explanations about the prevailing views of African-American men as emasculated, dominated by women, and lacking positive self-esteem. Staples also examines the socialization process and problems of African-American youth. He offers an alternative perspective to the traditional deprivation model generally applied to African-Americans.

Like Staples, Mosher and Sirkin (1984) examine childhood as a precursor to adult hypermasculinity. They point out that during early and middle childhood, the parental use of contempt and humiliation to socialize the emotions of fear and distress in boys is hypothesized to be of major importance in fostering an exaggerated masculine style. The hypermasculine boy experiences shame and self-contempt when he fails to attain the masculine ideals of courage and stoicism through inhibiting his fear and cry of distress. Enculturation of the masculine value of heroism continues through adolescence during participation in male peer group activities, including sports and less acceptable, dangerous, delinquent, or aggressive behaviors. The view of masculinity as heroic is joined with a conception of women as dominion and as sexual objects who exist as reward for the conquering hero (Mosher and Sirkin, 1984). A set of beliefs and attitudes becomes bonded to emotions, particularly interest-excitement, that motivate a hypermasculine style and hypermasculine actions.

This position is supported by the literature that examines the experiences of African-American males. Generally, this literature suggests that adolescent identity formation among African-American males is substantially influenced by high rates of father-absent families, poverty, and differential exposure to a significant number of male role models who associate manhood with toughness and sexual conquest (Hannerz, 1969; Perkins, 1975; Franklin, 1985; Wilson, 1987 and Anderson, 1990). Although these authors generally offer philosophical considerations in the development of an identity for African-American men, they do not offer empirical evidence. Either sample sizes are small, represent postadolescent ages (for example, young adults), or data are absent all together.

Similar work on sex roles and identity formation has been offered by Taylor (1989), and Hare and Hare (1987). Taylor's work with African-American college students offers insights concerning the important role that fathers or images of fathers play in the development of an identity for males. The Hares's work on "rites of passage" helps to establish important rituals that compensate for negative images projected by society in general. Both works have an important place in the literature. However, the theoretical frameworks of these works could be strengthened by empirical studies.

A recent report by Majors and Billson (1992) suggest that African-American men adapt to a hostile environment by being cool or adopting a "cool pose." They suggest that African-American men use the cool pose as a strategy to make sense of their everyday lives. They believe that coolness as a strength may be linked to pride, self-respect, and masculinity. At the same time, a persona of coolness provides a mask that may contribute to problem outcomes such as dropping out of school, getting into trouble, sliding into drug and alcohol abuse, and being sucked into delinquent or criminal street gangs. Majors's and Billson's work on the dilemmas of Black manhood in America offers important ideas about how African-American men express themselves. However, this work does not include experiences during adolescence.

The adolescent years are precursors to adult outcomes and have to be taken into consideration when attempting to explain adult outcomes.

Peer Influences

During the adolescent period, youth generally look to their peers for social acceptance and popularity. The messages peers project, overt and symbolic, represent the contextual experiences of African-American youth in American society. As described by Chestang (1972), societal inconsistencies represent the contradictions between professed societal beliefs and actual experiences. According to Wilson (1991), the transitional nature of adolescence is problematic for African-American adolescents, particularly as they struggle to define themselves and find their way in the confusing and distracting context of an oppressed, exploited, African-American community and a dominant, hostile, racially oppressive, and exploitative European-American-dominated society.

The adolescent's social contexts or microsystem-level experiences afford a buffer to societal inconsistencies. Parents, peers, schools, religious and social institutions have the potential to enhance youths' understanding of societal phenomena. Such transformative opportunities direct youth into using more proactive (that is, versus reactive) styles of coping with inequalities in the United States. The manner and magnitude in which microsystem variables can assist adolescents differ by race and gender. Boys spend more of their leisure time with friends compared to girls, who spend more leisure time with family (Coates, 1987). The dynamics of the difference have good and bad consequences. Group membership during adolescence is rewarding because of the opportunities that it provides for social comparisons (Erwin, 1993). Similarities between group members are seen as providing a consensual validation of the adolescent's thoughts, feelings, and behavior. Groups tend to validate the individual's identity and, in fact, are inclined to make their members more similar to each other and different from the out-group. Ethnographic work by Fordham and Ogbu (1988) reports on youth's coping with academic alienation by labeling academic achievement-oriented behavior as "acting White." There is pressure to conform to group expectations and standards because of concerns over group acceptance (Sherif and Sherif, 1953).

Overall, the literature on sex-role acquisition is influenced by philosophical works. Although these works are important for developing

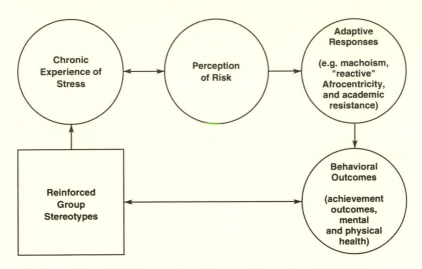

Figure 1   Identity processes as adaptive coping.

a theoretical framework, they lack the incorporation of empirical evidence. Additionally, much of the literature is problem-behavior-oriented, and lacks the inclusion of contextual variables that are important for establishing normative data. In many of the studies cited above, researchers who have incorporated contextual variables into a developmental perspective have done so with samples that include young boys (under ten) and adult men (over eighteen). Theoretically undergirded empirical research on African-American adolescents is sparse. Figure 1 offers a variation of a phenomenological variant ecological systems perspective (see Spencer, 1994) that provides a particular integration.

Among others, an important aspect of the model described in Figure 1 is that not only is it contextualized, but it is linked to normal comparative processes and identity pursuits. The benefit of more contemporary models of theoretically driven empirical studies, particularly during adolescence, is that they include critical contextual variables. Consequently, such a model could significantly influence policy and aid in developing interventions which would prevent many problematic outcomes of African-American adolescent males (see Markstrom-Adams and Spencer, 1994).

Longitudinal Research Project: One

Design and Methods

In our initial longitudinal study of urban children in the southeastern United States, a sample of African-American children was assessed on measures of self-esteem on two occasions separated by three years (Spencer, 1984). The sample included two groups: The younger transition group was made up of children who were observed from 1978 to 1979 initially as three- or five-year-old preschoolers or kindergartners (Time One), and again three years later in 1981 to 1982, during their transition into primary school as six- and eight-year-olds (Time Two). The older transition group was made up of youngsters who were observed initially when they were either seven- or nine-year-old early primary schoolchildren (Time One), and again assessed as they entered into early adolescence as ten- and twelve-year-olds (Time Two).

At Time One, the sample of 384 subjects was equally divided by socioeconomic status, age, and sex. A total of 150 children of the original sample was followed up at Time Two. There were slightly more lower-income youth included on the follow-up. Contrary to popular assumption, lower-income families were much easier to locate later than were middle-income families. The Primary Self-Concept Test (Mueller and Leonetti, 1974) was used for both the younger and the older group at both Time One and Time Two; due to the age limitations of the instrument, the Thomas Self-Concept and Value Test (Thomas, 1967) was used at both times for the younger transition group only. Both tests are used to assess general feelings about oneself and one's feelings about "self as a learner" (Spencer 1984, 1988).

Findings for the Global Self-Esteem Measure (Thomas Self-Concept Test)

Consistent with research findings by Hare (1985) and others, at the follow-up the overall mean self-esteem score for males was higher than the mean score for females at either Time One or Two. In general, self-esteem was positively correlated with age. The transition from Time One to Time Two resulted in no change in self-esteem for females and a pattern of increase in overall self-esteem for males.

Gender differences by self-esteem attribute were patterned. For example, for the attribute "happy," no difference between Time One and Two was apparent for girls, while boys obtained significantly higher scores at Time Two.

For the younger "transition into the primary school" group, both boys and girls obtained higher scores at Time Two for perceptions of self as having a "lot of ability"; the relationship was significant for girls although just barely evident as a pattern for boys. Similarly, both boys and girls showed a decrease in perception of "being accepted" by adult males at Time Two. The relationship was not significant for boys but appeared as a pattern for girls. It is difficult to determine whether the finding is linked to the fact that a significant number of children were from families in which women are the main wage earners and socialization agents.

Suggesting an aspect of personal health awareness and hygienic practice, both boys and girls viewed themselves as generally "more clean" at Time Two, although this difference could be called a significant response pattern for boys only. On the other hand, this early transition was associated with a significant increase in the self-perception of girls as "healthy"; the relationship was only slightly apparent for boys as they entered the early primary school years. The finding is particularly important given both the consistent finding of a lack of positive health orientation for males generally and the problem-plagued health findings for minority males specifically.

The response to "fear of things" appeared particularly gender-linked. Although not significant for either boys or girls, boys generally demonstrated a decrease in their stated "fear of things." The reverse was evident for girls. They indicated a pattern of increased fearfulness. On the other hand, although the overall mean score for girls was lower on the attribute "attractiveness," it did not decrease further at Time Two. However, the reverse was true for males and, in fact, represented a patterned response. Boys viewed themselves as much more attractive at Time Two. The mean change approached significance for boys as they made the transition into the early primary grades.

Findings from the Academic and Personal-Social Self-Concept Measure (Primary Self-Concept, Mueller and Leonetti, 1974)

In general, there was a patterned decrease discernible in the mean score for the "Student Self Dimension" for male youths at Time Two; that is, in general, boys saw themselves as *less competent* as students when compared with African-American girls. Measures for girls indicated a slight pattern for an increase in "student self" perception. The general trend for a lowered "student self" at Time Two was more pronounced for the older transition group, indicating an unmistakable decrease in academic self-esteem as African-American youth are entering adolescence.

Similarly, for the dimension "intellectual self," boys show somewhat of a pattern for lower scores. Importantly, although there is no change for girls, the overall effect appears to be contributed to by the older transition youth: The *decrease* in "intellectual self" for youth entering adolescence was highly significant. On the other hand, relative to the "personal/social self," females demonstrated a slight pattern for a lower self-evaluation, which was not evident for boys. These findings suggest a particular "youthful state" for early adolescent African-Americans as they begin their transition into puberty.

Discussion of First Longitudinal Study Themes

This research points to specific aspects of the development of African-American males that are relevant to the creation of intervention programs. First is the discrepancy between the youths' more *general* self-esteem, as opposed to their *specific* perception of their "student selves." Second is the issue of health consciousness.

The findings reported suggest that the transition into primary school for African-American children is associated with perceptions of self as having "a lot of ability." This finding is consistent with previous research that suggests the important "inoculating" or protective role of African-American families (see Spencer, 1983). Further, as supported by research findings on social cognitive development and "self-representational" processes (see Spencer, 1982), the Black child's normal experience of cognitive egocentrism appears to serve as a psychological protector against low self-esteem. While low self-esteem has been assumed to be directly linked with minority status, that assumption has not withstood empirical tests (see Spencer, 1988). In comparison studies with nonminority youth, African-American children consistently show positive self-esteem.

On the other hand, boys showed an increase from Time One to Time Two in overall mean self-esteem and in the qualities "happy," "having a lot of ability," and "more clean." On the the other hand, they showed a decline in measure of both "student self" and "intellectual self." The trend for a lower mean score for both "student self" and "intellectual self" was even more apparent for the older transition group than for the younger. Whereas positive perceptions of general ability appear to be in place quite early, the more specific perception of competence in school seems to be increasingly eroded the longer African-American males remain enrolled in traditional American schools. The observations underscores the salience of recent speculations by Fordham and Ogbu (1988).

The pattern for girls shows more consistency between perceptions of self as "having a lot ability" and "student self"; increases in perceptions of both ability and "student self" are apparent for African-American girls. The findings appear consistent with data compiled by Irvine (1990) and Washington (1988), who suggest that African-American girls experience fewer school-based problems than African-American boys. The boys may be more often viewed and interacted with—especially given media-supported stereotypes—as "dangerous [short adult] males" as opposed to "education-seeking" youth.

Significant gender differences were evident for the "perception of self as healthy"; boys' scores were significantly lower than girls'. It is important to ask whether this early pattern of health orientation and awareness has implications for the consistent differences observed in mortality and morbidity rates between males and females across the life course.

Given the special health needs and problems of minority group males, the issue has important program and policy implications and is presently being investigated by the authors. More specifically, the current project is a longitudinal study of nearly six hundred subjects—mainly male early and middle adolescent youth—who are being followed into early adulthood. The project examines the development of competence and resilience of African-American boys (Spencer, 1988).

Longitudinal Research Project: Two

Design and Methods

In the design of the second longitudinal, five-year project, approximately three thousand youth across four middle schools in a large, southeastern urban city completed a twenty-minute self-report survey. From this pool of subjects, 562 students were randomly selected from the school rolls and given parental permission forms for continued project participation. The original sample consisted of 390 boys and 172 girls in sixth, seventh, and eighth grades. Due to the high retention rate for Blacks in the several school districts, initially, the participants' ages ranged from eleven to fifteen years (they are currently fifteen- to nineteen-year-olds).

Out of the four schools, active consent was obtained for over eighty percent of subjects in two of the schools; the other two schools had return rates above seventy percent. Three of the four schools have student populations that are over ninety percent African-American, with over sixty percent in the fourth school. The data were collected during the 1989 to 1990 academic year. From self-report family income information, it was determined that 58 percent of the subjects' families met federal poverty guidelines (that is for a family size of four, the criterion for poverty was annual family income of $13,950 or under).

Instruments

Each student was given three surveys and an adolescent interview during the school year. The Personal Attributes Questionnaire (PAQ) was part of a survey. The surveys were administered in a group setting with a proctor reading each question aloud while monitors walked about to answer questions and to make sure that students answered at the same speed that the proctor read. The Racial Attitude Identity Scale (RAIS) and the Machismo Measure were given as part of the individually administered interview.

The (PAQ) was used to measure sex-role development. The PAQ is a self-report subscaled instrument that taps limited types of abstract personality traits that stereotypically have been shown to be gender-differentiating (Spence, Helmrech and Stapp, 1975). It consists of three eight-item scales. The PAQMAS scale may be described as containing socially desirable expressive traits more characteristic of men than of women. The PAQFEM scale is described by the original authors as containing socially desirable expressive traits more characteristic of women than of men. The PAQMF scale contains items for which social desirability differs for the two sexes. In content, the PAQMF scale contains two instrumental items (aggressive and dominant), the other items suggesting (lack of) emotional vulnerability.

Racial identity is measured by The Racial Attitude Identity Scale (Parham and Helms, 1981). The thirty-item scale assesses attitudes associated with four stages of Black identity development (preencounter, encounter, immersion-emersion, and internalization). Preencounter represents a pro-White/anti-Black perspective and is conceptualized as stage one. The encounter stage is characteristic of social experiences associated with a transition from anti-Black cultural beliefs. The immersion stage, conceptualized as stage three, represents a reactively Afrocentric individual; one who is strictly pro-Black while simultaneously withdrawing from other ethnic groups. The fourth and final stage, internalization, typifies an own-group orientation with a more pluralistic, nonracist perspective of others.

To assess a bravado attitude or hypermasculinity orientation, the Machismo Measure was used. The Machismo inventory consists of thirty forced-choice items designed to measure the three components of the macho personality constellation (callous sex attitudes, violence as manly, and danger as exciting) with ten items each. Examples of items, reflecting the above order with the macho alternative listed first, are: (a) get a girl drunk, high, or hot and she'll let you do whatever you want; or: It's gross and unfair to use alcohol or drugs to convince a woman to have sex; (b) I still enjoy remembering my first real fight; or: I hope to forget the fights that I've been in; (c) I like to drive fast, right on the edge of danger; or: I like to drive safely, avoiding all possible risks.

Second (Adolescent) Longitudinal Study Results

Adolescent males who exhibit less socially appropriate male traits and/or devalue female traits have higher bravado attitudes as their age increases. Correlations between a supermasculine (machismo) attitude and socially appropriate masculine (PAQMAS) and feminine (PAQFEM) orientations were statistically significant ($r = -.14$, $p < .01$); $r = -.22$, $p < .001$, respectively). Subscales of machismo attitudes (callousness towards women, danger as exciting, and violence as manly) were correlated with sex-role attitudes. Significant correlations were found between the machismo and the sex-role subscales.

Callous attitudes were negatively correlated with both socially appropriate male orientations ($r = -.23$, $p < .001$) and males who devalue feminine traits ($r = -.22$, $p < .001$). Significant correlations were found between negative male and female traits (PAQMF) and ideas of violence as manly ($r = .15$, $p < .01$). Youth who viewed danger as exciting also devalued feminine roles ($r = -.14$, $p < .01$). In the same manner, there were trend results for males with less socially appropriate male sex-role traits ($r = -.09$, $p < .10$).

Correlations between bravado attitudes and racial identity suggest that boys use reactive forms of coping. Specifically, the correlation between an overall machismo score and immersion racial attitudes (that is, "reactive/racist" Afrocentricity) was significant ($r = .22$, p < .001). Significant results were found between immersion and each of the machismo subscales: Violence as manly and immersion, $r = .19$, p < .001; danger as exciting and immersion, $r = .14$, p < .01; and callous sex attitudes towards women and immersion, $r = .18$, p < .001. Similar significant results are noted with preencounter attitudes having positive correlations with machismo and each of the related subscales. In correlating the racial identity scales with machismo subscales, the data show internalization (that is, culturally pluralistic) racial attitudes as having a significant, inverse relationship with machismo ($r = -.14$, p < .01), danger ($r = -.13$, p < .01), and callous attitudes ($r = -.16$, p < .01). Evidence of more pluralistic, positive racial attitudes as associated with less reactive sex-role attitudes is noted with the positive correlation between PAQMAS (positive masculine values) and internalization ($r = .18$, p < .001) and a reverse relationship with preencounter attitudes ($r = -.19$, p < .001).

Age was correlated with bravado attitudes and sex-role orientations. Significant results were found between age and males who expressed less socially appropriate attitudes ($r = -.15$, p < .01). Trend results were obtained between age and a general bravado attitude ($r = .13$, p < .10), the violence as manly subscale ($r = .13$, p < .10), and the callous sex attitudes subscale ($r = .09$, p < .10).

Multiple regression analyses were used to determine whether overly assertive or exaggerated masculine attitudes (bravado) could be predicted from respondent's orientation of sex roles. Males who devalued the female role expressed an exaggerated "macho" attitude ($t = -2.90$, p < .01), had more callous attitudes about girls ($t = -2.0$, p < .05), and tended to associate violence with being a man ($t = -3.3$, p < .01). The notion that violence is manly increased with age for males ($t = 2.2$), p < .05). Similarly, a positive trend is noted with age for those reporting that they found danger to be exciting (p < .09).

Since age appeared to have an effect on all bravado subscale scores, it was used as a dependent variable. The overall model with bravado variables as predictors was significant, $F(3, 6.19)$, p < .05. Specifically, boys with less socially appropriate male attitudes obtained higher ($t = -2.00$, p < .05) bravado scores.

Discussion of Second Longitudinal Study Themes

A life course developmental perspective was used to assess the relationship of personality attributes with sex-role and ethnic identity formation. Adaptive strategies are required for coping and psychological survival due to the contextual experiences of impoverished African-Americans. Though these strategies are relevant across the life course, the possible problematic consequences are of particular salience during adolescence.

The analyses suggest that the relationship between personality attributes and bravado coping attitudes are more salient for older youth, although influential in the formation of overly assertive male attitudes for all adolescent males. The analyses offer support for Erikson's theory of identity formation, which suggests that experiences prior to adolescence appear influential for attitude formation. Consequently, exaggeration of male coping attitudes is more salient as boys get older, accrue more life experiences, and form adult identities. Additionally, males who develop accepting orientations for the social roles of males (PAQ-MAS) and of females (PAQFEM) exhibit more pluralistic racial identity attitudes.

Hypermasculine coping attitudes associated with behaviors that devalue socially acceptable feminine orientations included callous sex attitudes and violence as manly beliefs; in addition, danger as exciting approached significance. Each of these have implications for school experiences, male/female relationships and ultimately life course decisions.

Moreover, these results suggest that boys grow up in a society where men express callous attitudes towards women. These chauvinistic attitudes are seen at the trend level for boys who express socially appropriate male behaviors. Furthermore, high-profile media events and recent court decisions seem to support these attitudes (for instance, the Clarence Thomas hearings and the William Kennedy Smith rape trial). American society accepts that men who seemingly express overt socially appropriate male behaviors and have middle-class actions and values can treat women in a derogatory manner; but such acceptance is not consistent across economic status.

One of the most striking results was the finding of violence as manly as a coping style. Boys' responses that devalued the female role, and maturation (growing older) were the best predictors of a violence as manly coping style. Moreover, the statistical trend suggests that even boys who express socially appropriate male traits (PAQMAS) view violence as manly, whether exaggerated sex-role attributes exist or not. This stereotype of manhood is frequently expressed in American society. Consequently, boys are being reared to perceive manhood as incorporating a series of violent acts. Such perceptions, however, may not emanate from the home, but from outside influences such as television, school, and peer groups. However, youths' home experiences with significant role models may serve as a deterrent.

In sum, adolescent males who exhibit less socially appropriate male traits and/or devalue female traits have higher machismo attitudes which increase with age. These attitudes are influenced by contextual experiences and are expressed as male youths arrive at their personal identity as men.

It is important to note that gender biases are prevalent in the experiences of adolescents and are compounded by their cognitive awareness of racial biases. The relationship between high immersion and machismo attitudes has implications for future academic and psychosocial outcomes, particularly for males among this age group. Because immersion attitudes represent a celebration of one's own race with the total exclusion of other races, consequently association with "outside" groups will be met with much resistance. This particular ethnic attitude, in conjunction with a devaluing attitude toward more traditional female roles, place such youth at extreme risk for poor academic experiences and maladaptive life course outcomes.

For example, since the public school system is primarily comprised of White female teachers, boys who devalue feminine behaviors and have anti-White attitudes may have a harder time respecting or cooperating with female authority figures. The result could be boys who are perceived by teachers and administrators as exhibiting problematic behaviors. It is apparent, however, that maintaining Eurocentric attitudes negatively influences the expression of socially acceptable male attributes. This insight appears critical for potentially offsetting negative academic and, ultimately, survival outcomes.

Reactive sex-role and racial attitudes represent two coping strategies for functioning in an environment perceived to threaten one's sense of competence or violate one's trust. This is exacerbated for males living in households with limited financial resources. They are burdened with the same sex-role expectations imposed upon all adolescent males, along with the promise of a better life. However, lacking is societal evidence to support the attainability of an improved quality of life. In essence, unemployment remains high, businesses in the Black community remain sparse, and legitimate apprenticeship, mentoring, and work opportunities for African-American adolescents remain limited. Social, educational, economic, and health policy recommendations could benefit from the findings described, and from research efforts generally that take more normative and contextualized approaches to understanding minority youths' development.

Future research on males should examine the effects of gender and racial identity processes on manifested behavioral outcomes and health risks. More carefully designed projects and associated findings would offer policy makers, practitioners, and research scientists an enhanced understanding about coping strategies and adaptive processes used by adolescents to offset threats to their sense of competence.

References

Anderson, E. C., 1990. *Street Wise: Race, Class and Change in an Urban Community.* Chicago: University of Chicago Press.

Biller, H. B., 1968. "A Note on Father Absence and Masculine Development in Lower-class Negro and White boys." *Child Development* 39 (3), 1003–1006.

Bronfenbrenner, U., 1989. "Ecological Systems Theory," *Annals of Child Development.* Greenwich: JAI Press.

Cazenave, N. A., 1984. "Race, Socioeconomic Status, and Age: The Social Context of American Masculinity." *Sex Roles* 11, 639–656.

Chestang, L., 1972. "The Dilemma of Biracial Adoptions." *Social Work* 17, 100–105.

Coates, D. L., 1987. "Gender Differences in the Structure and Support Characteristics of Black Adolescents' Social Networks." *Sex Roles* 17, 667–687.

Cooley, C. H., 1902. *Human Nature and the Social Order.* New York: Charles Scribner's Sons.

Erikson, E., 1959. "Identity and the Life Cycle." *Psychological Issues,* 1, 1–171.

Erikson, E., 1968. *Identity, Youth and Crisis.* New York: Norton.

Erikson, E., 1980. *Identity and the Life Cycle: A Reissue.* New York: Norton.

Erwin, P., 1993. *Friendship and Peer Relations in Children.* New York: Wiley and Sons.

Fordham, S. and Ogbu, J. U., 1988. "Black Students School Success: Coping with the Burden of Acting White." *Urban Review* 18, 176–206.

Franklin, C. W., 1985. "The Black Male Urban Barbershop as a Sex-Role Socialization Setting." *Sex Roles* 12, 965–979.

Freud, A., 1936. *The Ego and Mechanisms of Defense.* New York: International University Press.

Freud, S., 1949. *An Outline of Psychoanalysis.* New York: International University Press.

Gibbs, J. T. and Hines, A. M., 1989. "Factors Related to Sex Differences in Suicidal Behavior among Black Youth: Implications for Intervention and Research." *Journal of Adolescent Research* 4 (2), 152–171.

Gibbs, J. T., Huang, L. N., *et al.,* eds., 1989. *Children of Color.* San Francisco: Jossey-Bass.

Hare, B. R. and Castenell, L. A. Jr., 1985. "No place to run, no place to hide: comparative status and future prospects of Black boys," in *Beginnings: the Social and Affective Development of Black Children.* Eds. Spencer, M. B., Brookins, J. K., Allen W. R. Hillsdale: Erlbaum.

Hare, N. and Hare, J., 1987. *Bringing the Black Boy to Manhood: The Passage.* San Francisco: Black Think Tank.

Hannerz, U., 1969. *Soulside: Inquires into Ghetto Culture and Community.* New York: Columbia University Press.

Hetherington, E. M., Cox, M., Cox, R., 1985. "Long-term Effects of Divorce and Remarriage on the Adjustment of Children," *Journal of American Academy of Psychiatry* 24, 578–530.

Irvine, J. J., 1990. *Black Students and School Failure.* New York: Greenwood Press.

Kagan, J., 1958. "The Concept of Identification." *Psychological Review* 65, 296–305.

Kohlberg, L., 1966. "A Cognitive-Development Analysis of Children's Sex-Role Concepts and Attitudes," in *The Development of Sex Differences* (pp. 82–113). ed. Maccoby, E. Stanford: Stanford University Press.

Ladner, J. A., 1972. *Tomorrow's Tomorrow: The Black Woman.* New York: Doubleday Press.

Majors, R. and Billson, J. M., 1992. *Cool Pose: The Dilemmas of Black Manhood in America.* New York: Lexington Books.

Markstrom-Adams and Spencer, 1994. "A Model for Identity Intervention with Minority Adolescents," in S. Archer, ed., *Interventions for Adolescent Identity Development.* Newbury Park, Sage Publications.

McCandless B. R. and Evans, F. D., 1973. *Children and Youth: Psychosocial Development.* Detroit: Dryden Press.

Mead, G. H., 1934. *Mind, Self and Society.* Chicago: University of Chicago Press.

Millham, J. and Smith, L. E., 1981. "Sex-Role Differentiation among Black and White Americans: A Comparative Study." *Journal of Black Psychology* 7(2), 77–90.

Mishel, W., 1966. "A Social Learning View of Sex Differences in Behavior," in *The Development of Sex Differences* (pp. 56–81). ed. Maccoby E. Palo Alto: Stanford University Press.

Mosher, D. L. and Sirkin, M., 1984. "Measuring in a Macho Personality Constellation." *Journal of Research in Personality* 18, 150–164.

Mueller, D. G. and Leonetti, R., 1974. *The Primary Self-Concept Inventory Test Manual.* Boston: Teaching Resources, Inc.

Parham, T. A. and Helms, J. E., 1981. "The Influence of Black Student's Racial Identity Attitudes on Preferences for Counselor's Race." *Journal of Counseling Psychology* 28, 250–257.

Perkins, E., 1975. *Home is a Dirty Street* Chicago: Third World.

Phinney, J. S. and Rotheram, M. J. eds., 1987. *Children's Ethnic Socialization.* Newbury Park: Sage Publications.

Rubin, R. H., 1981. "Attitudes about Male-Female Relations among Black Adolescents." *Adolescence* 16(61), 159–174.

Rubin, R. H., 1974. "Adult Male Absence and the Self-Attitudes of Black Children." *Child Study Journal,* 4(1), 33–46.

Secretary's Task Force on Black and Minority Health. 1986. Washington, DC: U.S. Government Printing Office.

Sherif, M. and Sherif, C. W., 1953. *Groups in Harmony and Tension: An Integration of Studies in Intergroup Relations.* New York: Harper and Row.

Spence, J. T., Helmreich, R. L., and Stapp, J., 1975. "Ratings of Self and Peers on Sex Role Attributes and their Relation to Self-Esteem and Conceptions of Masculinity and Femininity." *Journal of Personality and Social Psychology* 32, 29–39.

Spencer, M. B., 1982. "Preschool Children's Social Cognition and Cultural Cognition: A Cognitive Developmental Interpretation of Race Dissonance Findings." *Journal of Psychology* 112, 275–296.

Spencer, M. B., 1983. "Children's Cultural Values and Parental Child Rearing Strategies." *Developmental Review* 4, 351–370.

Spencer, M. B., 1984. "Resilience and Vulnerability: Black Children's Evolving Self and Society," In *Congressional Black Caucus Foundation Research Conference*. Washington, D.C.

Spencer, M. B., 1988. "Self-Concept Development," in *Perspectives in Black Child Development: New Directions in Child Development* (pp. 59–72). Ed. D. T. Slaughter. San Francisco: Jossey-Bass Press.

Spencer, M. B., 1994. "Old Issue and New Theorizing about African American Youth: A Phenomenological Variant of Ecological Systems Theory," in R. L. Taylor, ed., *African American Youth: Their Social and Economic Status in the United States*. New York: Praeger Publishers.

Spencer, M. B. and Dornbush, S. M., 1990. "Challenges in Studying Minority Youth," in *At the Threshold: The Developing Adolescent*, ed. S. S. Feldman, G. R. Elliott. Cambridge, MA: Harvard University Press.

Spencer, M. B. and Markstrom-Adams, C., 1990. "Identity Processes among Racial and Ethnic Minority Children in America." *Child Development* 61(2), 290–310.

Spencer, M. B., Dobbs, B., and Swanson, D. P., 1988. "Afro-American Adolescents: Adaptational Processes and Socioeconomic Diversity in Behavioral Outcomes." *Journal of Adolescence* 11, 117–137.

Staples, R., 1978. "Masculinity and Race: The Dual Dilemma of Black Men." *Journal of Social Issues* 34 (1), 169–183.

Thomas, W. L., 1967. *The Thomas Self-Concept Values Test Manual*. Chicago: E. Clement Stone.

Taylor, R., 1989. "Black Youth, Role Models and the Social Constructions of Identity," in R. L. Jones Ed., *Black Adolescents*. Berkley, CA: Cobb and Henry Press.

Washington. V., 1988. "Historical and Contemporary Linkage Between Black Child Development and Social Policy." *New Directions for Child Development* 42, 93–105.

Wilson, W. J., 1987. *The Truly Disadvantaged*. Chicago: University of Chicago Press.

Wingard, D. L., 1987. "Social, Behavioral and Biological Factors Influencing the Sex Differential in Longevity." Background paper prepared for the National Institute on Aging. Washington, DC: U.S. Government Printing Office.

3

In Search Of Blackness and Afrocentricity: The Psychology of Black Identity Change

William E. Cross, Jr.

Introduction

In this chapter we are going to discuss the stages of Black identity change. Of course, it is possible for a Black person to be socialized from early childhood through adolescence to have a Black identity. At adulthood, such persons are not likely to be in need of change; that is, they do not need to "discover" their Blackness, for it is already a fully developed aspect of their psyche. Not everyone is so fortunate. Many African-Americans will experience a dramatic shift in their identity *after* they have reached adolescence or *after* they have become adults. We refer to this as the psychology of *Nigrescence*. Nigrescence is a French word that means the process of becoming Black, and over the last twenty years, Black researchers have been able to map out the four or five stages Black people go through when they tear down their "old" identity and replace it with one that is more Black-oriented. Such people grow up with a "non-Black identity," or the identity to be changed (stage one), then they have some sort of experience or *encounter* (stage two) that makes them feel they need to change; next they plunge into an intense period, during which the the old and new identities are at war (stage three), and finally, if all goes well, they grow comfortable with their new sense of self (stage four), and may even dedicate themselves to helping solve problems in the community (stage five). Elsewhere (Cross, 1991), I have labeled these five stages *Preencounter; Encounter; Immersion-Emersion; Internalization;* and *Internalization-Commitment.*

Stage One: Preencounter

Preencounter—low salience attitudes: Persons in the Preencounter Stage hold attitudes toward race that range from low salience, race neutrality, to anti-Black. In the case of persons who hold *low salience* views, they do not deny being physically Black, but this "physical" fact is thought to play an insignificant role in their everyday life. Being Black and knowledge about the Black experience has little to do with their *perceived* sense of happiness and well-being, and it (Blackness) contributes little to their purpose in life. In a sense, preencounter persons place value in things *other* than their Blackness; it may be their religion, their lifestyle, their social status, their profession, and so on. Thus, they *do* have values and they *do* experience meaningful existence, but little emphasis is given to Blackness. As long as their preencounter attitudes bring them a sense of fulfillment, meaningful existence, and an internal sense of stability, order, and harmony, such persons will not likely be in need of any type of identity change, let alone movement toward Afrocentricity.

Some low salience types have not given much thought to race issues, and appear dumbfounded and naïve during such discussions. They often see personal progress as a problem of free will, individual initiative, rugged individualism, and the personal motivation to achieve. Others have taken a more conscious route toward neutrality and see themselves as having reached a higher plane (that is, abstract humanism), beneath which lies what they see as the vulgar world of race and ethnicity. When pressed to give a self-referent, they may respond that they are "human beings who happen to be Black," or, "I am an American who happens to be Black."

Preencounter—social stigma attitudes: A variant of the low salience perspective can be found in the Black person who, while sharing the low salience orientation, also sees race as a problematic or stigma. Thus, race, by default, is attributed some significance, not as a proactive force or cultural issue, but as a social stigma that must be negotiated from time to time. The only "meaning" accorded race is its tie to issues of *social discrimination;* from this perspective, race is a hassle, a problem, a vehicle of imposition. Such people may have a surface interest in Black causes, not as a way of supporting Black culture and the exploration of Black history, but in joining with those who are trying to destroy the social stigma associated with Blackness. The need to defend oneself against Blackness as stigma can be found in preencounter persons who otherwise have very little knowledge of Black history and culture. Consequently, when you ask such people to define their Black identity, they invariably respond by telling you what it is like to be oppressed.

Preencounter—antiblack attitudes: The extreme racial attitude pattern to be found within the Preencounter Stage is anti-Blackness. There are some Blacks for whom being Black is very important, not as a positive force, *but as a negative reference group*. Blackness and Black people define their internal model of what they dislike. They look out upon Black people with a perspective that comes very close to that which one might expect to find in the thinking of White racists. Anti-Black Blacks loath other Blacks, they feel alienated from them and they do not see Blacks or the Black community as a potential or actual source of personal support. Their vision of Blackness is dominated by negative, racist stereotypes, and on the other side of the coin, they may hold positive racial stereotypes of White people and White culture. In viewing Black people to be their own worst enemy, anti-Black Blacks often explain the "race problem" through the prism of some variant of the "victim-blame perspective." When in positions of leadership, anti-Black Blacks can be very effective in weaving an ideology that bashes Black leaders, Black institutions, Black studies, the Black family, and Black culture.

Thus, the first stage, Preencounter, covers a broad range of attitudes from low salience, and Blackness as stigma, to the extreme of anti-Blackness and self-hatred. These preencounter tendencies may be combined with other characteristics, such as varying levels of miseducation; a Eurocentric cultural frame of reference; *Spotlight* or "Race-Image" Anxiety; and assimilationist attitudes.

Miseducation: In being formally educated to embrace a Western cultural-historical perspective, preencounter Blacks cannot help but experience varying degrees of miseducation about the significance of the Black experience. In fact, preencounter Blacks are frequently "average" products of a formal education system that is very White-oriented. One reason the need for Nigrescence is so common in the Black community is that it is very difficult for *any* Black American to progress through the public schools without being miseducated about the role of Africa in the origin of Western civilization and world culture, and the role of Blacks in the evolution of American culture and history in particular. This miseducation does not automatically lead to self-hatred, but it most certainly can distort how Black people discuss Black cultural and historical issues. Preencounter Blacks do not oppose Black Studies because of some "unconscious anti-Black or self-hatred complex"; rather, their *cultural bias* blinds them to the fact that there are other histories besides "American History"; that there are other cultural experiences besides "Western civilization." The most damning aspect of miseducation is not necessarily poor mental health, but the development of a worldview and cultural-historical perspective which can block one's knowledge about, and thus one's capacity to advocate and embrace, the cultural, political, economic, and historical interests of Black people.

Anti-Black Blacks suffer from the type of extreme miseducation which, in fact, *can* result in self-hatred. They tend to have a very distorted interpretation of Black history and thus a very distorted image of the historical, cultural, economic, and political *potential* of Black people. They believe that Black people came from a strange, uncivilized, "dark" continent, and that slavery was a civilizing experience. From their vantage point, there is nothing to be gained from the study of the slavery period—thus, "real" Black history begins at the end of the Civil War. Amongst poor Blacks, anti-Black Blacks actually develop the belief that Blacks somehow deserve the misery that comes with poverty. Extreme miseducation can result in a great deal of skepticism about the abilities and capacities of Black leaders, Black businesses, and Black professionals, and an equal degree of romanticization and near mysticism concerning the capacities and talents of Whites. That is, if Blacks are thought to be intellectually inferior and technologically backward, Whites are seen as intellectually superior and technically mystical.

Eurocentric cultural perspective: As a further extension of the miseducation concept, we note that preencounter persons have frequently been socialized to favor a Eurocentric cultural perspective. It is a perspective in which notions of beauty and art are derived from a White and decidedly Western aesthetic, as reflected in the content, themes, vehicles of emphasis, colorations, and modes of expressions in numerous cultural and academic preferences. Afrocentricists frequently interpret the preencounter person's preference for Western art as an expression of self-hatred, but this is in error. In rare instances, some preencounter Blacks have been raised in a manner that leaves them nearly ignorant of the existence of any other than Eurocentric cultural perspectives. However, most preencounter persons have been socialized to be *bicultural;* that is they know about and sometimes appreciate both Black and White artistic expressions. However, the low salience person, in particular, is more likely to give higher status to Western art. For example, preencounter parents tend to socialize their children to place greater emphasis on "high culture," or "classical art forms" (that is, ballet, classical music, modern dance, and so on), while classes in jazz, African dance, and Black literature are seldom considered. Although they may personally enjoy Black music and art, they may depict Black art as that which is "ethnic," "lowly," "less important," and something to be lost along the way toward acceptance and assimilation into the mainstream. Thus, it is not always the case that preencounter Blacks lack knowledge about or experience with Black art; rather, what separates them from people in more advanced states of Blackness are the *attitudes* they hold toward Black art forms, and the priority and preferences they accord Western versus Black art.

Anti-Black Blacks take the pro-White cultural bias to an extreme and wrongly put White and Black art on the same continuum, with White art defining that which is positive, rational, and highly developed, and Black art connoting that which is exotic, emotional, and primitive. Thus, classical music, ballet and Western theater define "good art," while jazz, the blues, African dance, and so on, are seen as interesting but less well developed, if not primitive and inferior imitations of (White) classical artistic expression. In its more vulgar expression, anti-Black Blacks may even prefer light skin, "flow" hair and European facial features.

Finally, it would be a mistake to think that this is solely a "problem of the Black middle class." Even in the inner city or "ghetto," where purer forms of Black expression can readily be found, one discovers the inner-city resident referring to the blues or jazz as something low, bad, or sexy. Sometimes such descriptions capture the Black urban resident's notion of that which is earthy, funky, and soulful, but at other times the terms suggest a negative perspective toward Black art, Black life, and Black culture. The "White is fine" attitude can be found in preencounter persons of varied socioeconomic standings.

Spotlight or race image anxiety: Most Black people, with the exception of those who are anti-Black in perspective, manage to keep from internalizing extremely negative stereotypes that racist Whites have of Black people. But while preencounter Blacks do not believe in these stereotypes, they are often overly sensitive to the fact that many White people *do* accept such images. This can lead to a hypersensitivity toward racial issues in which one is constantly on the lookout for the portrayal of (negative) Black stereotypes. This sensitivity can help the person flush out instances of social discrimination and racism. However, there is also the irony that this "sensitivity" to discrimination and stereotypes can also lead to an anxiety over things being "too Black." Even though a preencounter person may be married to a Black person, and even though he or she may live in a Black community, there are times when the preencounter person feels that a situation is *too Black-oriented,* or "not integrated enough." Things are thought to get out of hand when Blacks act too loud or disorderly. I refer to this anxiety about being too Black as *"Spotlight Anxiety."* It is an anxiety which is often only felt when the person is in the company of Whites, or when the situation is somehow construed as being in the "spotlight." When Whites are around, the person may check him or herself to determine whether he or she, or some other Black who is present, is acting *too* Black, and thus failing to project the best *race image.*

Anti-Black Blacks are beyond any anxiety about the race's image; for them, the negative stereotypes White people hold in reference to Blacks are taken as truth. They feel enslaved in a body and community they hate. They feel nothing but a sense of imposition, alienation, and inferiority, and their sense of Blackness is clearly that of a mark of oppression.

Assimilation-integration: In being socialized to see the system as adequate, in suffering various degrees of miseducation about the origin of Black problems, and in having a basic faith in the system, preencounter Blacks are predisposed to accept a victim-blame analysis of Black problems, and a race-conflict-resolution perspective that stresses assimilationist-integration themes. They feel that if Blacks can "overcome" their own "self-made" problems, and become a part of the system, as they perceive has happened to previously disadvantaged (White ethnic) groups, the race problem could be solved. The message is generally framed with greater sophistication when articulated by well-educated preencounter Blacks, but it can be stated crudely by others. White racism is viewed as a surface-level problem, one that exist alongside the basic strengths and race-neutral opportunity structures and culture of the society. Once one has managed to work through discriminatory obstacles, so their thinking goes, the weight is on Blacks to prepare themselves in a fashion that will lead to their acceptance by Whites. The emphasis is on *one-way change* in which Blacks learn to fit in, while Whites are asked simply to stop discriminating. No real demands are placed on White attitudes, White culture, and White institutions, since, as stated previously, the problem of racism is at the surface level of White institutions and society. Consequently, unlike pluralistic notions of integration or concepts of multiculturalism, the preencounter Black is often wedded to an assimilationist vision of race-conflict-resolution and social mobility.

Summary: Whether of the low salience or anti-Black varieties, the spectrum of preencounter attitudes can be found among poor and well-to-do Blacks. Class status may affect how preencounter attitudes are expressed, but the central messages, priorities, or preferences embedded in both middle- and lower-class Black expressions are generally the same. Thus, low salience can be found in a middle-class Black professional for whom Blackness has little meaning, as it can in an inner-city resident whose primary vehicle for meaning and purpose in life is the Christian church. At the more negative extreme of preencounter, anti-Black Blacks can be the middle-class Black youth who has joined the ranks of a White-dominated, punk street group, or they can be found in the inner-city youth who, as a member of a "Black" street gang, pushes dope on other Black kids. Preencounter-oriented people can be rich or poor, light-skinned or ebony-hued, living in Vermont or in Harlem, attending overwhelmingly White schools or all-Black institutions.

In the past, oppression and miseducation have been the main factors determining the social production of preencounter attitudes. However, today we note that such attitudes are evolving as a result of the *success* of the Black sixties. In other words, Black success, as well as White oppression, can produce preencounter attitudes. Over the last twenty years, some Blacks *have* experienced, as nearly as possible, that which by any standard would be called success within the American system. They are rich, they live in exclusive communities and neighborhoods, they manage in and sometimes head major corporations, and their children attend the finest educational institutions money can buy. They are major contributors to organizations that advocate Western culture, and in the overall scheme of things, they are practically invisible to the Black world. Thus their success, and not experience with oppression, has led them to embrace preencounter attitudes. Of course, not all successful middle-class and wealthy Blacks can be categorized in this fashion. Besides, the point being made here is not the negative stereotyping of the wealthy and the middle class, but to remind the reader that preencounter attitudes in Black people can be caused by a variety of situations and circumstances. As is the case with all the stages, Preencounter is an attitude or perspective, not an inherited or divinely ordained trait, and people who come to share the same preencounter frame of reference do so through a variety of social experiences and circumstances, inclusive of instances of both success and oppression.

It would be a mistake to presume that preencounter is a form of mental illness. While anti-Black Blacks may very well evidence poor mental health, the great majority of preencounter Blacks are probably as mentally healthy as Blacks in the more advanced stages of Nigrescence. The key factors that separate preencounter Blacks from those who are Afrocentric is not mental illness, but value orientation, historical perspective, and worldview. Preencounter Blacks are part of the diversity of the Black experience and must be understood as such. The complexity of the American economy means that there are all sorts of ecological niches within which Blacks are socialized, and each of these niches may support the growth of unique ideas on what it means to be Black, including those which downplay Blackness altogether.

On the other hand, whenever life's circumstances result in the social production of a Black person for whom "race" has limited importance, or, in the case of the anti-Black Blacks, extremely negative meaning, the scene has been set for a possible identity conversion experience. Such people are "sitting ducks" for an encounter that may cause them to rethink their positions on Blackness.

Stage Two: Encounter

In most instances, the preencounter identity is the person's first identity, that is, the identity shaped by one's early development. This socialization has involved years of experiences with one's family, extended family, one's neighborhood and community, and one's schools, covering the periods of childhood, adolescence, and early adulthood. It is a tried and fully tested identity, which serves the person day in and day out. It helps the person feel centered, meaningful, and in control, by making life predictable. The person's identity filters incoming experiences so that the information "fits" into his or her current understanding of him or herself and the world in which he or she lives. Therefore, any fully developed identity, let alone a preencounter identity, is difficult to change.

Since the person's ongoing identity will defend against identity change, the person usually has to experience some sort of *encounter* that has the effect of catching the person off guard. The encounter must work around, slip through, or even *shatter* the relevance of the person's current identity and worldview, and at the same time provide some hint of the new direction the person must now take.

Sometimes the encounter can be a single, dramatic event. In the late 1960s, the death of Martin L. King, Jr., hurled thousands of preencounter Negroes into a search for a deeper understanding of the Black Power movement. Likewise, being personally assaulted, or witnessing a friend being assaulted by the police, televised reports of racial incidents, or discussions with a friend or loved one who is further advanced into his or her Blackness may "turn a person on" to her or his Blackness. Middle-class Blacks who have somehow managed to avoid or escape racial incidents at an earlier point in their life often begin Nigrescence after an unexpected racial episode in college, or still later, at their place of employment. Having worked so hard at being the "right kind of Negro," racist encounters can completely shatter a preencounter person's conception of him or herself, and his or her understanding of the state of Black America. For lower-class preencounter Blacks, encounters with the law and imprisonment can be a turning point. While on the street, doing his or her "thing," the preencounter Black may be oblivious to discussions about Blackness, but incarceration may so traumatize the person, that he or she becomes receptive to different interpretations of the meaning of his or her life. Malcolm X is the most famous of a long list of Black men and women whose search for Blackness followed on the heels of their imprisonment.

In many instances, it is not a single event that constitutes a person's encounter, but a series of smaller, eye-opening episodes, each of which chips away at the person's ongoing worldview. These small encounters have an accumulative effect, and at a certain point something happens to "break the camel's back," so to speak, and the person feels pushed toward becoming Black.

Looked at more closely, we see that the encounter entails two steps: first, experiencing the encounter, and second, personalizing it. By this two-step analysis, I mean to split a hair. That is to say, one must make the distinction between being in the path or being the object of an encounter event or activity, versus actually personalizing it or being "turned around by it." As a case in point, in April of 1968, not every Black person who first heard about the death of Martin Luther King,

Jr., was transformed into a Black Power advocate. They "experienced" the event, but it did not lead to metamorphosis. On the other hand, others, experiencing the same event (that is, hearing the news of King's death), were *personally traumatized* by this encounter, and it became the basis for calling into question the continued embracement of an "integrationist ethos." For them, the void created in doubting their current worldview was simultaneously filled by the increasing credibility of something called Blackness. Using a more contemporaneous example, two Blacks working in different but similar White-dominated corporations may each encounter a potentially powerful, racist situation. One may respond with the attitude that one must learn to "roll with the punches," while the other person may describe the event as having helped him or her see, for the very first time, that racism is still an important obstacle in life. *In effect, an encounter must personally impact the individual in a powerful way.* In the course of a year, let alone a lifetime, just about every Black person is exposed to information or some sort of racist situation which has the potential of an "encounter," but unless the person, for what ever the reason, personalizes the encounter, their ongoing worldview or attitudes about "race" may go unchanged. One last point; the encounter need not be negative, that is, a racist event. It may, instead, revolve around exposure to powerful cultural-historical information about the Black experience, previously unknown to the person. Giving credence to (that is, personalizing) this information may challenge the person to radically rethink his or her conception of Black history and Black culture. Even in such instances, however, a negative flavor of the encounter is often introduced, for it is almost inevitable that the person will quickly become enraged at the thought of having been "previously miseducated by white racist institutions."

While an encounter may eventually steer the person toward Nigrescence, the person's initial reaction may be one of confusion, alarm, and even depression. It can be a very painful experience to discover that one's frame of reference, worldview or value system is "wrong," "incorrect," "dysfunctional," or, more to the point, "not Black or Afrocentric enough." However, such reactions are generally temporary. Somehow the person picks himself or herself up, and he or she begins to cautiously and perhaps even fearfully test the validity of their new perceptions.

The encounter stirs up a great deal of emotionalism, such as *guilt, anger,* and *general anxiety.* On the one hand, the middle-class person feels guilty for having denied the significance of race; the lower-class person feels guilt and shame for having degraded Blackness through street-hustle and exploitation. Simultaneously, the person, regardless of class background, feels angry at those perceived to have "caused" their predicament—White people and all the White world. Furthermore, each person feels anxious at the discovery that there is another level of Blackness to which he or she should aspire. Inner-directed guilt, rage at White people, along with the anxiety about becoming the right kind of Black person, combine to form a psychic fuel or energy that flings the person into a frantic, determined, obsessive, extremely motivated search for Black identity. The preencounter person or "Negro" is dying, and the "Black American" or "Afrocentric" person is beginning to emerge.

Stage Three: Immersion-Emersion

During the first phase of Immersion-Emersion Stage, the person *immerses* him/herself in the world of Blackness. The person attends political or cultural meetings that focus on Black issues, joins new organizations and drops membership in preencounter groups, goes to Black rapping sessions, attends seminars and art shows that focus on Blackness or Afrocentricity. Everything of value must be Black or relevant to Africanity, for the person is being swept along by "a sea of Blackness." The experience is an immersion into Blackness and a liberation from Whiteness. The person perceives him or herself being uprooted from the old self, while drawn into a different experience. This immersion is a strong, powerful, dominating sensation, which is constantly being energized by rage (at White people and culture), guilt (at having once been tricked into thinking Negro ideas) and a third and new fuel, a developing sense of pride (in one's Black self, pride in Black people and pride in Black culture). Superhuman and supernatural expectations are conjured concerning anything Black. The person accepts his or her hair and brown skin, and one's very being is now "beautiful." That the person exists and is Black is an inherently wonderful thing. The person may spend a great deal of time developing an African and/or Black "urban" hairstyle, and such concerns are carried over to one's style of dress. Converts give themselves African names or drop their "American" names, as did Malcolm X; children are named after African heroes. Of course, an intense interest in "Mother Africa" becomes evident, and this is especially true of persons associated with the more contemporary variant of Nigrescence, the "Afrocentricity Movement." The label "Negro" is dropped, as a self-referent, and preference is given to Black, Black-American or African.

Black literature is passionately consumed, and, in some instances, people who never before had an interest in reading, teach themselves to read and write. In fact, their new orientation causes them to process all types of information that focus on the Black and African experience (film, press, radio). In a related development, a person or group may decide there is need for a new periodical, journal, newsletter, rap song, television program, and so on, in which case the person may try to produce a new information outlet that does justice to their emerging Black and Afrocentric perspective.

The new convert's attention may be drawn to other than political issues, and during the Immersion-Emersion Stage, some may experience a creative burst in which they feel "driven" to write poetry, essays, plays, rap songs, novels, and literary confessionals. A segment may turn to the plastic arts or painting. People who never before sought or experienced creative activity discover they are able to express themselves in a totally new mode. Established artists speak of a radical shift in the direction of their art, as happened to LeRoi Jones (Imamu Amiri Baraka) or Gwendolyn Brooks or Don L. Lee (Haki Mutabiti). In explaining this change, these artists state that although they were born to a Black situation, their overall socialization and artistic training caused them to look for inspiration and content *outside* the Black experience. For example, some wanted to be "pure" and "free," creating art for art's sake, or others admitted that their artistic sensibility was once decidedly Eurocentric. With the realization of their Blackness, the professional artist is awakened to a vast and new world of rich colors, powerful dramas, irony, rage, oppression, survival, and impossible dreams—and it is all there within reach. The artist (or scholar) has simply to look in the mirror (those familiar with the Black sixties will recall that the Black Arts Movement was one of the most powerful reflectors of Black identity change).

For new converts, confrontation, bluntness, directness, and an either/or mentality may be the primary mode of communications with other people, Black or White. This communication style is associated with the much discussed "Blacker-than-thou" syndrome. As a prelude to passing judgment on whether or not a person has the appropriate level of Blackness, Black people are classified into neat groups or categories such as "Uncle Tom," "militant," non-Afrocentric versus Afrocentric, "together," "soulful," "middle-class," "intellectual snob," and so on. Labeling and passing judgment on others helps the person clarify his or her own identity, but this name-calling, with its attendant ideological fractionation, can produce disastrous results, as in the Californian Black-Panther-versus-US murders of the sixties or the well-documented split between Malcolm X and the Nation of Islam. The more contemporary variant of Blacker-than-thou comes from the Afrocentricity movement, in which some converts see themselves being "more Afrocentric than others." They often describe Blacks who disagree with their perspective as insane, crazy, mentally ill, confused, unreliable, dangerous, and incapable of making a positive contribution to Black life. Often such converts mean well, as they merely seek the means of promoting greater consensus within the Black world, but their zeal for ideological correctness can lead to coercive and even fascist tactics.

The name-calling and Blacker-than-thou propensities are all part of the new convert's anxiety that his Blackness be "pure and acceptable." We can refer to this anxiety as *Weusi Anxiety*. *Weusi* is the Swahili word for Black, and *Weusi* Anxiety is the anxiety the new convert experiences, when one worries about being or becoming Black enough. Should the person be left to his or her own devices to work out all aspects of the identity crisis, such *Weusi* Anxiety could lead to considerable personal chaos. Generally, this is not the case, as most converts will seek and find the social support of others by joining certain organizations and groups. The groups joined provide a counterculture to the identity being replaced (the "Negro" or non-Afrocentric identity), by entangling the person in membership requirements, symbolic dress codes, rites, rituals, obligations, and reward systems that nurture and reinforce the emerging, new (Black or Afrocentric) identity. This can lead to a great deal of conformity on the part of the new recruit. In fact, it is one of the paradoxes of conversion that, while rebelling against the larger society, the new convert may willingly conform to a number of the demands of certain Black organizations. Again, we should keep in mind that the person's new identity is still emerging and has not been internalized; consequently, the person is anxious to be put in a position which allows him or her to demonstrate, in some fashion, that he or she is developing into the "right kind" of Black person.

Much that goes into the demonstration of one's level of Blackness takes place within the confines and privacy of Black organizations, and is part of the overall theme of the Immersion-Emersion Stage, involving the need to turn inward, while simultaneously withdrawing from everything perceived as being or representing the White world. Yet, ironically, there also develops a need to confront the "man" as a means of dramatizing, concretizing, or proving one's Blackness. The confrontation, especially for Black leaders, is a manhood (or womanhood) ritual—a baptismal or purification rite. Carried to its extreme, the impulse is to confront White people in authority, frequently the police, on a life-or-death basis. Such impulses tend not to define reality and action. Brothers and Sisters *dream* about or give a heavy rap about the need for physical combat, but daydreams and rhetoric are about as far as it goes.

Most converts do not get involved with paramilitary activities. Instead, the episodes of hatred they may feel toward Whites during the Immersion-Emersion Stage are worked through as daydreams or fantasies, such as the urge to rip off the first White person one passes on a particular day. During Immersion-Emersion, "kill Whitey" fantasies appear to to be experienced by Blacks—regardless of age, sex, or class background. Persons who fixate or stagnate at this point in their development are said to have a "pseudo"-Black identity because it is based on the hatred and negation of White people, rather than the affirmation of a pro-Black perspective, which *includes* commitment to the destruction of racism, but not the random killing of Whites.

Finally we note that, during this transition period, the person experiences a surge in altruism. A constant theme of selflessness, dedication, and commitment to the (Black) group is evident; the person feels overwhelming *love and attachment* to all that is Black. The person's main focus in life becomes this feeling of togetherness and oneness with the people. It is a religiouslike feeling, and clusters of new converts can create an atmosphere in which Blackness or Africanity has a spiritual and religious quality.

The first part of this transition stage is *immersion* into Blackness, an experience in which the person feels almost driven and compelled to act, think, and feel in a certain way. People are not out of control during immersion, but they often look back upon the episode as something akin to a *happening*, as if Blackness were an outside force or spirit that was permeating, if not invading, their being. The second part of the stage is *emergence* from the emotionality and dead-end, either/or, racist, and oversimplified ideological aspects of the immersion experience. The person begins to level off, and feel in control of his or her emotions and intellect. In fact, the person cannot continue to handle the intense emotional phases and concentrated affect levels associated with conversion, and is predisposed to find ways to level off.

Frequently, this leveling off is facilitated by a combination of the person's own growth, in conjunction with the person's observation that certain role models or heroes appear to be operating from the vantage point of a more advanced state of identity development. The first hint of this advanced state may be discovered during face-to-face interactions with role models who evidence a calmer, more sophisticated quality to their Blackness, or the person may infer it from having read the life and times of a person such as Malcolm X, in which Malcolm depicts moving *beyond* a rigid sense of Blackness, as a consequence of his experiences in Mecca. The story of how one gets over the hump of Immersion is likely to differ from person to person, but however it occurs, it results in the discovery that one's first impressions of Blackness can be romantic and symbolic, rather than substantive, textured, and complex. In fact, the person may find him or herself pulling away from membership in organizations whose activities seem designed to help one feel immersed in Blackness, and toward memberships in and associations with groups or persons who are demonstrating a more serious understanding of Black issues. When the grip of the immersion phase loosens, when the convert begins to comprehend immersion as a period of transition rather than a final point of development, and when the convert seems to understand that continued growth, perhaps of a less emotional nature, lies ahead, the person has reached the end of the transition stage, and is moving toward internalization of the new identity.

Negative consequences of transition: The previous paragraph depicts a person headed toward continued identity development. We should understand, however, that the ups and downs of the transition stage can very well result in regression, fixation, or stagnation, as well as forward movement. The events of the Immersion-Emersion Stage can inspire or frustrate an individual. Consequently, the degree of a person's continued involvement in Black affairs may prove significant or negligible. During the transition stage, the person embraces idealistic, if not superhuman, expectations about anything Black, in which case minimal reinforcement (when you are attracted to something, it does not take a great deal of reinforcement to sustain that interest) may carry the person over into advanced identity development (evolution into the next stage). On the other hand, failure to meet these expectancies may break the person's spirit and desire to change, in which case regression becomes a real possibility. For others, intense and negative encounters with White racists leads to their becoming fixated at Stage Three. They get stuck in a never-ending state of militancy and hatred. In still a third scenario, people may give all the appearance of having grown beyond the boundaries of the Immersion-Emersion Stage, that is, their behavior and attitudes suggest a great deal of internalization of the new identity, but for reasons that are not very clear, they cease involvement in the Black struggle. In effect, they drop out. Keeping in mind that not everyone moves forward, let us examine the experiences of those who are able to sustain growth.

Internalization

Key markers of internalization: If encounter and immersion-emersion usher in confusion and a roller coaster of emotions, then the Internalization Stage marks points of clarity and levelheadedness. The person feels calmer, more relaxed, more at ease. An inner peace is achieved, as *Weusi* Anxiety (tension over being the right kind of Black person) is transformed into *Weusi* Pride (Black Pride) and *Weusi* Self-acceptance (Black self-acceptance). The shift is from concern about how your friends see you ("Am I Black enough?"), to confidence in one's personal standards of Blackness; from uncontrolled rage toward White people, to controlled anger at oppressive systems and racist institutions; from symbolic, boisterous rhetoric, to serious analysis and quiet strength; from unrealistic urgency that can lead to dropping out, to a sense of destiny that enables one to sustain long-term commitment; from anxious, insecure, rigid, pseudo-Blackness based on the hatred of Whites, to proactive Black pride, self-love, and a deep sense of connection to, and acceptance by, the Black community.

In being habituated and internalized, Blackness becomes a backdrop for life's transactions. It can be taken for granted, freeing the person to concentrate on issues that *presuppose a basic identification with Blackness.* One *is* Black, thus one is free to think about matters beyond the scope of one's personal sense of Blackness (organizational development, community development, problem-solving, conflict resolution, institution building, and so on).

One of the most important consequences of this inner peace is that the person's conception of Blackness tends to become more open, expansive, and sophisticated. As general defensiveness fades, simplistic thinking and simple solutions become transparently inadequate, and the full complexity and inherent texture of the Black condition becomes the point of departure for serious analysis.

The person perceives him or herself to be a totally changed person, with both a new worldview and an equally revitalized personality.

However, research findings show that Nigrescence tends to have more of an effect on the group-identity or reference-group component of the Black self-concept than it does the general personality. The person's personality is most certainly put under stress during immersion-emersion, and there is a great deal of emotionality associated with conversion, but with internalization and the easing of internal psychological stress, the basic core of the person's personality is reestablished. For example, if a person was an effective (or ineffective) leader at preencounter, his or her leadership profile will go unchanged at internalization. Likewise, this pattern is likely to be replicated in countless other examples: shy at preencounter, shy at internalization; outgoing and gregarious at preencounter, outgoing and gregarious at internalization; introverted and mildly uncomfortable around large groups at preencounter, introverted and uncomfortable in groups at internalization; calm, rational, and deliberate at preencounter, calm, rational, and deliberate at internalization; anxious and neurotic at preencounter, anxious and neurotic at internalization; relatively normal and happy at preencounter, relatively normal and happy at internalization, and so on. In fact, research suggests that during immersion-emersion one's basic personality strengths act as a *psychological cushion* or relative backdrop of stability for the intense struggle taking place within the group-identity level of the Black self-concept. (Conversely, personality weaknesses may make Nigrescence more stressful to the person, although the point being made here is that successful completion of Nigrescence rides or floats on whatever are the person's extant personality strengths.) At internalization, when the conflict surrounding reference-group and worldview change has been resolved, the person is able to fall back on his or her basic personality traits, which, though greatly stressed, perturbed, and excited during immersion-emersion, helped him or her negotiate the group-identity change in the first place.

For the fraction of people who were anti-Black at preencounter, Nigrescence may enhance their general level of self-esteem, but again, the person's characteristic personality attributes beyond self-esteem are likely to remain the same. As a form of social therapy, Nigrescence is extremely effective at changing the importance of race and culture in a person's life; however, it is not a process that lends itself to the needs of personality therapy.

What makes the person feel completely "new" are the changes experienced at the level of one's group identity. In moving from preencounter to internalization, the person has moved from a frame of reference where race and culture had low salience, to a perspective that places high salience on Blackness in everyday life. With this change in salience comes membership in new organizations, changes in one's social network, changes in one's manner of dress and personal appearance, changes in one's self-referents, changes in what one reads or views on television, changes in how one socializes one's children, changes in one's internal image of the capacity and efficacy of Blacks as a group, changes in one's cultural and artistic preferences, changes in one's historical and cultural perspective, changes in the causes and social problems that engage one's activism, and perhaps even changes in one's name. These types of changes define what is important in *adult life,* and that's why the person feels totally new. Left unnoticed to the person is the fact that his or her basic personality profile is the same as it was during preencounter.

Salience and ideology: While advanced Black identity development results in the person giving high salience to issues of race and culture, not every person in internalization shares the same degree of salience for Blackness, as this is likely to be determined by the nature of one's ideology. Persons who construct a strong nationalistic framework from their immersion-emersion experiences may continue along this ideological path at internalization, while others may derive a far less nationalistic stance. The former can lead to total salience on Blackness, and the latter, less so. For example, *vulgar* nationalists (person's who believe Blacks and Whites are biogenetically different, with Blacks being of "superior" racial stock, and Whites being an "inferior" mutation of Black stock) and traditional nationalists (persons who frame their nationalistic perspective with other than biogenetic constructs) have saliencies about race and culture that in some instances can border on the obsessive. The traditional nationalist presents the most healthy alternative, as his or her high salience and frame of reference are subject to rational analysis and debate, while the vulgar nationalist's reactionary racism, which is usually steeped in an odd mixture of pseudoscientific myths, historical distortions, and outright mysticism, offers a salience and orientation beyond the reach of normal discourse. Although vulgar and traditional nationalists are African-Americans by history and culture, both tend to stress a singularity to their cultural emphasis, and in some instances, they may even *deny* that there is anything American or Eurocentric about their being. In this sense, their internalized Black nationalist identity, though far more sophisticated than the version espoused during immersion-emersion, carries with it, in varying degrees, themes of conflict on how to relate to the other half of their cultural-historical makeup.

Other Blacks reaching internalization derive a *bicultural* reference-group orientation from their Nigrescence experience. From their vantage point, internalization is a time for working through and incorporating into one's self-concept the realities of one's Blackness as well as the enigmatic, paradoxical, advantageous, and supportive aspects of one's Americanness.

Taking this a step further, others may embrace a *multicultural* perspective, in which case their concern for Blackness is shared with a multiplicity of cultural interests and saliencies. Consequently, the cultural identity of the Stage Four person can vary from that of the monocultural orientation of the extreme nationalist to the identity mosaic of the multiculturally oriented Black person. Each ideological stance incorporates certain strengths and weaknesses, and there are times when the holders of one perspective may find themselves at odds with those who share another variant of Blackness. This means that Nigrescence may increase the salience of race and culture for all persons who successfully reach the advanced stages of Black identity development, but internalization does not result in ideological unity. One can look upon this variability as ideological fractionation, or as healthy, ideological diversity.

Stage Five: Internalization-Commitment

After developing a Black identity that services their personal needs, some Blacks fail to sustain a long-term interest in Black affairs. Others devote an extended period of time, if not a lifetime, to finding ways to translate their personal sense of Blackness into a plan of action or general sense of commitment. Such people characterize the fifth and final stage of Nigrescence: Internalization-Commitment. Current theory suggests there are few differences between the psychology of Blacks in the fourth and fifth stages, other than the important factor of sustained interest and commitment. Consequently, other than to repeat what has already been said about internalization, a more differentiated look at internalization-commitment awaits the results of future research.

Parham's concept of recycling: A complete Nigrescence cycle involves traversing all four or five stages, and as originally conceived,

Nigrescence was thought to be a "one-time event" in the life of a person. Recently, the young, brilliant Nigrescence theorist, Thomas A. Parham, who completed his dissertation under the tutelage of another key figure in the field, Janet E. Helms, has extended the implications of my model across the life span. Parham has noted that, for those who have completed their original Nigrescence cycle at an earlier point in the life span (say, for example, adolescence or early adulthood), the challenges unique to another life span phase (middle age or late adulthood) may induce *recycling* through some of the stages. For example, a young man might go through Nigrescence at the age of twenty, when he is single and a college student. During this first cycle, he is able to successfully address those identity questions that are important to early adult functioning. Subsequently, his marriage may trigger new questions about Blackness, and still later, the raising of his progeny may cause him to discover "gaps" in his thinking about Blackness. These new questions and the discovery of gaps in one's thinking, or a powerful racist incident at work or in the community, represent a new encounter episode, leading to the need to recycle (in all likelihood, recycling does not involve the Preencounter Stage). In recycling, the person searches for new answers and continued growth in his or her thinking about what it means to be Black. Depending on the nature and intensity of the new encounter, recycling may vary from a mild refocusing experience to passage through full-blown Encounter, Immersion-Emersion, and Internalization Stages.

References

Cross, W. E. *Shades of Black*. Philadelphia: Temple University Press. 1991.
Parham, T. A. "Cycles of Psychological Nigrescence." *The Counseling Psychologist*, 17(2): 187–226, 1989.

4

Biracial Identity—Asset or Handicap?

Elaine Pinderhughes

"Mommy," pleaded a four-and-a-half-year-old who is African-American, Native American and White, "If I'm part Indian now, when was I a whole Indian?" (Young, 1982). Some young, racially mixed children look at parts of themselves "to see whether they are different colors to reflect parts of each parent" (Root, 1992, p. 343). Such confusion has been viewed as typical of the reality and psychological state of biracial people. For generations the societal view of biracial or racially mixed people has labelled them not only as confused and bewildered, but as weirdos, misfits, degenerates, moral deviants, tormented and pathological souls (Spickard, 1992; Nagashima, 1992; Kich, 1992). Studies on biracial children have reported that problems commonly occur with racial identity confusion, low self-esteem, ambivalence toward family, parental rejection, and problems in both psychological and behavioral areas (Gibbs, 1989; Faulkner and Kich, 1983; Ladner, 1977). My personal experience as a clinician did not appear to refute such impressions. Consider the following:

1) Henry J. was referred to me in a state of panic. Now employed as a psychologist in an outpatient children's center, he had been warmly welcomed as an African-American male to work with the large numbers of Black children in the caseload. Mr. J., now twenty-eight years old, was biracial, the offspring of an Anglo-Saxon mother and Black father whom he never knew. In his family, which resided in a completely White area, there were three other siblings, whose fathers were White. In appearance Mr. J. was unmistakenly African-American.

   Totally unfamiliar with African-American culture, the community, or any individuals within, he became immobilized with anxiety upon being assigned the case of an biracial child whose African-

American father had abandoned the family. Of particular note was the fact that Mr. J.'s blood pressure, which had always been high, was found to be at a dangerous level.

2) Lisa S., age fifteen, was Caucasian in appearance except for her fuzzy hair. She came for treatment because her parents could not handle her acting-out behavior. Both her African-American father and her Polish-Irish (third generation) mother were in treatment with different clinicians because of serious marital problems. A major battleground in their ongoing conflict was the discipline of the children, with Mr. S. appearing overly rigid and authoritative and Mrs. S., overly permissive. While Lisa and her two siblings were in fairly close contact with grandparents and extended family on both sides, Mrs. S.'s family rejected Mr. S. Mr. S's family was intensely disapproving of Mrs. S.'s permissiveness, and Mrs. S. herself was extremely threatened whenever her husband's family attempted to expose the children to African-American culture and the community. A major battle took place, for example, when Mr. S.'s sister took Lisa to an African-American hairdresser because she had been unable to manage her hair.

3) Mr. and Mrs. Y. and Jane, their twenty-one-year-old biracial daughter, were seen in family therapy after Jane precipitously left college and threatened suicide. The Y.'s, who are White, had adopted Jane, who was biracial, when she was three months old. Along with a biological son, three years older, the Y.'s resided in an affluent suburban neighborhood. Jane was reported to have been successful with friends and at school, and essentially without problems ("a little intense, sometimes, perhaps") until, as a teenager, she found that her girlfriends became more distant and her male classmates would not date her. She had become infuriated when told she should date students in the program that bussed in students of color from the inner city. In an interview with her family, Jane became overwhelmed with rage as she accused her parents of ignoring her needs by living far away from the African-American community and failing to teach her how to deal with being Black. The depth of her feeling was such that this ordinarily sufficiently controlled young woman was on the verge of striking her mother.

The conflict and pain in these cases can easily be construed as an affirmation of the fate that automatically awaits biracial people in our society. Are these cases typical of the struggle that awaits the biracial child? Is it inevitable that they will be doomed to marginality, unable to deal with dual cultures, becoming torn, confused, not accepted by the cultural groups from which they spring, outcasts and targets of the anger of both parents' groups and of their hatred for one another (Root, 1992, p. 173)?

Currently researchers and others, including biracial individuals themselves and their parents, are now challenging these assumptions. Irrespective of their claims, a study of the issues involved in biracial identity can make clear a number of issues related to social systemic process, intra- and intergroup relations, and the processes of identity development and human resilience. Although this chapter focuses primarily on biracial children of White and African-American mixtures, the discussion on identity development has relevance for children of all interracial pairings. In this chapter, I will present recent research findings and the opinions of experts, to examine healthy biracial identity development in terms of the aforementioned issues. I will then discuss implications for clinical intervention.

Biracial identity is a dynamic, changing phenomenon shaped not only by the parents' racial identity and their attitudes about it, but by the child's interaction with a variety of persons in the systems with which he or she must interact, including peers, extended family, and his or her community. Through these interactions, experiences of recognition, acceptance, and belonging occur which can facilitate healthy biracial self-acceptance (Kich, 1992). The usual ongoing process of mutual recognition and belonging which takes place between the individual and the ethnic group, and which contributes to the development of the ethnic group as well as validating an individual's ethnicity, is complicated for biracial persons. Their developmental task mastery must occur in the context of powerful social systemic processes that have prevented the recognition of their dual ethnic-group heritage and have denigrated the minority heritage that has traditionally been reinforced for them (Kich, 1992; Root, 1992).

Social System Factors

The notion of race and categorization based on race are ambiguous concepts, since they are based on the notion of objectively absolute gene pools (Spickard, 1992). Despite the fact that there is no such thing as a pure race, even in the most homogeneous-appearing groups, racial categorization does exist in the U.S., and is seen as a strategy to preserve the purity of the White race, along with its power and domination in our society. The very clear racial boundaries which are deemed necessary to maintain the social, economic, political, and psychological organization of our nation in the interest of White domination are seriously threatened by the presence of biracial persons (Nagashima, 1992; Spickard, 1992).

Fear of racial mixing is also thought to be related to psychological factors as well, such as the White male's fear about his own sexual prowess and the perceived greater sexual prowess of Blacks (Hernton, 1965; Brown, 1990); an underlying suspicion that White women are attracted to the Black male (Barron, 1972; Brown, 1987); and the guilt of the White male related to his exploitation of the Black female during the period of African-American enslavement and afterwards (Pinderhughes, 1982).

To maintain these boundaries, and thus to control the threat posed by racial mixing and the presence of biracial persons, rigid, irrational policies, attitudes, and practices have been employed. One such practice is the doctrine of hypodescent, which holds that individuals whose lineage is both White and non-White are to be categorized within the non-White group. Thus, when an individual's lineage is mixed, identity is derived by membership in the "lesser" group. As a result of such categorization, there exist within non-White groups all levels of racial mixture (Nagashima, 1992), whereas the White and dominant group remains "pure." It is important to note, however, that a significant proportion of persons who identify themselves as white also have multicultural origins (Root, 1992; Pinderhughes, 1982). Currently up to seventy percent of African-Americans are multiracial, as are virtually all Latinos and Filipinos and the majority of American Indians and Native Hawaiians. The irrationality inherent in the exercise of this doctrine of hypodescent is also manifest in the fact that it is more rigidly applied to White/non-White mixtures than to mixtures of different non-White groups. The intermixing of persons of color with other persons of color—such as American Indians, Latinos and Blacks—does not conventionally threaten the border between White and non-White (Root, 1992).

Some experts are quick to note that treasuring clear and tight boundaries is practiced by people of color too. For example, the African-American community accepts persons of all degrees of racial mixture as embodied in the "one drop of Black blood" concept, provided that they do not assert their multiracial identities (Nagashima, 1992). Seen by some to mean collusion in the reenforcement of White domination and acceptance of the White definition of Whiteness (Root, 1992), racial categorization is also seen by others as a consequence of political expediency and the need for solidarity in the battle of people of color for respect from and access into the social system.

The doctrine of hypodescent and the lack of a visible mechanism to claim both their heritages may prevent racially mixed people from moving back and forth between color lines, a process which is now seen as necessary for adopting a healthy, biracial identity (Root, 1992; Johnson, 1992). The requirement to deny one part of their heritage makes biracial individuals vulnerable to a sense of disloyalty to one parent. This phenomenon, along with the denial of one side of the family, can create a psychological cutoff which causes stress in family structure and functioning due to the consequent intensification of emotional processes (Bowen, 1978). It also places stress on other relationships, and may compromise the development of a healthy identity.

Biracial persons (and some experts) now call for a liberation from this system that so narrowly categorizes them and then devalues the limited option. Among their demands are recognition of their dual heritage, the development of multidimensional models of ethnic/racial identity that do not emphasize "dichotomous or bipolar schemes that marginalize their status" (Root, 1992), and acknowledgment of the dynamic complexities embedded in the realities with which they must negotiate in their struggle for a healthy sense of identity (Thornton, 1992; Stephan, 1992).

What are the Facts?

Currently there are over a million interracial marriages of all types in the U.S. In 1992, 246,000 of these marriages were Black/White, while 883,000 were between Whites and other persons of color (U.S. Census, 1992). The number of interracial children is not known, but experts agree that it is rapidly escalating.

Despite the denigration of non-White status and the lack of recognition of biracial persons, research on biracial persons in the U.S. and in Britain suggests that the attainment of a healthy biracial identity is possible. This more positive and more complete perspective on racial identity, so different from findings in earlier studies that focused on pathology, is related to several factors. First, by using "normal" populations rather than "problem" populations, recent studies have been based more on ecological, non-Eurocentric models which are seen as more appropriate to the biracial person; and second, it is now recognized that low self-esteem need not be correlated with minority identification, since self-esteem and reference-group orientation operate independently (Spencer, 1987). This represents a major shift in the perception that self-esteem automatically suffers when an individual is connected to a denigrated group. In these studies on young children, adolescents, and adults, the majority of the subjects appeared comfortable with themselves and their social identity as biracial persons, and had established positive relations with both Whites and persons of color, including other mixed-race and minority peers. They saw themselves as attractive, citing the benefits of being connected to two cultures and heritages, of receiving the best qualities of each, along with their unique capacity for understanding people from a variety of backgrounds (Jacobs, 1992; Johnson, 1992; Kich, 1992; Stephan, 1992; Cauce, Hiraga, Mason, Aguilar, Ordonez, and Gonzales, 1992; DeAndre and Riddell, 1991; Logan, Freeman, and McRoy, 1987; McRoy and Freeman, 1986; Poussaint, 1984).

Researchers expressed surprise at the sophistication and awareness of some children. Even as young as six, children were found who could discuss the confusion and illogical criteria embodied in racial categorization, and who demonstrated a capacity to identify and examine their socially defined racial identity in terms of negative as well as positive evaluations and stereotypes (Jacobs, 1992 p. 206; Wilson, 1987).

For biracial children to achieve a healthy identity, two barriers must be transcended:

1) the continuing denigration in our society of the minority group to which they are connected; and
2) the nonexistence of a multicultural ethnic group to which they can feel connected, causing the "invisibility" of biracial existence.

Primary factors in producing a positive growing-up experience for interracial children include:

1) geographic location—having a community where the sense of being different or unacceptable is minimized, which, for the biracial child, means a community of diverse people of a variety of backgrounds;
2) the degree and quality of parental understanding and help in dealing with racial issues—children must have help to cope with the idealization of White and the denigration of color;

3) sense of support from school networks, grandparents, relatives, friends, and the larger community. Parents must help marshal these resources;

4) having both parts of their racial heritage accepted and confirmed, this can be done by maintaining positive connections with individuals from both ethnic groups—a situation always threatened by divorce (Jacobs, 1992; Kich, 1992; Miller and Miller, 1990; Gibbs, 1987).

Healthy Biracial Identity Development

The stages identified by researchers proceed from recognition, through acceptance, to belonging, in a process where transition occurs from a confused, denigrated sense of self, to one in which a secure and valued biracial identity has been achieved. The primary task is to separate the evaluations of others including "various perjorative and grandiose labels and mislabels, from their own experiences and conceptions of themselves" (Kich, 1992, p. 306), and to resolve the experience of dissonance and the longing to belong somewhere. The significance of an ecological approach to understanding how biracial identity evolves in each of these stages cannot be underestimated. Differing outcomes regarding self-definition are determined by the social meaning that exists for the child and family, the social cognition of the child (the ability to see the self from the perspective of others), and the socialization processes undergone by the child (Johnson, 1992). Specific factors in the outcome of this developmental process are physical appearance, personality, surname, the status of the groupings, the individual's acceptance by his or her heritage groups (including the extended family), parental attitude toward and management of the child's biracial identity, racial composition, and the attitudes of school, other institutions, and groups, including the availability of role models from both groups (Stephan, 1992; Miller, 1992; Bradshaw, 1992).

Between the ages of three to four and a half years, the child can accurately identify her own skin color, as demonstrated by choosing a doll or picture close to her own skin color (brown or tan). At this point there is no recognition of the permanency of skin color and no connection to racial group, that is, children see racially different individuals with similar skin color tone as being like themselves (Jacobs, 1992; Johnson, 1992; Wilson, 1987). Whereas Black children develop racial awareness six months to one year earlier than Whites, some experts think the biracial child's awareness may be either later or in between. Although the findings of studies on biracial children's skin color preference for White identity tend to be conflicting, there is now recognition that there are more complexities involved than previously believed. By the age of six the child begins to understand the nonchangeability of skin color and its meaning, that is, the denigration of color identity, and its significance for the roles with which the child is becoming familiar (Jacobs, 1992; Wilson, 1987; Logan, Freeman, and McRoy, 1987), and now becomes ambivalent about his or her racial status. A sense of differentness is felt as negative and discrepant.

In my research the experience of differentness was found to be fraught with anxiety and pain for most people, irrespective of cultural background (Pinderhughes, 1989). Nonetheless, the situation of the biracial child creates a unique experience of difference, since the child experiences difference not only from peers and others, but from parents as well. There is a sense of being "both yet neither" (Kich, 1992). At this stage, which is a necessary component of the process, ambivalence usually takes the form of White preference and Black rejection, and later may be reversed. Jacobs (1992) emphasizes that, if the child is allowed to maintain his ambivalence, identity development moves forward to the level where discordant elements begin to be reconciled in a unified identity. An internalization occurs of a biracial label which the child tries to use cognitively to build racial identity.

Not to be underestimated is the importance of parents supplying open communication about race and offering an interracial label (McRoy and Freeman, 1986; Jacobs, 1992). Through providing support, comfort, and opportunity to process feelings, experiences, and facts (Kich, p. 308), and through an emphasis on cultural practices from both groups, a foundation is laid for subsequent identity resolution.

Wilson (1987) describes a somewhat similar process. In her research she found that by the age of nine, children either were preoccupied with conflict concerning where they were in the Black/White dichotomy, or else had now accepted definition of selves as non-White and were exploring how Black/mixed-race identity fit in with their experiences. If they were not comfortable with biracial identity, the identity conflict was expressed in one of three ways: they *fantasized* they were White; defensively retreated to a Black identity; or were unable to choose between the two. If differentness is negatively connoted within the family, a sense of not belonging is created and *results* in the beginning internalization of experiences embodying ambiguity and rejection (Kich, 1992; Wilson, 1987). Under such circumstances, conflict *will* occur. Researchers agree that the biracial child, by age eight or nine, can now separate skin color from racial group membership. For example, while she may appear Caucasian, she also recognizes connection to a people-of-color group.

During adolescence, although ambivalence may appear resolved for some, "the restructuring of sexual identity may require that racial ambivalence again be worked through" (Jacobs, 1992, p. 203). There is some disagreement concerning the duration of the adolescent stage in which an ethnic identity is chosen; from three to four years, to well into adulthood (Kich, 1992). Several studies indicate the achievement of healthy ethnic identity between the ages of thirteen to eighteen (DeAndre and Riddell, 1991) or by college age (Poussaint, 1984). The child may experience this process consciously, as whether or not to choose an identity, and which one. Major issues concern how important cultural identity is, who is the reference group, and where they belong in these groups (Gibbs and Hines, 1992; Hall, 1992). Resolution means not only accepting and valuing both heritages and being comfortable in both the minority and majority community, but having the flexibility to accept that others may identify them as minority, majority, or biracial (Logan, Freeman, and McRoy, 1987). Those unable to reconcile their dual identifications into an integrated sense of self and group connection, wherein both heritages are positive, will not resolve this developmental stage, and will become trapped in conflict (Gibbs, 1987; McRoy and Freeman, 1986).

What appears particularly helpful is development of the ability to separate personal identity preferences from the larger society's definition (Root, 1992); for example, identifying oneself as biracial when one is identified as a person of color only. From a developmental perspective this means being well differentiated as an individual within the family and resolving the psychological struggles related to separation. Biracial identity is a dynamic construct which changes over time in relation to the specific social situations which biracial persons experience. For example, at home with parents, on a visit to Caucasian extended family members, or in school in an all-White classroom, the biracial Black/White individual may experience herself as biracial, White, and Black respectively (Miller, 1992). Such dynamicism of perceived identity may complicate the developmental task of separation and individuation. Moreover, since physical appearance and ethnicity do not necessarily coincide with an individual's chosen identity (Root,

1992, p. 6), how an individual feels about her identity and how she identifies herself may differ considerably from how others see her. A multiracial Black-Indian-European person who looks African-American may identify as multiracial, while someone of similar heritage identifies as African-American. The minority versus majority issue must be negotiated particularly in association with the denigrated meaning. As noted above, key in success are the availability of the minority parent, how the child identifies with that parent's history, experiences, and values, and the significance of the minority group in the child's socialization experience, that is, the child's acceptance of its cultural institutions and the group's acceptance of the child. The child's physiognomy and personality are mediating factors in this process (Johnson, 1992).

If tension exists in the form of loyalty to parents versus longing for acceptance outside, this can lead to a tendency to separate home and school (for example using ethnic behaviors or eating ethnic foods at home but not at school). Such separation of family and outside social life is only a temporary solution, since the reality of being biracial continues to assert itself, and fear of exposure creates pressure to end the discomfort and conflict. The presence of loyalty conflict becomes manifest in confusion as to which parent to identify with. Ambivalence toward the parent who is most different and overidentification with the other parent are common (Root, 1992, pp. 18–19). If parents do not help with this conflict, feelings of embarrassment, disappointment, and self-doubt will be hidden behind frustration, anger, longing, guilt, and a sense of inferiority. Only by moving back and forth between a sense of connection to first one and then another reference group, first one and then another side of the extended family, or between personal preferences and capacities, can biracial people struggle to integrate the differing aspects of themselves and their histories (Kich, 1992).

Confronted with highly charged acceptance and rejection experiences, "a heightened ability to negotiate this mine field" is developed (Kich, 1992, p. 311). Sometimes self-definition will be in terms of nationality or ability, such as being American, an athlete such as U.C.L.A.'s "twin killer" who excels in both volleyball and basketball (Jenkins, 1993); or a super student, as in the case of Mr. J, but this too is temporary. Trying to "pass" through exaggerated attempts to fit in constitutes another attempted solution. Eventually active exploration of both sides of their heritage will occur before final recognition that they belong in a different ethnic/racial category from either parent. For example, a young African-American biracial female whose mother was Jewish used fellowship funds to study in Israel and Africa. It is readily apparent that the task of differentiation within the family and psychological separation from the parents is more complex for the biracial person.

Stable self-acceptance occurs when the definition of self is no longer determined by others' definition. There is now greater acceptance of parents, extended family, ethnic heritage, and history, an enhanced understanding of the dilemmas implicit in others' prejudice, mislabelling, ignorance, or confusion, and a willingness to educate them. Self-expression rather than defensiveness marks this stance, which is also characterized by knowing when to fit in, when to expose or confront distortions, and by possessing a unique ability to gain acceptance by different groups. Also achieved is an integration of the disparate aspects of self and the ongoing contradictory heritages, histories and parents, messages from society in general and the community (Kich, 1992, p. 315). While some resolution is achieved, the process remains ongoing, since future experiences may require reworking.

As noted earlier, the factors which support positive identity development include strong peer and family relationships and multiethnic group connections (DeAndre and Riddell, 1991; McRoy and Freeman, 1986). If the child fails to acquire the emotional flexibility required to negotiate the processes outlined above, and/or does not have available supports and models—both parental and environmental—a conflicted, ambivalent, confused, and negative sense of identity will emerge. Five major areas of functioning will be affected: dual identity, social marginality, sexuality and impulse management, psychological autonomy and individuation, education and work aspirations. These dynamics will be manifest in extreme behaviors, such as those associated with the devalued social status of the denigrated group, for example, sexual acting out, rebelliousness, delinquency, and underachievement; or in extreme behaviors such as those associated with the idealized group, for example, superachievement and overconformity (Overmeir, 1990; Gibbs, 1987). Identity confusion may extend to gender confusion and ambiguity about sexual identity or orientation. The more serious the problem of racial identification, the more serious may be the problem of sexual identification (Teicher, 1968).

All experts emphasize the significance of the environment in the biracial child's identity task mastery. Miller examines this in relation to the biracial Black-White child:

> It is social content that determines whether an individual will be marginalized or unaffiliated, have a unique role in several social groups, adopt a monoracial social label or create a new label. Parent,

> peer, and community socialization influences will guide the content of available identity options. The Black-White child raised by the Black parent in the Black community may be socialized almost exclusively toward a Black identity; this child's developmental experience will mirror the experiences described in models for Black Identity Development. The same child raised by both parents in an interracial community may be socialized to a multiracial identity, experiencing a developmental process not reflected in current models. (Miller, 1992, p. 32)

Peer standards are especially significant in the shaping of ideas and perceptions. In monocultural environments, where the usual expected and valued conformity becomes compounded, causing them to be perceived as not fitting in, biracial adolescents are vulnerable to experiencing rejection, exclusion, and isolation. In such environments this vulnerability is heightened for females, since they generally experience greater anxiety about being accepted socially. This is particularly true in relation to dating, where the lack of opportunity for females to take the initiative contrasts with that of males, who "perceive that they have a wider selection of girls from a variety of backgrounds" (Overmier, 1990; Gibbs, 1987, p. 270). If a teen is rejected by peers because of race, it is imperative that there be support from parents and peers to process the experience. Without such, the usual transition stress of adolescence will become compounded.

Wilson (1987) found that among mixed-race British families the identity which the parent encouraged the child to adopt was critical. The few (twenty five percent) biracial children in Gibbs's study who were insecure in their self-identity had parents who were more likely to express a desire for them to have Black friends, at the same time that the racial labels preferred by these teenagers for themselves were somewhat different from those attributed to them by their parents. These youngsters were more likely to avoid socializing with Blacks and more likely to be ambivalent about labeling themselves as Black.

The socialization needed by the biracial child is similar to that of the minority child. Miller and Miller (1990) examine this issue in relation to the biracial Black-White child who, according to them, must be socialized to function in the American mainstream and in the African-American community. Functioning within the African-American community means being comfortable with the differences in values and behavioral styles in the areas of "spirituality, harmony, movement, verse, affect, communalism, expressive individualism, oral expressiveness, and time" (Miller and Miller, 1990, p. 172). The child must also be able to cope with his or her minority status. The latter means being able to deal with the denigrated status of being African-American, which involves the following:

1) learning how to handle racism without feeling "personally stigmatized, which facilitates a "protected sense of personal worth and a unified identity" enabling active coping with "the racially defined incidents that the child inevitably confronts" (Miller and Miller, 1990, p. 172);

2) belonging to organizations such as churches and social clubs which support identity development and offer alternative role models to mainstream culture, and belonging to other organizations which promote personal empowerment through activities that aim to alter racism;

3) learning to "successfully negotiate mainstream" systems while also "having the pride and skills necessary to attempt to fight structural racism" (Miller and Miller, 1990, p. 172). It is critical that biracial children be able to function in the mainstream while at the same time not colluding in the perpetuation of racism;

4) "being able to view the status of people of color as a function of systems that support and maintain discrimination as opposed to viewing these as flaws and failures of minority people" (Wilson, 1987).

The Parents

In several studies of normal biracial Black children, the parents were very concerned that "both races be offered as equal components in the child's heritage and identity" (Jacobs, 1992, p. 266). Overt encouragement of the Black biracial child's view of self as Black or mixed race seemed to foster a positive identity, whereas the view that the child was colored or only just non-White appeared more conducive to identity conflict (Wilson, 1987). One can speculate that the problem with the label "non-White" is that it encourages avoidance of acceptance of the Black part of the child's heritage and offers nothing affirmative. In terms of attitudes to educational opportunity, the parents whose children were most successful were mothers who presented racism as a reality to children, which seemed to allay anxiety and minimize social identity conflict; mothers who stressed individual effort, on the other hand, tended to heighten child's desire to be White (and thus to deny their heritage of color). Finally, a strong cultural awareness or enthusiasm for the Black parent's culture seemed to strengthen the child's mixed-race identity if the parents were simultaneously encouraging a mixed-race identity. If parents fail to offer the necessary support and structure around cultural identity, definition, and meaning, the child will feel compelled to hold in feelings, will fail to develop a healthy sense of curiosity about his or her dual heritage, and will not develop the mandatory capacity to self-explore. As noted earlier, a balance must somehow be struck between acknowledging the unfairness of the system and encouraging the children to fulfill their potential as *individuals*. The parents in one study who were most successful in achieving this balance were those who separated the Black community's struggle against racism from the child's personal struggle to get on in life (Wilson 1987). They encouraged their children to strive for success for their own benefit as people, rather than to prove that they can do as well as White children. The unfairness of the system was admitted freely, but the children's frustrations were channeled into Black people's fight against injustice, rather than being allowed to damage their motivation and self-esteem. The parents' actions focused on system-changing which teaches and promotes personal empowerment (that is, actively changing racism in the school through PTA-sponsored educational initiatives) (Miller and Miller, 1990).

The vulnerability of mixed-race children to identity conflict and its sequela places great responsibility on school and mental health personnel, who must be able to assess real or potential problems in racial identity and assist parents, peers, and community residents to help in resolution (McRoy and Freeman, 1986).

Implications for Treatment

The assessment of problems that underlie the conflicts which biracial clients bring should be based on an ecological approach which incorporates the use of the genogram, eco map, and cultural continuum (Logan, Freeman, and McRoy, 1987). These tools clarify the following dynamics as related to the client's mixed-race situation: the relationships, values, and attitudes within the immediate family, extended family, neighborhood, school, and community, and the ways in which these support or interfere with positive racial identity formation, identifying where conflict, nonacceptance, and negativity occur (Logan, Freeman,

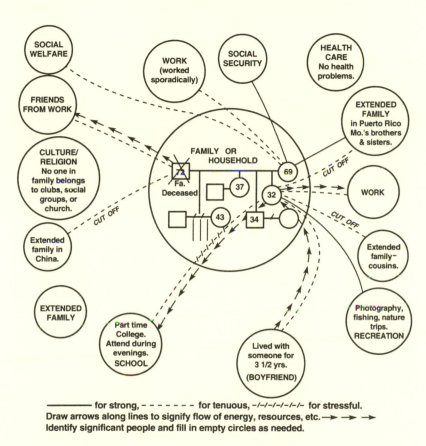

Figure 1 Logan, S., Freeman, E., and McRoy, R. 1987. *Journal of Intergroup Relations* XV (2).

and McRoy, 1987). They facilitate determining whether or not the parents' messages are positive and confirming, or uncertain, confusing, and negative; whether there a conflict between the parents regarding cultural values, their perception of the child, and/or how to help her; the degree to which there is acceptance of the child by the neighborhood, school, and/or community; and how much value conflict there is between the family and these institutions (see Figure 1).

It is critical to differentiate between the normal strains of adolescence in the context of the biracial situation and more severe problems, as manifest in behavior that is emotionally rigid, overachieving or underachieving, overaccommodating or antisocial and alienated (Gibbs, 1991; Overmeir, 1990). Positive individual, family, and network connections must be identified as fundamental supports to be enhanced during treatment.

A variety of approaches may be used: family, parent group, teen-biracial group, and individual treatment. Family work might focus on:

1) the entrapment of the child in the dynamics of the family and the role of racial difference in this entrapment;
2) identification of differences between parents and between parents and child in attitude and expectation;
3) education concerning the needs of bicultural children and of their parents as well.

An effective treatment modality delivers treatment to a group of biracial families.

Use of the cultural continuum (Logan, Freeman, and McRoy, 1987) helps biracial clients identify their adaptations to their situation and the consequences of their responses and alternatives. The choices include:

1) denial of cultural significance;
2) denial of minority identity and emphasis on majority identity;
3) the reverse;
4) acceptance of a biracial, multicultural identity (see Figure 2—Continuum).

Experts emphasize the importance of validating biracial clients' feelings about their biracial identity and its meaning; building self-esteem through supporting strengths and competence in a variety of areas; helping them to connect their problems in behavior or development with their confusion concerning cultural identity; and actively exploring their dual heritage on both sides with the goal of establishing a more positive, cohesive identity. Particularly useful strategies should include: focused discussions which facilitate further clarification and working through of issues which impact racial identity; bibliotherapy in which readings are used to explore personal issues related to the racial situation; homework assignments requiring them to interact with persons who are important in resolving their identity problems—for example, connecting them with a multiethnic peer group or reference group and role-playing; the use of diaries; and the expression of feeling

THE CULTURAL CONTINUUM

X————————————X————————————X————————————X

	Denial of the importance of race and culture (color-blind perception).	Complete assimilation within the dominant culture.	Complete assimilation within the relevant minority culture.	Bicultural or multicultural.
A D V A N T A G E S	Avoidance of pain associated with working through racial identity issues.	Greater acceptance by and blending in with dominant culture when successfully assimilated.	Greater group support, maintenance of the minority culture, and possibility of positive racial identity.	Increased ability to function effectively in two or more cultures, access to resources in the dominant culture as well as those of minority culture, and cultural maintenance.
D I S A D V A N T A G E S	Lack of connection with and support from any culture, denial of self, and failure to handle conflictual views of society about racial identity.	Loss of culture, traditions, and group support from the rejected cultural group.	Limited access to resources available in dominant culture and loss of opportunities to learn about the positive effects of cultural diversity.	Risk of failing in two or more cultures, and emotional stress associated with adapting to more than one culture.

Figure 2 Logan, S., Freeman, E., and McRoy, R. 1987. *Journal of Intergroup Relations* XV (2).

through creative activities such as storytelling (Gibbs, 1991; Overmeir, 1990; Logan, Freeman, and McRoy, 1987; McRoy and Freeman, 1986).

Assistance to Parents

Educational groups constitute a helpful medium for work with parents to enable them to raise biracial children with strong positive identity (Hill and Peltzer, 1982). The following activities have been identified as useful: open discussion on mutual concerns; readings; movies; speakers (particularly biracial individuals or their parents who have been successful in their adaptation). One group invited several speakers whose varied experiences and resolutions helped to emphasize the personal aspects of people's experiences and choices and how they differed from one another, a Black speaker who discussed institutional racism in schools and community; and White speakers on experiences with personal and institutional racism. There were also planned role-plays of incidents to help parents deal effectively with personal racial incidents.

Nearly every researcher echoed the following in emphasizing the parents' attitude toward race as a factor in the child's development of biracial identity:

> It is crucial for White parents of Black children to be aware of their own racism and engage in a conscious, continuous effort to eliminate their personal racism. Without this introspection, the White parent may consciously or unconsciously express racist attitudes to his or her Black child as well as define their Black child's behavior according to racial myths and stereotypes. (Hill and Peltzer, 1982, p. 564)

Examining their own self-esteem and self-concept issues, identifying their own personal racism, the racism of others, institutional racism per se, and understanding how it impacts their lives become mandatory activities for parents. Toward these goals therapeutic groups have been found more effective than educational groups (Hill and Peltzer, 1982). A primarily therapeutic format was found to promote the development of trust on a deeper level than did educational groups, so that members could share their own beliefs and experiences concerning racism, and begin to deal with it. Especially for White parents, this format was deemed more helpful in developing an awareness of their own self-concepts, an awareness of how their self-concepts affected the parenting of a minority child, and an awareness of their personal racial attitudes which could affect their children in negative ways (Hill and Peltzer, 1982).

Work with School and Community

The critical part played by teachers and the educational system must be recognized. Preparation must be mandatory that will enable them to function effectively in their interaction with biracial pupils as supports and role models. Educators should appreciate that these youngsters must negotiate unique developmental challenges, and can do so successfully, partly with their help. Clinicians who are expert in biracial families can help teachers learn to identify signs of difficulty, such as identity diffusion, negative identity, and identity foreclosure, along with other behaviors stemming from biracial status. They can also provide relevant workshops and programs in the school setting.

Schools can facilitate the search of biracial children for cohesive identity through the creation of a supportive environment by developing peer support groups and programs providing peer counseling, a format in which trained adolescents function as counselors (Gibbs, 1991).

Churches, agencies, and community groups which offer spiritual, social, and recreational programs can be valuable resources providing support to biracial families which, along with schools, form a critical network.

The changes occurring in research and in activities sponsored by biracial people and their families should make clinical work with them much easier. In 1989 more than thirty organizations existed to help multiracial (primarily Black/White) persons affirm their heritages. Among them were Multiracial Family Network of Boston, Interracial/Intercultural Pride in Berkley, Multiracial Americans of Southern California (L.A.), the Biracial Family Network in Chicago, and a national umbrella organization called AMEA (Association of Multi-Ethnic Americans) (Grosz, 1989).

The push by the multiracial community for liberation from the systemic processes that entrap biracial people centers on pressure to have, by the year 2000, a census form that will not "perpetuate the forced-choice nature" and the "please choose my dilemma" of most forms. What is being demanded is that people be able to choose more than one category "under race and under ethnicity" to truly reflect multiple heritage.

That the biracial experience can be and must now be seen as valuable and positive is a priority. Biracial people say they have been identified as the "children of the future," the natural "bridges" between the artificial boundaries that divide the humans of the world (Nagashima, 1992, p. 173). Whether or not this is true, their numbers are rapidly increasing, as must our knowledge, soundly grounded in research, concerning what constitutes healthy development and how to reinforce it.

References

Barron, M. 1972. *The Blending of America: Patterns of Intermarriage.* Chicago: Quadrangle Books.

Bowen, M., 1978. *Family Therapy in Clinical Practice.* New York: Jason Aronson.

Bradshaw, C. 1992. "Beauty and the Beast: On Racial Ambiguity," in *Racially Mixed People in America,* ed. Root, M. Newbury Park: Sage Publications.

Brown, P. 1990. "Biracial identity and social marginality." *Child and Adolescent Social Work,* 7: 319–337.

Cauce, A. Hiraga. Y., Mason, C., Aguilar, T., Ordonez, N., and Gonzales, N. 1992. "Between a Rock and a Hard Place: Social Adjustment of Biracial Youth," in *Racially Mixed People in America.*

DeAndre, D. 1984. "Bicultural Socialization: Factors Affecting the Minority experience." *Social Work,* 29: 101–107.

DeAndre, D. and Riddel, V. 1991. "Ethnic Identity, Self-esteem and Interpersonal Relationships among Multiethnic Adolescents." *Journal of Multicultural Social Work,* 1(1): 83–98.

Faulkner, J. and Kich, F. 1983. "Assessment and Engagement Stages in Therapy with the Interracial Family." *Family Therapy Collections,* 6:78–90.

Gibbs, J. 1987. "Identity and Marginality: Issues of Treatment of Biracial Adolescents." *American Journal of Orthopsychiatry,* 57: 265–278.

Gibbs, J. 1989. "Biracial Adolescents," in *Children of color: Psychological interventions with minority youth.* Eds. Gibbs, J.T., Huang, L. N., *et al.* San Francisco: Jossey-Bass.

Gibbs, J., 1991. "Clinical and Cultural Issues in the Treatment of Biracial and Bicultural Adolescents." *Families in Society* 72, 579–592.

Gibbs, J., and Hines, A. 1992. "Negotiating Ethnic Identity: Issues for Black-White Biracial Adolescents," in *Racially Mixed People in America.*

Grosz, G. 1989. "From Sea to Shining Sea . . . A Current Listing of Interracial Organizations and Support Groups across the Nation." *Interrace,* 1: 24–28. 1989

Hall, C. 1992. "Coloring Outside the Lines," in *Racially mixed people in America.*

Hernton, C. 1965. *Sex and Racism in America.* Garden City, NJ. Doubleday. 1965

Hill, M. and Peltzer, J. 1982. "A Report of Thirteen Groups for White Parents of Black Children." *Family Relations,* 31: 557–565.

Jacobs, J. 1992. "Identity Development in Biracial Children," in *Racially Mixed People in America.*

Jenkins, S. 1993. "Twin killer." *Sports Illustrated,* 79: 34–38.

Johnson, D. 1992. "Developmental Pathways: Towards an Ecological Theoretical Formulation of Race Identity in Black-White Biracial Children," in *Racially Mixed People in America.*

Kich, G. 1992. "The Developmental Process of Asserting a Biracial, Bicultural Identity," in *Racially Mixed People in America.*

Ladner, J. 1977. *Mixed Families.* Garden City, NY: Anchor/Doubleday.

Logan, S., Freeman, E., and McRoy, R. 1987. "Racial Identity Problems of Biracial Clients: Implications for Social Work Practice." *Journal of Intergroup Relations,* 15: 11–24.

McRoy, R. and Freeman, E. 1986. "Racial Identity Issues among Mixed Race Children." *Social Work in Education,* pp. 164–174.

Miller, R. and Miller, B. 1990. "Mothering the Biracial Child: Bridging the Gap between African-American and White Parenting Styles." *Women and Therapy,* 10: 169–180.

Miller, R. 1992. "The Human Ecology of Multiracial Identity," in *Racially Mixed People in America.*

Nagashima, C. 1992. "An Invisible Monster: The Creation and Denial of Mixed-race People in America," in *Racially Mixed People in America.*

Overmeir, K. 1990. "Biracial Adolescents: Areas of Conflict in Identity Formation." *Journal of Applied Social Sciences,* 14(2): 157–176.

Pinderhughes, E. P. 1982. "Black Geneology: Self Liberator and Therapeutic Tool." *Smith College Studies for Social Work*, 52: 93–106.

Pinderhughes, E., 1989. *Understanding Race, Ethnicity, and Power*. New York: Free Press.

Poussaint, A. 1984. "Study of Interracial Children Presents a Positive Picture." *Interracial Books for Children*, 15: 9–10.

Root, M. 1992. "From Shortcuts to Solutions," in *Racially Mixed People in America*.

Root M. 1992. "Introduction" in *Racially Mixed People in America*.

Spencer, M. B. 1987. "Black Children's Ethnic Identity Formation: Risk and Resilience of Castelike Minorities," in *Children's ethnic socialization: pluralism and development*. Ed. Phinney, J. and Rotherman, M. Newbury Park, CA: Sage Publications.

Spickard, M., 1992. "The Illogic of American Racial Categories," in *Racially Mixed People in America*.

Stephan, C. 1992. "Mixed Heritage Individuals: Ethnic Identity and Trait Characteristics," in *Racially Mixed People in America*.

Teicher, J. 1968. "Some Observations on Identity Problems in Children of Negro-White Marriages." *Journal of Nervous and Mental Disorders*, 146: 249–256.

Thornton, M. 1992. "The Quiet Immigration: Foreign Spouses of U.S. Citizens, 1945–1985," in *Racially Mixed People in America*.

U.S. Bureau of the Census. 1992. Statistical abstract of the United States.

Wilson, A. 1987. *Mixed Race Children: A Study of Identity*. London: Allen and Unwin.

Young, D. 1982. *Interracial Children: Considerations for Counseling*, Unpublished manuscript.

5

Transracial Adoptions and the Continuing Debate on the Racial Identity of Families

Ezra E.H. Griffith and
Ina L. Silverman

Introduction

Transracial adoptions of Black children, where typically a Black child is placed with White adoptive parents, continue to make news across the country (Bates, 1991; McCalope, 1991; Orwig, 1993; Sowell, 1992). What are usually private legal proceedings become public when, typically, a White family wishes to adopt a Black child, and an adoption agency or a special interest group steps in to prevent or delay the adoption so that an attempt can be made to find potential Black adoptive parents. Heartrending images of a dark-skinned toddler screaming for his or her foster parents, as a social worker carries the child out of the White foster family's home to a waiting car and an unknown and insecure future, continue to be evoked by these stories. The events remain newsworthy and of interest because there is still considerable disagreement about whether the best way to consolidate the togetherness of a given family unit is to follow tradition and assure that the family has a single racial identity. Transracial adoptions obviously tear at the heart of this culture-bound view of traditional family structure. But, in addition, transracial adoptions evoke the frightening question, with its political ramifications, of whether such multiracial families ultimately dilute or alter the individual racial identities of the Black members of these mixed families.

There is therefore no surprise that the transracial adoption debate continues to provoke heated discussions. The arguments and counterarguments over the policy questions have been summarized by a number of scholars (Bartholet, 1991; Griffith and Adams, 1990; Griffith and Duby, 1991; Mahoney, 1991; Silverman, 1993). Furthermore, Bartholet (1992) has distilled the arguments in a recent commentary on the debate that was accompanied by responses from Allen, Griffith, Hollinger, and other colleagues (1992). But the transracial adoption subject evokes such passion that these scholarly summaries still have not tamed the discussion or the rhetoric. Special interest groups, such as the National Association of Black Social Workers (NABSW), continue to publicize their positions and to agitate for public policy directions that may have no strict relationship to results of recent scientific research or to judicial arguments. For example, the NABSW (1991), as recently as three years ago, was still formally advocating "same-race, same-culture" placements for Black children awaiting adoption, and arguing that such placements provided a "least restrictive or less limiting family setting." While this language was less hostile and provocative than their 1972 claim that "a white home is not a suitable placement for black children" (NABSW, 1972), the two political positions are fundamentally similar, and both ignore research in the field.

There are those at one end of the spectrum who would prohibit all transracial adoptions, either for racist reasons, or because they honestly believe that the best interests of minority children require that these children be brought up by parents of the same race (see, for example, NABSW, 1972). Then there are those at the other end of the spectrum who believe that adoptions should be color-blind; for them, race is an irrelevant issue when placing an adoptive child with a permanent family (see, for example, Bartholet, 1991, 1992). There are others who promote a compromise position, in which racial homogeneity within families is preferred if a minority child can be placed relatively quickly in a family with similar racial characteristics (see, for example, Rita Simon's opinions in the commentary by Allen *et al.,* 1992).

This paper will review, after outlining basic adoption data, recent developments in this ongoing debate, first by highlighting the latest research findings concerning transracial adoptees and their families. Then consideration will be given to the status of the law governing transracial adoptions. Finally, attention will be focused on political efforts seeking to modify present transracial adoption policy.

Statistics on Transracial Adoption

In a recent article, Stolley (1993) reminded us there are still no comprehensive national data on adoption collected by the federal government. She also pointed out that "there is a marked lack of information about the prevalence and particularities" (p. 29) of informal adoption arrangements involving networks of real and fictive kin that are said to be widespread in the Black community. From various statistical sources, Stolley (1993) estimated that in 1986 there were about 104,088 total domestic adoptions in this country, a number that apparently rose to about 118,529 in 1990. Of the 1986 total, it was estimated that about 51 percent were related adoptions and 49 percent were unrelated adoptions. Related adoptions "include stepparent adoptions and those cases in which a child is adopted by a nonparent relative" (Stolley, 1993, p. 29). In providing estimates derived from the 1987 National Health Interview Survey, Stolley (p. 34) suggested that transracial adoptions, where parents and children were of different races, were about eight percent of all adoptions. White women adopting Black children accounted for one percent of all adoptions, in contrast to White adoption of children from races other than White or Black, numbering about five percent of all adoptions. Mothers of other races adopting White children occurred about two percent of the time. Stolley (1993) did note that these estimates included foreign-born children, which would suggest that the actual rate of transracial adoption of U.S.-born Black children is quite low.

The 1990 U.S. Bureau of the Census (1992) estimate put the total U.S. resident population at about 249 million people; African-Americans represented about twelve percent of the population or about thirty million people. Of those, there are about ten million children under the age of eighteen years. In light of this backdrop, the data about the racial background of children who are adopted are interesting. Tatara (1993), in his recent review, presented data collected by the American Public Welfare Association on the characteristics of children in the public child welfare system who were in out-of-home placements as of the end of the fiscal year 1989. The data submitted by thirty-two states showed that 383,000 children were in out-of-home placements, and 34.3 percent of them were Black children. By out-of-home placements is meant that permanent caretakers (relatives or others) can no longer care for the children, so a public agency takes responsibility for the children on a temporary basis. Goals for these children may be returning them to their parents, preparing them for adoption, or sending them to long-term institutions. Finalized adoptions for that year numbered 16,000; 28.9 percent of these adoptions were of Black children, and 54.9 percent were of Whites. Of the 383,000 in out-of-home placements, twenty thousand were legally free for adoption, although they were still in placement. Of this group, 42.2 percent were

Black and 47.0 percent were White. There were another eighteen thousand children living in nonfinalized adoptive homes, 35.8 percent of whom were Black and 51.9 percent were White. Such statistics show that while about a third of those children in out-of-home public placements are Black, a somewhat lower percentage (29 percent) of finalized adoptions is represented by Black children. Bartholet (1991) has suggested that Black children wait twice as long as White children to be adopted, and the wait for the White child is about a year.

It is evident that the transracial adoption of Black children by Whites, estimated at the rate of one percent of all adoptions, is not a very frequent occurrence. But we shall see that the practice, relatively rare though it may be, generates substantial commentary and thought, possibly because it forces us to confront the basic question of how we link families and racial identity.

The Research Evidence and Outcome

The research evidence focusing on the outcome for Black children transracially adopted into White families has been reviewed in recent years by several authors (Silverman and Feigelman, 1984: Griffith and Adams, 1990; Bartholet, 1991; Silverman, 1993), and the reader is referred to those reviews for a coherent analysis of the fundamental scholarship on the topic.

The important themes that do emerge concern first the outcome in early and middle childhood. Silverman (1993) most recently summarized once again the notion that the studies concluded that about seventy-five percent of transracially adopted preadolescent and younger children adjusted well in their adoptive homes. This success rate was also noted to be about as high as the success rate for traditional White inracial infant adoptions. Two subgroups emerged among those children with problems in adapting. One subgroup had problems with their health, with physical or intellectual handicaps, or with other family difficulties that seemed unrelated to their status as transracially adopted children. The second subgroup did appear to have problems that might be attributed to aspects of race and identity (see, for example, Grow and Shapiro, 1974).

As would be expected, observers and commentators have been most interested in the question of outcome as it pertains to transracial adoptees who have reached adolescence and adulthood. Furthermore, it is never surprising that, in legally contested cases of transracial adoptions, a burning question always arises as to what will happen to the transracially adopted child once he or she reaches adolescence or adulthood.

One relevant study worth recalling is that carried out by McRoy and colleagues (1982, 1984), who were particularly interested in studying the potential self-esteem and identity problems in a sample of transracial adoptees. They compared a group of thirty White families who had adopted Black children to a group of thirty Black families who had adopted Black children. Each family had a Black adopted child who was at least ten years old and who had been in the adoptive home at least a year; the mean age of the children in the study was 13.5 years and ranged from ten to twenty-one years. Eighty-seven percent of the White families lived in predominantly White areas, and their Black adopted children attended predominantly White schools; seventy percent of the Black families lived in predominantly Black areas and their Black adoptive children attended predominantly Black schools.

The results of this study showed there were no significant differences in the self-esteem scores of the transracially and inracially adopted Black children. On the other hand, the results regarding identity were more complex. The transracially adopted Black children were influenced by their parents' views. Consequently, parents who viewed the Black child as being mixed or part White tended to have the Black child voice the same view of his or her own identity. Some of the transracially adopted Black children who had little contact with Blacks also tended to devalue their Black heritage.

Another longitudinal study of transracial adoptees was performed by Shireman and Johnson (1986) and also reported in a later publication by Shireman (1988). Forty-two transracially adopted children under the age of three years were selected between 1970 and 1972, and slated for follow-up at age eight and again at age twelve. At age eight, twenty-six of the children were still in the study and at age twelve, twenty-one were still available. The transracial adoptees were also compared to control groups of Black inracial adoptees of single-parent and two-parent families. Parents of transracial adoptees reported academic or behavior problems in 33 percent of the group in comparison to 21 percent of the inracial group. However, the authors thought that this difference might have been explained by the excessive number of learning difficulties described in the transracially adopted group. On the other hand, the groups showed no difference in the areas of self-esteem or identity; and social distance scores showed that the transracially adopted group was more comfortable than the other groups with both Black and White Americans.

The same longitudinal technique has been applied by Simon and Alstein in their follow-up study of a cohort of transracially adopted children. These authors began their work in 1971 (Simon and Alstein, 1977) by interviewing 204 families who had transracially adopted a non-White child (Black, Native American, or other) and also inracially adopted forty-two White children. Most of the children were under the age of three years at the time of adoption. In 1979 (Simon and Alstein, 1981), there was follow-up of 71 percent of the original parents. In 1983 to 1984 (Simon and Alstein, 1987), eighty-eight families were reinterviewed. These authors found that about twenty percent of the transracial adoptive families had serious difficulties with the preadolescent children. But the majority of the parents and children felt good about themselves and their relationships with each other; and self-esteem scores of the Black transracially adopted adolescents were the same as the scores of the other control groups. Academic performance of the groups were similar (B for inracial adoptees; B minus for Black and other transracial adoptees). Among the families with problem children, most of the problems could be traced to learning disabilities and developmental delays in the children; and only in one case did a problem appear to be explicitly related to race.

Professor Simon (1993) recently summarized the results of the 1991 follow-up interviews of these now adults, who were first studied in 1972. The full description of the 1991 results will appear in a later publication (Simon, Alstein, and Melli, 1994). She reported that as adults the transracial adoptees were aware of and comfortable with their racial identity. Those who were Black laughed at the notion that only Blacks can raise Black children, and apparently were pleased at the possible cultural diversity of African-Americans.

Simon (1993), with these results of twenty years of observation and study in hand, directly took on and criticized the NABSW for their militant opposition to the transracial adoption of Black children. Simon even suggested that the phenomenon of transracial adoption led to the formation of families who were by definition fully ensconced in multiracial living, which in turn enriched the lives of the participants in the process.

Legal History and Recent Developments

A. *The Equal Protection Clause*

The equal protection clause in the Fourteenth Amendment of the United States Constitution prohibits racial discrimination. The equal protection clause has been cited by courts in numerous hotly debated cases, including those overturning laws making interracial cohabitation (*McLaughlin v. Florida,* 1964) and interracial marriage illegal (*Loving v. Virginia,* 1967). Laws enforcing segregation in public schools were found to be unconstitutional under the equal protection clause in *Brown v. Board of Education* in 1954. It has been only in the last forty years that the United States Supreme Court has enforced the principle of racial equality. Prior to 1954, the infamous "separate but equal" concept, in effect, sanctioned racial discrimination.

The simple phrase found in Section 1 of the Fourteenth Amendment, "No State shall make or enforce any law which shall . . . deny to any person within its jurisdiction the equal protection of the laws," has had an overwhelming impact on this country's Constitutional and social history. As a result of that phrase, a state cannot classify people by race without a compelling reason for doing so. In addition, the racial classification must be necessary for the state to accomplish its purpose. In general, racial differences cannot justify treating people of different races differently. The United States Supreme Court has also subjected the federal government to the equal protection guarantee, though in the Fourteenth Amendment it applies only to states, by holding that the due process clause of the Fifth Amendment is violated when the federal government uses discriminatory classifications. The standards under the due process and equal protection clauses are identical (see, for example, *Bolling v. Sharpe,* regarding segregated schools in the District of Columbia).

Despite the power and influence of the equal protection clause and the numerous court cases providing precedent for the unconstitutionality of racial discrimination, race is still a significant matching characteristic when children are adopted. Matching light-skinned children with light-skinned adoptive parents and dark-skinned children with dark-skinned adoptive parents would appear to be unconstitutional racial discrimination. There is probably no other area of community life in which racial classifications are made so openly. Several court cases have dealt with the issue of racial matching in the context of adoption. Many of these cases involve White adults attempting to adopt Black children. Even though the courts have upheld transracial adoptions, and prohibited race from being the sole determinant in an adoption placement, racial matching in public and private adoption agencies continues under different guises.

B. Palmore v. Sidoti

In *Palmore v. Sidoti* (1984), the United States Supreme Court reviewed a decision by a Florida state court divesting a biological mother of custody of her minor child because of her remarriage to someone of a different race. The biological parents, both White, were divorced and custody was awarded to the mother. The next year, the father sought custody because his ex-wife was living with a Black man, whom she later married. The Florida trial court awarded custody to the biological father despite finding that there was no issue as to either party's devotion to the child, adequacy of housing, or respectability of the new spouse of either parent. It took note of a court counselor's recommendation for a change in custody because the wife chose a lifestyle unacceptable to the father and to society. The trial court concluded that awarding custody to the father would serve the child's best interests.

The United States Supreme Court agreed to review the case because it raised important federal concerns arising from the Constitutional commitment to eradicate discrimination based on race. The state court had found that the child would be stigmatized by remaining in a racially mixed home and made no effort to place its holding on grounds other than race. The outcome clearly would have been different had the wife remarried a White man.

Classifications based on race are subject to "strict scrutiny." Such classifications, to be Constitutional, must be justified by a compelling governmental interest, and be necessary to accomplish a legitimate purpose. Granting custody based on the best interests of the child is a compelling governmental interest for purposes of the Equal Protection Clause. The United States Supreme Court stated that "private biases may be outside the reach of the law, but the law cannot, directly or indirectly, give them effect" (p. 433). The Court concluded that "the effects of racial prejudice, however real, cannot justify a racial classification removing an infant child from the custody of its natural mother found to be an appropriate person to have such custody" (p. 434). The Supreme Court reversed the Florida State Court.

Griffith and Duby (1991) in their recent review, pointed out that there remains considerable controversy over the scope of *Palmore,* particularly concerning whether *Palmore* applies only to custody matters or to custody and adoption policy. Griffith and Duby suggested that, in practice, adoption agencies were easily circumventing strictures possibly imposed by *Palmore* by arguing that, instead of being guilty of showing racial bias, their insistence on same-race placements of Black children was justified by their strong commitment to the best interests of Black children. Furthermore, the Fifth Circuit Court in *McWilliams v. McWilliams* (1986) and the Eighth Circuit Court in

J.H.H. and S.C.H. v. O'Hara (1989) disagreed clearly over the scope of *Palmore*.

C. The Minnesota Case: In the Matter of the Welfare of D.L.

Regardless of the developments in the judicial arena, adoption placement professionals have continued to match children with potential parents who have similar racial characteristics. There has often been an unwritten hierarchy for placements. The first choice would be a family in which both potential parents matched the race of the adoptive child. This often resulted in a longer wait in foster care for minority children, because minority adoptive parents were not represented on placement lists in the same numbers as White adoptive parents. Transracial adoptions were discouraged by adoption agencies in varying degrees, but in practice were often prohibited altogether.

Recent developments in Minnesota have provided a new twist to the task of considering the role of race in adoptive placements. Minnesota's Minority Adoption Act (1990) established a preference for placement of a minority child with a relative or with a family of the same race or ethnicity. The statute provided in relevant part:

> The policy of the state of Minnesota is to ensure that the best interests of children are met by requiring due consideration of the child's minority race or minority ethnic heritage in adoption placements. . . .
>
> In the adoption of a child of minority racial or minority ethnic heritage, in reviewing adoptive placement, the court shall consider preference and in determining appropriate adoption, the court shall give preference and in determining appropriate adoption, the court shall give preference, in the absence of good cause to the contrary, to (a) a relative or relatives of the child, or, if that would be detrimental to the child or a relative is not available, to (b) a family with the same racial or ethnic heritage as the child, or if that is not feasible, to (c) a family of different racial or ethnic heritage from the child that is knowledgeable and appreciative of the child's racial or ethnic heritage.

This statute was at the heart of a recent case heard by the Court of Appeals of Minnesota (*In re D.L.*, 1991) which resulted in the determination that this statute violated the Equal Protection Clause of the United States Constitution found in Section 1 of the Fourteenth Amendment. The United States Supreme Court explained the purpose of this clause as being the elimination of all governmentally imposed discrimination based on race (*Palmore v. Sidoti,* at 432, 1984).

The facts of the Minnesota case merit further review. D.L. was born in July 1989, and a few days later was turned over to White foster parents. D.L.'s mother, Debra, was Black, and her father, Jonathan, was White. Debra and Jonathan had two other children—a boy, who lived with Jonathan, and a girl, who lived with Debra's Black parents—and another child Debra had from a prior relationship. In February 1990, Debra's parents learned she was in jail in Minneapolis. They called Debra, who said D.L. was with good people, and she would get her back. In June 1990, Debra called her mother from jail to say that if she couldn't get out of jail, she was going to lose D.L. Debra's mother, D.L.'s grandmother left Virginia and went to Minneapolis to locate D.L. In October 1990, D.L.'s foster parents filed a petition to adopt D.L. In November 1990, the grandparents filed their own petition to adopt D.L.

January 1991 was set for trial. But before the trial commenced, the trial court limited the hearing to the issue of whether there was good cause not to approve the Black grandparents as D.L.'s adoptive parents. At the trial, the court made findings on the good health of the grandparents, their emotional and financial stability, the nurturing environment of their home, the presence in the home of D.L.'s two sisters, and the grandparents' willingness to supply necessary love and comfort to D.L.

Expert witnesses also testified that breaking the bond that had developed between D.L. and her foster parents would cause temporary harm. But they disagreed on the question of the harm's permanency. Of note was that one expert witness, a clinical social worker, testified that "African-American parents have a unique ability to pass along to their children the coping skills needed for a minority person to manage in this society" (*In re D.L.* at 411, 1991). The trial court granted the adoption petition of the Black grandparents, and found that this was consonant with the "relative" placement preference of the Minority Adoption Act. The court also separately found that it was in D.L.'s best interest to be adopted by her grandparents. The foster parents then appealed.

The appeal was brought on four major grounds: that the Minority Adoption Act impermissibly classified adoption children based on their race, thereby violating the Fourteenth Amendment's Equal Protection Clause; the trial court erred in refusing to consider the petition of the foster parents; the trial court was biased; and the trial court erred in permitting the testimony of a surprise rebuttal witness.

While the Minnesota Court of Appeals found that the state's Minority Adoption Act was unconstitutional, it nevertheless affirmed the trial court's decision granting a Black child's adoption by her maternal grandparents when the child's White foster parents had also petitioned to adopt her. The court declared the Minority Adoption Act unconstitutional because it imposed different standards for placing minority and nonminority children. However, the court applied a legislative and common-law preference for placing children with relatives and found that this relative, or family, preference existed apart from the unconstitutional state statute. Minnesota's long-standing common-law custodial preference for near relatives supported the trial court's decision to place the child with her grandparents. The Appeals Court did not agree that the trial court had made other errors claimed by the appellants.

One judge issued a dissenting opinion in this case, arguing that any common-law preference for relatives applied in custodial actions should not be extended to adoption proceedings. Family preference in the context of custodial issues fostered the goal of preserving family unity while parental rights continued. The adoption statute seeks to provide a permanent family relationship for children only after the biological parents' rights are terminated. The adoption statute severs all biological relations and creates an entirely new parent-child relationship with a new family and new relatives.

This case was appealed to the Minnesota Supreme Court (*In re D.L.*, 1992) which affirmed the Court of Appeals. The Supreme Court held that the adoption of a child by relatives is presumptively in a child's best interest unless good cause to the contrary can be shown or it is detrimental to the child. This court underlined the assumption that blood relatives will do more for the child's welfare than persons without biological ties. The Minnesota Supreme Court in fact avoided the Constitutional issue by relying on the state's established strong preference for placement with blood relatives. Indeed, it is noteworthy that the Court of Appeals issued its decision in February 1992. In April 1992, the Minnesota Legislature indicated its strong belief in a family preference by amending the Adoption Act to apply a primary family preference and secondary racial or ethnic matching preference in all adoptions and foster care placements regardless of the child's race. In addition, the Minnesota Department of Human Services directed its placement agencies to make special efforts to recruit relatives to become adoptive parents (*In re D.L.* at 380, 1992). The Minnesota Supreme Court noted this legislative change and indicated, however, that family preference was not automatic. Trial courts must still make detailed findings of fact to ensure the child's best interest is served.

This Minnesota case, and the response of the Minnesota Legislature, deserve reflection because the case apparently shifted the basis of the argument from ethnicity or race to a discussion about family preference. The Minnesota Supreme Court referred to "the common-sense notion that blood relatives are most likely to look out for one another's interests, through good times and bad" (*In re D.L.* at 380, 1992). It is hard to fault this language, which at first blush appears neutral and respectful of family ties. But behind the family-blood-tie argument was other, race-based logic. For one thing, the trial court judge had authored a newspaper article (see *In re D.L.* at p. 378, 1992) in which he criticized White Minnesotans for wanting to transform colored people into a reasonable facsimile of White people. So the trial judge may have had race on his mind when he was arguing for family preference. (Both the Appeals Court and the Supreme Court denied that the trial judge showed bias.)

Furthermore, at least one expert witness (the clinical social worker) argued on the basis of race for the adoption placement to be given to the Black grandparents. It should be emphasized, too, that the legislative preference list moves from family preference as a primary basis, to race and ethnicity as a secondary basis. One other point to be observed here is that the Appeals Court explicitly noted that D.L.'s mother and grandparents were African-American, but not her father. It would be interesting to know exactly what her skin color looked like then and what her skin color will look like as the years go by. Only time will tell, unless at the age of two she was already very dark-skinned, whether she was placed with a family she will ultimately resemble.

Political Considerations

A major player in the political arena of public policy development regarding transracial adoptions has been the National Association of Black Social Workers (NABSW). In 1972, the NABSW took a vehement stand against the placement of Black children in White homes for any reason (NABSW, 1972).

The NABSW argued that identity developed on the three levels of all human development—physical, psychological, and cultural; and they posited that developing self-identity was a prime function of the family, hence the obvious incongruence of a White family performing this function for a Black child (NABSW at p. 1, 1972). "One's physical identity with his own is of great significance . . . internal conflict is inevitable by (the transracial adoptee's) minority status within his own family. Such status is normal in school, employment and some communities but in one's most intimate personal group such oddity status is neither normal nor anticipated" (NABSW at p. 2, 1972).

The position statement went on to discuss the importance of socialization in one's cultural heritage, and stated that the developmental needs of Black children were significantly different from those of White children. "Only a black family can transmit the emotional and sensitive subtleties of perception and reaction essential for a black child's survival in a racist society" (NABSW at p. 2, 1972).

Further, they claimed that White parents of Black children engaged in special programming which put normal family activities in the form of special family projects to accommodate the odd member of the family (NABSW at p. 3, 1972). The statement concluded by suggesting that more be done to place Black children with members of their own extended families, even if financial assistance was necessary to accomplish this. This might require easing the "obstacle course of the traditional adoption process" used to screen out likely Black adoptors by emphasizing "high income, educational achievement, residential status and other accoutrements of a white middle-class life style. . . . (p. 3) We stand firmly . . . on conviction that a white home is not a suitable placement for black children and contend that it is totally unnecessary" (p. 4).

In 1991, the NABSW reaffirmed its position against transracial adoption (NABSW, 1991). The Association affirmed ". . . the inviolable position of African American children in African American families where they belong physically, psychologically and culturally in order that they receive the total sense of themselves and develop a sound projection of their future" (NABSW at p. 25, 1991). The NABSW also argued that even the most loving and skilled White parent could not avoid doing irreparable harm to an African-American child (NABSW at p. 30, 1991).

The NABSW suggested the Indian Child Welfare Act be amended to include a National African-American Heritage Child Welfare Act or similar legislation that would provide guidelines for considering race and ethnic origin in foster care and adoption placement. A child placement agency would be expected to make special efforts to place the child with relatives, or secondarily with a family of the same racial or ethnic heritage as the child, or thirdly with a family of different racial or ethnic heritage from the child but knowledgeable and appreciative of the child's racial or ethnic heritage.

The NABSW's position, in a nutshell, is that Black families are willing and able to adopt Black children but are often discriminated against and discouraged from adopting. The problem of so many Black children in the child welfare system is not due to the shortage of Black homes or diminished transracial placements, but rather to the difficulties in getting the children out of the agencies. A main concern for NABSW is that Black children not lose their cultural identity by being reared in a White home.

The claims made by the NABSW *en route* to their conclusions obviously do not withstand serious scrutiny, as the research data on outcome studies do not support the logic used by the NABSW. On the other hand, their ultimate recommendations about adoption preferences, as described in the proposed National African-American Child Welfare Act, are similar to those articulated by the Minnesota Legislature.

The National Association for the Advancement of Colored People (NAACP) addressed the transracial adoption issue in an emotionally charged process that began in 1991 with a proposed resolution (Resolution on Transracial Adoption, 1991). The Resolutions Committee worked on the proposal during its May, 1992 meeting and it went before about four thousand delegates to the National Convention held in July, 1992 in Nashville, Tennessee.

In relevant part, the proposed resolution was based on preliminary arguments that conceded several points: studies of transracial adoption have revealed that Black children placed in White homes suffered no psychological damage and were not confused by their racial identity; about forty percent of the half million children in foster homes are minority children, and this percentage has increased dramatically in the last few years, such that there are more Black children waiting to be adopted than may be placed with Black families; matching children with families based on race was rooted in segregationist policy; and that adoption, as opposed to foster care, constitutes a permanent home for children conducive to stability and security. The resolution itself then advocated the following adoption preference procedures: if Black families are available and suitable under the criteria of advancing the "best interest" of the child, Black children should be placed with these Black families. If Black families are not available, transracial adoption ought to be pursued as a viable and preferred alternative to foster care.

Four thousand delegates almost unanimously approved this resolution. However, all resolutions must be ratified by a majority of the sixty-four members of the NAACP Executive Board. In October 1992, this Board revised the resolution to support the NABSW proposed legislation to amend the Indian Child Welfare Act. The final resolution passed by the Board (Transcultural Adoption Resolution (Revised), 1992) emphasized the importance of attempting to preserve natural families, and stated that Black children should be placed with suitable Black families in advancing the best interest of the child and that barriers to such placements be removed. More intense efforts should be made to place Black children with extended family members. Transracial adoption would only be an alternative if all efforts for same-race placement had been exhausted and only if Black lay and professional "monitors" presumably agreed that all possible efforts had been made to find Black families and had been futile. There was no limit placed on the length of time that should be allowed to find an appropriate same-race placement.

The resolution finally ratified was quite different from the resolution approved by delegates at the National Convention. The positive language about transracial adoption present in the resolution passed by the delegates disappeared from the final document. The more stringent rules regarding transracial placements became the policy position of the NAACP for the purposes of lobbying efforts in Congress and the development of legislative policy.

In July 1993, the NAACP National Convention took place in Indianapolis, Indiana, where the Minneapolis Suburban Branch reintroduced a resolution that was similar to the one that had been passed at the July 1992 Convention. This time, the resolution was overwhelmingly defeated, thereby apparently leaving the NAACP with a policy position that, while not being straightforwardly anti-transracial adoption, in practice would allow the professionals to search as long as they wished to find a same-race adoptive family.

The pathway ploughed by Minnesota and the NAACP has not had the field all to itself. The Texas Legislature (General and Special Laws of Texas, 1993) recently passed a bill to take effect on September 1, 1993 that prohibits the denial or delaying of an adoption on the basis of the race or ethnicity of the child or the prospective adoptive parents. This crisp language is precisely what is being sought on the national level by advocates of transracial adoption. But to date they have not been successful.

In July 1993, Senator Howard Metzenbaum (Democrat of Ohio) introduced Senate Bill 1224 that would prohibit the delaying or denying of the placement of a child for adoption "solely because of the race, color, or national origin of the adoptive parents or the child." However, the bill also permitted consideration of race, color, or national origin if such factors were relevant to the best interests of the child involved, and were considered in conjunction with other factors. Not surprisingly, advocates of transracial adoption have criticized two critical aspects of this proposed national legislation. First, they dislike use of the word "solely" as a modifier of the prohibition against use of race and color in the adoption process. The advocates think this modifier dilutes the prohibition and makes the bill weaker than the Texas Legislation. Second, the advocates regret the permissible consideration of race, color, or national origin if these elements are factors relevant to the best interests of the child. The advocates think such language will allow agencies that are against transracial adoptions to hide their intentions.

The Senate Labor and Human Resources Committee approved a substitute for Senator Metzenbaum's original bill that more clearly favors transracial or multiethnic adoptions over long-term foster care. The bill also prohibits the disqualification of prospective adoptive parents from initial consideration based on race. The bill passed the Senate on March 21, 1994. Drafts of the bill unfortunately place no time limit on the search, which in a practical sense is seriously problematic.

Discussion

It should be clear, in reviewing recent developments in the transracial adoption arena, that the debate continues, particularly regarding the major question about how one should construct the racial identity of families. Still, what have the recent developments reviewed here shown us?

First, the longitudinal outcome data reported by the longest running and most recently reported study (see Simon, 1993) show that the transracial adoption of Black children by White families can be, in the vast majority of cases, a successful undertaking. The transracially adopted children can thrive and grow into confident adults who know who they are, who feel good about themselves, who perform well at school and work, and who remain well connected to their adoptive parents. It would therefore be an important and progressive step to have professionals in the adoption field understand these outcome data. We also urge that these studies be continued and replicated, because the factors involved in these studies are complicated and numerous. So improvement of the study design could be continually effected. But dissemination of the results in these studies is crucial if the expert testimony given in adoption cases is to improve, and if the experts are to stop uttering claims about the unique, magical abilities of African-American parents to impart special coping skills to Black adopted children (see *In re D.L.* at 411, 1991).

Regardless of the outcome findings derived from the scientific studies, the Minnesota court case and legislative response analyzed here suggest powerfully that many people in this country have a reflex response about the nature and structure of families. We do not believe it is a purely racial argument that persuaded the Minnesota Supreme Court to take the position that blood relatives will do more for a child's welfare than persons without biological ties. And so, at first blush, the State Supreme Court's position in that case, and the Minnesota Legislature's response that relatives should first be sought in the adoption quest, all seem reasonable—even though it was additionally convenient that the grandparents granted the adoption were of the same race as the child.

We must emphasize that certain potential issues in the Minnesota case were lost from sight because the litigants were White, nonrelative, foster parents on the one hand and Black relatives on the other. Using the court's arguments about family, what would they have decided had the litigants turned out to be the non-Black father's parents on the one hand and the Black mother's parents on the other? And what would the court do with children born of biracial families who look more like their White relatives than their Black relatives? So the preference for relatives easily carries the day when the contest is between qualified nonrelatives and qualified relatives. But where White relatives and Black relatives are competing for the child born of a biracial marriage, we can see the NABSW rearing its head to argue the child is automatically Black, although the grounds for such a position remain baffling, even if traditionally convenient.

Ultimately, it seems hard to us to take the position that argues for the racial integrity of families and for same-race placements in the adoption context. Such an argument inevitably brings us face to face with an example where the argument, when applied, seems ludicrous. For example, the recent Jenkins case reported by a Texas newspaper proves the point (Orwig, 1993). Four-year-old Christopher Jenkins, a Black child, had lived all his life with White foster parents. But a Black family sought to adopt Christopher, and the contest between qualified

White and Black nonrelatives was on. Under the Minnesota rules, since no relatives were in this contest, the secondary preference would apply. So the Black family, being of the same racial heritage as the child, would win the contest. In fact, the Texas judge ordered that the White family retain care of the Black child they had raised for the preceding four years.

As a society, we apparently believe that racial discrimination is acceptable in the context of establishing families, although we will generally not tolerate racial discrimination in other contexts. Segregated schools and segregated water fountains patently offend, but the everyday reality suggests it is expected that children share the characteristics of skin color and ethnic heritage with parents who have given them up.

We continue to argue that color-blind adoptive placements of Black children still make the most sense in the large majority of cases. We concede that family preference is logical in the context where, all other factors being equal, nonrelatives are competing against relatives to adopt a child. We have no objection to agencies being encouraged to seek relatives to adopt their children. However, a reasonable, but strict, time limit needs to be put on the amount of time allowed for a search. And under no circumstances should the search for relatives be confused with a preference for same-race placements.

So once the search for relatives is concluded, the task must be to pursue a color-blind placement. The community value of the same-race family and the professional norm of same-race placements in the adoption context must give way to the hard-won judicial standard that outlaws racial classifications. We think Senator Metzenbaum's bill would have been improved had he sought to facilitate, as a first step, the search for adoptive relatives in a time-limited period. Then, beyond that, the task ought to be to find an appropriately qualified adoptive family without regard to the race, color, or national origin of the adoptive parents or of the child.

Our position puts little stock in the age-old belief that requires all family members to be of the same racial stock or the same ethnic background. We also think it clearly confirmed by the research findings that members of a given family can have different racial origins and still grow up to be healthy and productive members of society, without feeling inferior to the dominant group in the society.

References

Allen, A., Griffith E. E. H., Hollinger, J. H., *et al.* 1992. "Responses to Bartholet." *Reconstruction,* 1(4): 46–54.

Bartholet, E. 1992. "The Politics of Trans-racial Adoption: A Special Report against Racial Matching." *Reconstruction,* 1(4): 22–43.

Bartholet, E. 1991. "Where Do Black Children Belong? The Politics of Race Matching in Adoption." *University of Pennsylvania Law Review,* 139: 1163–1256.

Bates, K. G. 1991. "Are You My Mother?" *Essence,* April, p. 49.

Brown v. Board of Education, 347 U.S. 48J (1954).

Bolling v. Sharpe, 347 U.S. 497 (1954).

General and Special Laws of Texas, Acts 1993, 73rd Leg., Ch. 189.

Griffith, E. E. H. and Adams, A. K., 1990. "Public Policy and Transracial Adoptions of Black Children," in *Family, Culture and Psychobiology,* ed. Sorel E. Ottawa: Legas Press, pp. 211–233.

Griffith, E. E. H. and Duby, J. L., 1991. "Recent Developments in the Transracial Adoption Debate." *Bulletin of the American Academy of Psychiatry and the Law,* 19: 339–350.

Grow, L. J. and Shapiro, D., 1974. *Black Children—White Parents: A Study of Transracial Adoption.* New York: Child Welfare League of America.

In re D.L., 479 N.W. 2d 408 (Minn. App. 1991).

In re D.L., 486 N.W. 2d 375 (Minn. 1992).

J. H. H. and S. C. H. v. O'Hara, 878 F. 2d 240, 242 (8th Cir. 1989).

Loving v. Virginia, 388 U.S. 1 (1967).

Mahoney, J. 1991. "The Black Baby Doll: Transracial Adoption and Cultural Preservation." *University of Missouri-Kansas City Law Review,* 59: 487–501.

McCalope, M., 1991. "Should White Families Adopt Black Children?" *Jet,* January 28, p. 12.

McLaughlin v. Florida, 379 U.S. 184 (1964).

McRoy, R. G., Zurcher, L. A., Lauderdale, M. L., and Anderson, R. N., 1982. "Self-esteem and Racial Identity in Transracial and Inracial Adoptees." *Social Work,* 27: 522–526.

McRoy, R. G., Zurcher, L. A., Lauderdale, M. L., and Anderson, R. E., 1984. "The Identity of Transracial Adoptees." *Social Casework,* January: 34–39.

McWilliams v. McWilliams, 804 F. 2d 1400, 1403 (5th Cir. 1986).

Minority Adoption Act, Minn. Stat. Sect. 259. 28, subd. 2, (1990).

National Association of Black Social Workers. 1972. *Position Statement on Trans-Racial Adoptions.* New York: National Association of Black Social Workers, September.

National Association of Black Social Workers. 1991. *Preserving African American Families: Research and Action Beyond the Rhetoric.* Detroit: National Association of Black Social Workers, April.

Orwig, G., 1993. "Christopher Becomes a Jenkins." *Abilene Reporter-News,* February 27, pp. 1A and 8A.

Palmore v. Sidoti, 466 U.S. 429 (1984).

Resolution on Transracial Adoption, 1991. reported by Thorwald Esbenson, Chair, Political Action Committee, Minnesota Suburban Branch of the NAACP, December 4.

Shireman, J.F., 1988. *Growing Up Adopted: An Examination of Major Issues.* Chicago: Chicago Child Care Society.

Shireman, J.F. and Johnson, P.R., 1986. "A Longitudinal Study of Black Adoptions: Single Parent, Transracial, and Traditional." *Social Work,* 31: 172–176.

Silverman, A.R., 1993. "Outcomes of Transracial Adoption." *The Future of Children,* 3(1): 104–118.

Silverman, A.R. and Feigelman, W., 1984. "The Adjustment of Black Children Adopted by White Families," in *Adoption: Current Issues and Trends,* ed. Sachdev, P. Toronto: Butterworth and Company, pp. 181–194.

Simon, R., 1993. "Transracial Adoption: Highlights of a Twenty-year Study." *Reconstruction,* 2(2): 130–131.

Simon, R.J. and Alstein, H., 1977. *Transracial Adoption.* New York: John Wiley.

Simon, R.J. and Alstein, H., 1981. *Transracial Adoption: A Follow-up.* Lexington, MA: Lexington Books.

Simon, R. J. and Alstein, H., 1987. *Transracial Adoptees and Their Families.* New York: Prager Publishers.

Simon, R.J., Alstein, H. and Melli, M., 1994. *The Case for Transracial Adoption.* Washington, DC: American University Press.

Sowell, T., 1992 "Adoption Apartheid." *The Washington Times,* November 21, p. C1.

Stolley, K.S., 1993. "Statistics on Adoption in the United States." *The Future of Children,* 3(1): 26–42.

Tatara, T., 1993. *Characteristics of Children in Substitute and Adoptive Care: Based upon FY 82 through FY 89 Data.* Washington, DC: American Public Welfare Association, May.

Transracial Adoption Resolution (Revised). 1992. ratified at NAACP Board Meeting, October.

U.S. Bureau of the Census. 1992. *Statistical Abstracts of the United States: 1992 (112th edition).* Washington, DC: U.S. Government Printing Office.

6

Coping with Stress through Art: A Program for Urban Minority Children

Ian A. Canino

Introduction

In My World

In my world there would be no illegal drugs
In my world there would be no physical or
    sexual abuse towards children . . .
In my world there would be no hate for people
    from different races . . .

In this world there are fatal illegal drugs
In this world there is mistreatment of
    innocent children
In this world there is no harmony between
    countries or races
Oh! how I wish I could have my world.

by Rhina (*Like Open Bright Windows*, p. 60, 1991)

This poem was written by an urban adolescent in a program called Poets in the Schools (Klahr and Oskam, 1988). As a participant in a writing workshop, she learned to express herself through poetry. The program exemplifies three core issues: exposure to stressful life events, discrimination, and a need to develop empowering coping mechanisms.

The Art Project at the Museo del Barrio has attempted to address all these issues. It is located within the community of a large, inner-city area, one block away from the public school of the children it serves. The area is constituted mainly by Latino and African-American children. The staff of the Museo Art Project reflects this ethnic diversity as well. Helping children cope with stress by developing ethnic and individual empowerment through art is the objective of this program.

El Museo Art Project

Introduction

Presently one in five American children lives in poverty. Among African-American and Latino children younger than six years of age living in female-headed households, nearly three out of four are poor (S.O.S. America, 1990). Poor teenagers are four times more likely than nonpoor teens to have below average basic skills, and are three times more likely to drop out of school (S.O.S. America, 1990). It is estimated that there are two million children in New York City, sixty percent of whom are poor. Of these, the great majority are ethnic minorities. An estimated 245,000 children suffer from emotional disorders, of whom twenty thousand are severely emotionally disturbed (The Commissioner's Task Force Report, 1991). Nationally, it is estimated that seventy to eighty percent of the approximately 7.5 to 9.5 million children with emotional problems are not getting the help they need (Select Committee on Children, 1990).

History and Description of the Program

In view of these findings, and the paucity of culturally sensitive primary prevention programs in the community, a dialogue was established in 1989 with a well-known community art museum called El Museo del Barrio. The museum, located amidst a primarily Latino and African-American urban community, is well known for its dedication and support of Latino art. It is housed in the same building as many after-school and adult education programs. The museum has ample space to hold groups, and maintains an excellent relationship with the public school in its area. In addition, it supports an Artist in Residence Program, which allows young minority artists to be funded while they develop their work. The museum's staff had expressed concern about the multiple stressors to which the community's children were exposed. Concomitantly, the Department of Child Psychiatry at Columbia University felt strongly that their child psychiatry trainees needed to immerse themselves in the culture of the children they were treating, learn ethnically sensitive group approaches, and develop skills in primary prevention techniques. For the joint project between the museum and Columbia to proceed, two problems needed to be addressed: identification of funds for the project, and the legal issues of treating children who were not patients. A nonprofit organization, "CARING at Columbia," was formed. Its Board of Directors identified private donors for the program and supplied a volunteer. The funds supported the artist in residence, who would become the coleader of the group, and allowed for the purchase of art materials. The program was designed to produce workshops teaching children about ethnic art and about better ways of dealing with stressful events. It was an educational activity, not a therapeutic one, thus resolving the legal issues.

El Museo Art Project is presently a community rotation for Columbia's Child Psychiatry residents, in which a trainee joins an artist and a volunteer in conducting group art sessions for children. The workshops last one and a half hours weekly. Each workshop continues for a total of three months. The public school across the street serves as a referral. After receiving parental permission, the school allows the children to attend these workshops during lunch and recreational time. The average age of the children is between nine and eleven years of age. The children attending the workshops were represented by the following demographic characteristics: forty-three percent were African-American, forty-one percent were Latinos, four percent were Black-Latino, four percent were African, four percent were White-Latino, and four percent were other. Thirty-four percent of the children were males and sixty-six percent were females. Forty-four percent of the children lived with both of their biological parents, while thirty percent lived with their mother only. The rest had other living arrangements. Both parents were alive for the vast majority of children (ninety-six percent). Thirty-four percent of the children's parents had divorced. In sixty-seven percent of the families, both parents were working in low-paying jobs. Approximately fifteen percent of the families were not working at all. The rest of the families consisted of one working parent.

The size of groups ranges from eight to twelve children. The group is selected to reflect the reality of the ethnic, religious, and racial diversity of the neighborhood. Missed appointments are virtually non-existent.

The majority of children have no identified psychiatric problems, but have been exposed to a variety of stressors. A demographic and modified Life Events Checklist (Johnson and McCutcheon, 1980) is administered in the first session to guide the group leaders to the specific profile of each group. This checklist allows the subjects to rate whether an event has occurred to them in the previous twelve months, whether they thought it was a good or bad event, and how much effect it had in their lives. Items are rated on a scale of 1 to 4. "No effect" is rated a 1, and "great effect" is rated a 4. Some items are deleted as not applicable to this age group, and some spaces are added to let the children identify their own categories of other important life events.

Among the most frequently negatively endorsed life stressors were the following: drug and alcohol exposure in the neighborhood and at home, death and illness in the family or friends, failing grades, witnessing violence in the school, home, or neighborhood, and being "put down" because of their color or their race.

The group activity is designed to utilize an artistic modality, such as drawing, painting, or sculpting, as the ultimate expression and the concluding effort of each group session. The first part of the group consists of a discussion led by the therapist regarding the most prevalent stressor affecting the group. Children are able to express their concerns and fears, and are then supported to identify better and more effective approaches to diminish the impact of the stressor. The second part of the group consists of a creative activity, during which the children continue to discuss their concerns. The art project is chosen beforehand so as to elicit discussion relevant to the needs of each group, and to support and consolidate ethnic pride and empowerment.

Through this group process, each idea is explored for its meaning and for its pertinence to the growth of each individual member. Gradually, and through the contribution of all the group members, one final, large artwork is produced, reflecting the final, collective, and integrated idea of the whole group. During the process of creating this large artwork, the children are exposed to issues of leadership and cooperation, ethnic pride, activity and passivity, fear of failure and success, and themes of competition, jealousy, and envy. Topics evolve regarding individual response styles to stress, current societal concerns, needs, and expectations, and the necessity of curtailing impulsivity and developing frustration tolerance for the actual success of the group and its social goal. The children are helped in their social comprehension skills, are supported in their self-esteem, and, through the group, are taught to be adaptable and to solve problems more effectively.

Once the large artwork is finalized, the children are able to evaluate and visualize the synthetic and integrated result of their group effort as well as the pictorial message reflecting their sociocultural environment. The artwork is later shown in a group exhibit at the end of the year, to which members of the community at large are the guests. The artist and participating children are the hosts. At the end of each workshop, the children are administered a brief series of questions to assess their own evaluation of the project.

Theoretical Principles

A. Stress and Coping

All children and adolescents face multiple life stressors. Some are natural, others are man-made. Some involve loss, while others involve threat. Some are likely to be recurrent, while others are not likely to reappear. Some are situation-specific. Many minority children in urban areas are also exposed to the stressors of migration, acculturation, poverty, urban violence, and discrimination.

The relationship of stress to symptom development has been and is presently being researched. Rutter (1981) noted that the term "stress" related to a wide range of events, and that because of their heterogeneity, different types of events may well have different psychopathological consequences. Loss events tend to evoke depressive psychopathology, while threatening events evoke anxiety. Some studies have found that children who experience loss events are at greater risk of suicidal attempts (Cohen-Sandler, *et al.,* 1982) and somatic complaints (Hodges, *et al.,* 1984). Exposure to violence has been associated with poor school performance in general (Dyson, 1990), as well as to lower performance in cognitive tasks (Emery, 1989; Dietrich, *et al.,* 1983). Research has documented that younger children tend to be more vulnerable to disaster stress (Gleser, *et al.,* 1981), hospitalizations (Rutter, 1985), or the birth of a sibling (Rutter, 1981). Adolescents seem to be more vulnerable to interpersonal stress (Compas and Wagner, 1991), and male children seem to be more affected psychologically by divorce (Rutter, 1981) and chronic illness (Lavigne and Routman, 1992).

In terms of those stressors associated with poverty, it seems that factors associated with the criminal background of the parents, the extent of family discord, and residence in overcrowded or dilapidated housing contribute more to predicting delinquency than parental occupation or income. Rutter (1975, 1979) described six familial risk factors that appear to correlate with childhood psychiatric disorders: severe marital distress, low social status, overcrowding or large family size, paternal criminality, maternal psychiatric disorders, and admissions of children into foster home placement. The cumulative frequency of these factors, more than any single one, creates the increasing possibility of negative outcomes. Homel and Burns (1989) focused on the home, the street, and the neighborhood separately to determine the effect of each when controlling for other sociodemographic factors. They concluded that children who reside in commercial and industrial areas of inner cities "stood out from all others in their feelings of rejection, worry, fear, anger, unhappiness and dissatisfaction with their lives and with their families in particular" (pp. 152–153).

While we await better social policies to protect these children, many children in urban areas cope with these stressors through strong family and community supports. Many are not so fortunate, and need to develop strong coping skills to avert the development of symptoms of distress. Still others may succumb to mental illness. Those children who can learn to develop a sense of locus of control, self-esteem and perceived competence, social orientation and comprehension, achievement motivation, problem-solving abilities, and humor comprehension seem to do best. Cultivating these characteristics in children exposed to stressful life events was one of the major reason for establishing the Museo Art Project.

The Museo Art Project teaches children exposed to stress how to learn better coping strategies. It is a primary prevention program that induces host resistance (Kaplan and Saddock, 1991) and specific protection (Goldston, et al., 1990). It is a psychoeducational approach that integrates Rutter's principles about resiliency (1987). It was designed to increase the children's self-esteem and self-confidence, to increase their belief in their own self-efficacy and ability to deal with change and adaptation, and to help them create a repertoire of problem solving strategies.

B. Ethnic Development

The term ethnicity includes group-shared patterns of rules of social interaction, values, social customs, behavioral roles, perceptions, and language usage (Barth, 1969; Ogbu, 1981). Ethnic patterns refer to well-documented differences in affective, attitudinal, and behavioral patterns across cultures (Whitting and Whitting, 1975).

Goodman (1964) and Porter (1971) state that children develop awareness of ethnic and color differences by the ages of three or four. Between the ages of four and eight, children develop an ethnic orientation (Goodman, 1964), strong social preferences with given reasons (Porter, 1971), consolidation of group concepts (Katz, 1976), and awareness of group affiliations (Aboud and Mitchell, 1977). By then they are aware of the more obvious ethnic cues, such as language utilization. Between the ages of eight and ten, children exhibit attitude crystallization (Goodman, 1964; Katz, 1976) and curiosity about other groups (Aboud and Mitchell, 1977). They realize the power, status, and economic resources of their own ethnic group, and sometimes may identify with another group. Such identification may stem from their conviction that they belong to another ethnic group, their wish that they did, or their admiration for the other group because of its higher status in the culture (Rotheram and Phinney, 1986). It may not be until adolescence and young adulthood that they think and behave differently from members of other ethnic groups in specific situations. In communities located in close proximity to other ethnic groups, adolescents may borrow or integrate other ethnic patterns into their behavior.

Rotheram and Phinney (1986) describe ascribed ethnic criteria in children as the way others see them, according to their physical characteristics of skin color and facial and body features. Performance criteria refers to the extent to which children feel and act as group members. Ethnic identity behavior may vary in children, and be more salient in some situations than in others. This depends on the status of the group, as well as on the degree of ethnic heterogeneity and homogeneity in the daily life of the youngsters (Canino and Spurlock, 1994). Ethnic attitudes may also vary across groups, according to other situational factors such as proximity, ethnic balance, density, frequency of contact, degree of vertical mobility, and changes in the political and economic structure (Levine and Campbell, 1972).

The coexistence of ethnicity and minority status trigger predictable social and psychological behaviors within the ethnic group and between that group and the majority culture. When the majority culture develops negative connotations which serve to channel hostilities towards the minority group, prejudice and discrimination result.

Gordon Allport (1954) defines ethnic prejudice as "an antipathy based upon a faulty and inflexible generalization. It may be directed toward a group as a whole, or toward an individual because he is a member of that group" (p. 10). The group or individual who becomes the object of prejudice most often experiences a position of disadvantage. Children exposed to negative images of their ethnic background, or those taught by teachers values that conflict with their families, may develop a sense of inferiority. They become mistrustful of an environment which they correctly perceive as rejecting and demeaning of themselves and their culture. For those who have been exposed to the belief that there is nothing they can do to change this, additional feelings of alienation and impotence develop.

Aware of the principles of ethnic identity development, the multiple ethnic groups surrounding these children, and the open expression of incidents of discrimination perpetrated against them and their families, the Museo Art Project is held in a culturally sensitive context. It utilizes techniques to enhance ethnic empowerment and pride, and teaches the children the importance of leadership, ethnic diversity, group participation, and prosocial behavior. This in turn serves to increase their self-esteem, consolidate their identity, and fortify their coping skills. Some current theories emphasize the benefits of socialization to more than one culture's group norms (Fitzgerald, 1971; McFee, 1968; Ramirez and Castenada, 1974) because the community consists of both Latino and African-American children. The Museo Art Project exposes the children to both groups' ethnic and creative history during group sessions. This enhances the children's appreciation of ethnic diversity and their own group's contributions to the greater society.

C. Group Artistic Expression

With the growth and prominence of group psychotherapy, and the concomitant emphasis on the understanding of group process as a tool for change, group art therapy has increasingly used the medium of joint projects as a way of helping individuals to externalize and examine their interrelationships and life experiences.

Edith Kramer (1973) states that art is a method of widening the range of human experiences by creating equivalents for such experiences. It is an area where experiences can be chosen, varied, and repeated at will. The artistic experiences take place in a world of symbols and conventions, which has the power to evoke genuine emotions, and are enjoyed without guilt and anxiety and without the urge for acting out. Kramer (1973) has also studied artistic sublimation in the works of children. She views this artistic expression as a replacement of the impulse to act out fantasies by creating equivalents for the fantasies through visual images. Dalley (1990) underlines the variety of emotional situations expressed through art and play. Through art sessions, children can be less verbal, and communicate in a less problematic and more spontaneous manner. Feelings, as in free play, can be expressed and contained in the session in a safe and nonthreatening way.

Particularly relevant to our culturally diverse urban children, Gruber (1981) supports the theory that creativity and the creative process can be understood as a systematic integration of a specific biopsychosocial potential interacting with a ripe domain at a particular moment in a unique sociohistorical context. Finally, Congdon (1985) sees all art as a communication system and as a heritage of many different groups. Through studying folk art, children can identify and recognize specific groups of people, alter and elaborate on barriers distinguishing minority and majority cultures, and, most of all, become aware of the similarities among cultures in expressing, through art, universal human needs and feelings.

El Museo Art Project, through its artist in residence and a child psychiatry trainee, utilizes culturally relevant art materials and subjects in a group setting, often inviting live community models, offering children ethnic snacks, and educating them about Latino and African-American art and artists.

Project Examples

A. Portrait Quilt

The group began the quilt project (Figure 1) by sharing their own cultural heritage. Throughout the first part of each session, the children told stories about their oldest living relative:

> Aunt Helen is my father's uncle's wife's mother. She is eighty-three. Helen cooks lemon pies and apple pies. She was on the march on Washington with Dr. Martin Luther King Jr. Great Aunt Helen goes to church and uses a cane. She lives in Washington, D.C.   L.T.

> The year before last I met my great grandmother Yeya. She lives in Santo Domingo, which is the capital of the Dominican Republic. She is very poor. She doesn't have a kitchen or a door or cold water.

Figure 1

She is ninety-six. She sits on the porch with the cat and the dog. She watches the sun set. Cousin Pedro lives next door.   S.G.

Ethel is my father's mother. She is seventy-three. She originally came from North Carolina. I often visit her. She likes the company because we play games and watch TV together. She goes away and she brings me stuff like toys, jewelry, and shoes. On my father's side there are two ethnic groups: Cherokee and Black. On my mother's side there are: Irish, Trinidadian, Spanish, English, Hawaiian, and Black.

G.C.

As the children told these stories, the artist in residence and the volunteer used the opportunity to discuss African-American history and religion (L.T.); Caribbean geography, poverty, the supportive nature of pets and family (S.G.); and the richness and diversity of a multicultural society (G.C.).

During the second part of each session the students worked in teams of two. They made contour line drawings of each other, transferred them on to fabric, painted the drawings with inks, and sewed the pieces together to make a quilt. The children learned about mixing colors to capture the beautiful subtleties of the many tones of their skin. In the process they discussed the differences in their personalities and how thoughts and feelings are reflected in a person's facial expressions and body language. They discussed how to better "read" their parents, and how hard it was to identify "sad" feelings and how easy to identify "angry" feelings.

The group leaders helped the children develop a sense of ethnic pride and empowerment. They strengthened their social inference skills by helping them identify emotional states in another person and empathize with their role and perspective. They supported the children's self-image, and helped them label their feelings. As the project was completed, the beauty and uniqueness of all the faces was underlined within the importance of maintaining connections with themselves, their peers, and their family of origin. The final quilt became the portrait of the multiethnic richness of their community.

B. Neighborhood Collographs

This group was based on the positive and negative aspects of street life. After a walk through their community and a visit to their neighborhood park, the children were asked to comment about what they saw and then turn their stories into pictures. These in turn eventually became cardboard plates or "collographs." These images were then printed into individual and group pieces. The childrens' comments about their individual pieces include the following:

> This is what happens every day in the streets of New York. There is a homeless man behind a tree doing what he has to do . . . people on the sidewalk shoot crack, people chase people, and old ladies take off their high heels to protect themselves (Figure 2).
>
> Child X

> When you go outside, there is always a lot of violence. People shoot other people, they shoot out the windows . . . people walk around with "machetes" (Figures 3, 4, 5)., , In the center of my picture there is a man yelling "STOP" as he sees all the violence.
>
> Child Y

Figure 2

During the group discussion, the children shared the hope that, working together, they could learn to make a difference in urban society. They shared their concerns that, since the homeless they saw were minority people, this might happen to their parents and themselves when they grew up. Through group discussion and the support of the group leaders, many topics were addressed: old women needed to learn to protect themselves through special programs, bystanders to violence should seek help, a strong message should be sent to politicians and the media to "STOP" crime and poverty by developing better schools and better job opportunities, and children should have good recreational facilities.

During this group, the history of many minority men and women who had made a difference was reviewed. The children also learned skills to seek out reliable adults if they sensed danger, and to inform the correct authorities in the school or at home if they themselves were exposed to violence. Techniques to avoid drugs and to immediately identify a drug pusher were discussed.

Through this psychoeducational model, the children strengthened their ability to identify a problem, generate an alternative, and evaluate the consequences of the new alternative. They were reminded how to identify the range of emotions evoked by a variety of stressful situations, and how to self-talk and access support from their peers and

Figure 3

available adults. The group leaders reinforced the importance of clear communication. The children taught each other how to identify a dangerous person by their nonverbal cues, and how to initiate conversations and ask appropriate questions for clarification. They were most of all taught how to elicit the memory of those minority men and women who had made a difference, and how to reward themselves with positive self statements when effective tasks were accomplished.

C. Papier-Mâché Figures

The group of children who participated in this workshop were sixthgraders, many of whom were underachieving, had little self-confidence,

Figure 4

and had difficulty working cooperatively. The *papier-mâché* figures (Figure 6) were created using the theme of self-empowerment. The artist and the volunteer began the group by discussing aspects of the childrens' lives, such as violence, drugs, and unemployment, which threatened their sense of well-being. The children then develop ideas about imaginary powers that would enable them to protect themselves and help other people in need. Each student created drawings of a personality in power, made armatures, shaped the figures with papier-mâché, and finally painted them. Examples of the personalities created included a man with a magical wand, a figure with wings, and a power dancer. The children during this project stated:

> Powerful. These figures are like the person you never could be. If you wanted to be your imaginary self, you could have special abilities

Figure 5

Figure 6

such as flying, super strength, and super vision. You wish you could have wishes that would last for a long period of time. You could use some kind of magic to stop a war. With your wish you could be a child for twenty years and not go to school. With the super abilities I would put the people that kidnap kids in jail.   S.V.

I would help the homeless by giving them food and putting them in a safe house. Give them an education and a job. Give them clothes. Take them to the doctor for a check-up.   Y.J.

Advice to rule the country. I'd put them in a biosphere. After two years I'd give them a safe home and a job. For the teenagers that dropped out of school and got on drugs, I would put them back in the right school level to recover their education.   T.D.

The figures in this workshop were representative of the hopes and need for empowerment in these children. These *papier-mâché* creations were clearly ethnic community characters with the power to lead, cause change, and protect. While the children constructed them they discussed their wishes and fears. The group leaders utilized the opportunity to discuss the need to develop rapid responsivity to danger, altruism, strength and hope, and information-seeking behavior, which are some of the resiliency techniques utilized by Mrazek and Mrazek (1987).

Conclusion

There are certainly many children of all races in the world affected by poverty, recurrent traumas, and stressful life events. These events are often associated with an increased likelihood of illness and with the timing of disease onset. In children they are often associated with increased physician visits, reports of physical health complaints, and number of school day absences (Johnson, 1986). In spite of this, many children develop or are born with an incredible resiliency. Others have strong family or community supports, while still others are fortunate to have access to good health care. Many, unfortunately, do not. Some develop symptomatic behavior and still others suffer psychiatric disorders.

These children, considered minorities in this country, constitute a majority in the world population. They come from diverse cultural groups with a variety of child-rearing practices, family norms, religious beliefs, and, more importantly, with specific assumptions about the etiology of illness and cultural patterns of health-seeking behavior. Some of these children have arrived here recently, and many have been here for a long time. Others were always here.

Multiple approaches and levels of intervention are necessary for these children. Better access to quality care is crucial. Effective, comprehensive, and culturally sensitive treatment and rehabilitative approaches need to be implemented with more frequency for those already manifesting illness. Children at risk must be addressed also, in order to reduce the incidence of new cases and contain both the financial and social costs to our society. Health promotion and specific protection strategies are thus equally important.

The art workshops in the Museo attempt to integrate primary prevention approaches within an ethnically empowering and culturally sensitive context for young urban children. Utilizing an art group psychoeducational approach, the Museo program teaches children strategies to develop resiliency against the future consequences of continuous stressful life events. The childrens' evaluations of their workshops consistently indicated that they had made better friends, enjoyed the art project, and better understood the things that bothered them.

They had learned to talk and understand their feelings, found new ways of dealing with their environment, and had learned about their culture. A program which incorporates families more fully is now under consideration to evaluate whether the preliminary results of this program can be enhanced. In the meantime, these workshops serve as one step towards enhancing the children's capacity for dealing with many of their concerns. Perhaps some day the wish captured in this inner-city youngster's poem will be realized. She wrote the following:

Ever since I came into this world,
    I wanted to shout.
If only someone else could see what
    I am about.
As days and days go by,
    I want to break down and cry.
I wish I could be me.
    Then I could be free.

by Trayshawn (*Paper Moon*, 1986)

References

This project was made possible through the able direction of Ms. Joan Yeshida, Director of Training of the Museo del Barrio in New York City, and the dedication of Ms. Robin Holder, the artist in residence and Mrs. Chiqui Williams from CARING. Special thanks are due to the children of PS 171 and to the child psychiatry trainees from Columbia University. This program could not have been implemented without the generous funding of CARING and the New York State Office of Mental Health Contract #COO4106.

Aboud, F. E. and Mitchell, F. G. 1977. "Ethnic Role Taking: The Effects of Preference and Self-identification." *International Journal of Psychology*, 12: 1–17.

Allport, G. 1954. *The Nature of Prejudice*. New York: Doubleday Press.

Barth, F. 1969. *Ethnic Groups and Boundaries*. Boston: Little, Brown.

Canino, I. A. and Spurlock, J. 1994. *The Treatment of Minority Children*. Guilford Press.

Cohen-Sandler, R., Berman. A. L., and King, R. A. 1982. "Life Stress and Symptomatology: Determinants of Suicidal Behavior in Children." *Journal of the American Academy of Child Psychiatry*, 21 (2): 178–186.

Commissioner's Task Force Report on Mental Health Services for Children and Adolescents. 1991. New York: New York City Department of Mental Health, Mental Retardation and Alcoholism Services.

Compas, B. E. and Wagner, B. M. 1991. "Psychosocial Stress During Adolescence: Intrapersonal and Interpersonal Process," in *Adolescent Stress Causes and Consequences,* eds. Colton, M. E. and Gore, S. New York: Aldine de Gruyter.

Congdon, K. G. 1985. "A Folk Group Focus for Multicultural Education." *Art Education,* 13–16, January.

Dalley, T. 1990. "Images and Integration: Art Therapy in a Multicultural School" in *Working with Children in Art Therapy,* Eds. Case, C. and Dalley, T. London: Butler and Tanner.

Dietrich, J. N., Starr, R. H., and Weisfield, G. E. 1983. "Infant Maltreatment: Caretaker-Infant Interaction and Developmental Consequences at Different Levels of Parenting Failure." *Pediatrics,* 72: 532–540.

Dyson, J. L. 1990. "The Effects of Family Violence on Children's Academic Performance and Behavior." *Journal of the National Medical Association,* 82 (1): 90–95.

Emery, R. E. 1989. "Family Violence." *American Psychologist,* 44: 321–328.

Fitzgerald, T. K. 1971. *Education and Identity: A Reconsideration of Some Models of Acculturation and identity.* New Zealand Council of Educational Studies, 45–57.

Gleser, G. C., Green, B. L., and Winget, C. 1981. *Prolonged Psychosocial Effects of Disaster: A Study of Buffalo Creek.* New York: Academic.

Goldston, S. E., Yager, J., Heinicke, C. M., *et al.,* eds. 1990. *Preventing Mental Health Disturbances in Childhood.* Washington, D. C.: American Psychiatric Press.

Goodman, M. E. 1964. *Race Awareness in Young Children* (rev. ed.). New York: Collier.

Gruber, H. E. 1981. *Darwin and Man: A Psychological Study of Scientific Creativity,* 2nd ed. Chicago: University of Chicago Press.

Hodges, W. F., Tierney, C. W., and Buchsbaum, H. K. 1984. "The Cumulative Effect of Stress on Preschool Children of Divorced and Intact Families." *Journal of Marriage and the Family,* 46: 611–617.

Homel, R. and Burns, A. 1989. "Environmental Quality and the Well-being of Children." *Social Indicators Research,* 21: 133–158.

Johnson, J. H. 1986. *Developmental Clinical Psychology and Psychiatry: Life Events as Stressors in Childhood and Adolescence,* vol. 8, California: Sage Publication.

———. and McCutcheon, S. 1980. "Assessing Life Stress in Older Children and Adolescents: Preliminary Findings with the Life Events Checklist," in *Stress and Anxiety,* vol. 7, ed. Sarason, I. G. and Spielberger C. D. Hemisphere Publishing Co, Washington, DC, 111–125.

Kaplan, H. I. and Saddock, B. J., eds. 1991. *Synopsis of Psychiatry,* 6th Edition. Baltimore: Williams and Wilkins.

Katz, P. A. 1976. "The Acquisition of Racial Attitudes in Children" in *Towards the Elimination of Racism,* ed. Katz, P. A. New York: Pergamon Press.

Klahr, M. and Oskam, B. 1988. *To Open A Door: Conducting Poetry Workshops for Populations with Special Needs. A Program Manual.* New York: Poets in Public Service, Inc.

Kramer, E. 1973. *Art Therapy in a Children's Community.* Springfield: Charles Thomas.

Lavigne, J. V. and Routman, J. F. 1992. "Psychological Adjustment to Pediatric Physical Disorders: a Metaanalytic Review." *Journal of Pediatric Psychology,* 17 (2): 133–157.

Levine, R. and Campbell, D. 1972. *Ethnocentrism: Theories of Conflict, Ethnic Attitudes and Group Behaviors.* New York: John Wiley Press.

McFee, M. 1968. "The 150% Man, a Product of Blackfeet Acculturation." *American Anthropologist,* 70: 1096–1103.

Mrazek, P. J. and Mrazek, D. A. 1987. "Resilience in Child Maltreatment Victims: A Conceptual Exploration." *Child Abuse and Neglect,* 11: 357–366.

No Place to Call Home: Discarded Children in America. 1990. Select Committee on Children, Youth and Families. U.S. House of Representatives, 101 Congress. Washington, D.C.: U.S. Government Printing Office.

Ogbu, J. 1981. "Origins of Human Competence: A Cultural Ecological Perspective." *Child Development,* 52: 413–429.

Porter, J. D. R. 1971. *Black Child, White Child: The Development of Racial Attitudes.* Cambridge, MA: Harvard University Press.

Ramirez, M. and Castaneda, A. 1974. *Cultural Democracy, Biocognitive Development, and Education.* New York: Academic Press.

Rhina. 1991. "In My World," in *Like Open Bright Windows,* ed. Plantenga, B. New York: Poets in Public Service, Inc.

Rotheram, M. J. and Phinney, J. S. 1986. "Introduction: Definitions and Perspectives in the Study of Children's Ethnic Socialization" in *Children's Ethnic Socialization Pluralism and Development,* eds. Phinney, J. S. and Rotheram, M. J. Newbury Park: Sage Publications.

Rutter, M. A. 1979. "Protective Factors in Children's Response to Stress and Disadvantage" in *Primary Prevention of Psychopathology,* vol. 3, eds. Kent, M. W. and Rolf, J. E. Hanover, NH: University Press in New England.

———. 1981. "Stress, Coping and Development: Some Questions and Some Answers." *Journal of Psychology and Psychiatry,* 22: 323–353.

———. 1985. "Resilience in the Face of Adversity: Protective Factors and Resistance to Psychiatric Disorders." *British Journal of Psychiatry,* 147: 598–611.

———. 1987. "Psychosocial Resilience and Protective Mechanisms." *American Journal of Orthopsychiatry,* 57 (3): 316–331.

———. Cox, A., Tripling, C., *et al.* 1975. "Attainment and Adjustment in Two Geographical Areas. The Prevalence of Psychiatric Disorder." *British Journal of Psychiatry,* 126: 493–509.

S.O.S. America; A Children's Defense Budget. 1990. Washington, D.C.: Children's Defense Fund.

Trayshawn. 1986. "Me," in *Paper Moon,* Eds. Halperin, J. and Radicella, J. New York: Poets in Public Service, Inc.

Whitting, B. B. and Whitting, J. W. 1975. *Children of Six Cultures: A Psychocultural Analysis.* Cambridge, MA: Harvard University Press.

7

Images Used by African-Americans to Combat Negative Stereotypes

Barbara A. Hudson

There is a long artistic tradition among the civilizations of Africa. In Yoruba traditions, for example, there is a deity of art and creativity, Obatala/Orisanla, "who models and sculpts people to life" (Nzegwu, 1992). For centuries the Mende of Sierra Leone have practiced the traditional art form of masquerades. In these masquerades the traditional mask, Sowo,[1] becomes an "artistic center around which revolves the intellectual, social, and spiritual life of the Mende community" (Boone, 1986, p. xxi). Some of these traditions and artistic impulses have informed the works of many artists of African ancestry. Throughout the African diaspora, from South America, to the Caribbean, to Central America, to North America, one can find evidence of African artistic traditions (Thompson, 1984). Although the Atlantic slave trade did much to disrupt civilization and culture as the forcibly enslaved Africans had known them, there was never a complete stripping of the African's cultural styles and forms. As Thompson writes in his book, *Flash of the Spirit:*

> a grand message of Yoruba Atlantic art wherever it is found . . . is this: sheer artlessness may bring a culture down but a civilization like that of the Yoruba, and Yoruba Americans, pulsing with ceaseless creativity richly stabilized by precision and control, will safeguard the passage of its people through storms of time. (1984, p. 97)

Indeed, artists of African descent have endured a multitude of storms. Among those storms has been the persistence of the view that artists of African descent are circumscribed primitives and exotics with limited skills in communicating more thoughtful and grand artistic ideals.

Recent scholarship has begun to challenge these criticisms and to examine the significance of African-American art, not as a subset of American art, but as American art. What did (do) African-American artists have to say about the experiences of Americans of African descent as well as all Americans? In examining the impact of artists of the Harlem Renaissance, Mary Schmidt Campbell (1987) asks "do they constitute just an exotic interlude in the history of American art? or do their images provide the seeds of an authentic artistic tradition?" Indeed it does seem that African-American artists have provided an essential perspective on the life of African-Americans which has gone beyond the glories of Afrocentricity and which indeed remained in line with authentic artistic traditions of Mother Africa; although those traditions have been modified by cultural displacement, enslavement, marginalization, and sociopolitical oppression. Nzegwu (1992) comments on the assumptions which are often made when an artist's work is described as African:

> It is often simplistically assumed that to say an artist's work is African is to imply that it portrays a well-defined set of features that are typically African or black. Of course, from this perspective, the very term "typically African" conjures up images that are replete with black faces, quixotic forms, and phantasmogoric scenes. The view of African art as exotic, neoprimitive and expressionistic derives from the popular racist view of Africans (and by extension Blacks) as unsophisticated and incapable of deep critical thought. It is a view that fails to acknowledge the range, breadth and diversity of works by African artists in diaspora. (1992, p. 32)

Early African-American artists had to contend with the same kinds of political and social exclusions as nearly all African-Americans. As artists, committed to the artistic endeavor, and understanding the power of image to construe a social reality, they were surely cognizant of the ways in which African-Americans were depicted by others who were not interested in celebrating African heritage nor in detailing the experiences of ordinary Black life in America. A major problem was the sheer prevalence of demeaning images of African-Americans which were used not only to sell products but also to maintain African-Americans as subjectively inferior. Frequently, African-American artists were unable to exhibit their art widely, and therefore faced tremendous obstacles to countering White racist art and artifacts, which were indeed more readily accessible and hugely popular. Additionally, their work was likely to be dismissed as interesting but primitive. Because the nature of feeling and being constitutes driving impulses toward creativity, it can be easily argued that racist distortions of a people's way of feeling and being can lead to creations which counter those notions. Nzegwu's comments in the following passage captures an aspect of being an artist of African ancestry, situating that being in a context which supersedes the aesthetic, spiritual, documentary, or political dimensions of artistic aims:

> . . . in the larger political sense . . . "being of African ancestry" implies a certain way of being, perceiving or inscribing space that can not be divorced from the actual experience of living in an institutionally marginalized location and that cannot be spelled out in abstraction. Race mediates art in a multiplicity of ways, not the least of which is the black person's non-stereotypical responses to events in a racially inscribed environment. . . . (1992, p. 32)

Throughout the history of artistic expression among African-Americans, their work conveying Black life more realistically has been hampered by the presence of White racist "artistic" depictions designed to reenforce notions of inferiority and primitivism and to drown out images which construed African-Americans as people going about their lives ordinarily despite extraordinary circumstances. Cornel West has correctly pointed out that Black artists are faced with "a modern black diasporan problematic of invisibility and namelessness" (West 1993b, p. 16) which "requires that black people search for validation and recognition in a culture in which white supremacist assaults on black intelligence, ability, beauty, and character circumscribe such a search" (p. 59). Despite attempts to cast the artist and his or her art into an abyss of namelessness and invisibility, African-American art has survived, and truly exhibits a rich diversity. Throughout this chapter I will cite specific examples to illustrate how a unique and powerful African-American artistic identity has emerged against a background of White racist stereotypic imagery.

What does this landscape, "Falls of Minnehaha" (photo 3) have to do with this subject, one may correctly ask? During the nineteenth century, most African-American artists created or painted in the prevailing style of the day. This painting, "Falls of Minnehaha," by Robert Scott Duncanson (1821–1872) is a good example of this; it was inspired by the Hudson River School of painting. In the early eighteenth century, a few completely self-taught artists, such as Neptune Thurston and

Photo 1   Anonymous
"Happy Coon," Early Twentieth Century (detail)
silver spoon, Souvenir of Atlanta Georgia
Collection of the Amistad Foundation
Wadsworth Atheneum, Hartford, CT

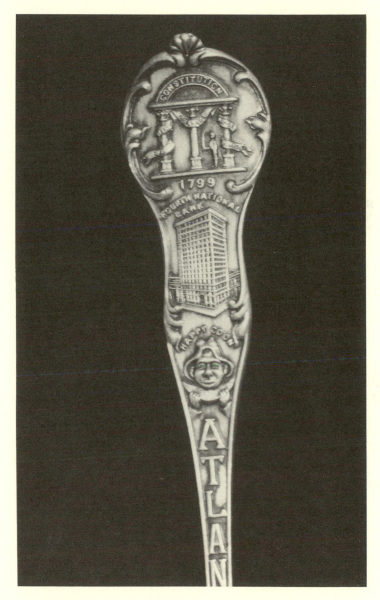

Photo 2   Anonymous
"Happy Coon," Early Twentieth Century (detail)
silver spoon, Souvenir of Atlanta Georgia
Collection of the Amistad Foundation
Wadsworth Atheneum, Hartford, CT

Photo 3 Robert S. Duncanson
"Falls of Minnehaha," 1862.
oil on canvas
National Museum of American Art, Smithsonian Institution
Washington, D.C.

Scorpio Moorehead, painted nonstereotypical images of African-Americans.[2] Unfortunately their productions were not widely known, and very few works remain from which we can get a clear perspective of their output.

Nineteenth-century Blacks had to contend not only with enslavement and later emancipation and reconstruction but also with the constant bombardment of stereotypic images such as this souvenir silver spoon, "Happy Coon" (photos 1 and 2), which conveyed overt messages of subhuman status, and denied the sociopolitical reality of Blacks during that era. Mary Edmonia Lewis[3] (1843–1912?) was not only the first Black woman in America to gain widespread recognition as an artist, but was also the first trained Black artist to use her heritage as subject matter. Born of mixed ancestry, African and Chippewa Indian, her neoclassical "Forever Free" shows an Indian girl kneeling in prayer next to a man with one hand raised containing a broken chain. Although the man's features are not identifiably African, he is thought to represent her father. Her sculpture, "The Old Arrow Maker" (photo 5) highlights her Native American heritage. "Hagar" (photo 4), named after the Egyptian wife of Abraham and sculpted in 1865 in white marble in neoclassical style, symbolizes the inner will and determination of oppressed people.

Henry O. Tanner[4] (1859–1937), the greatest of the nineteenth-century African-American painters, was born into a distinguished, free, Black family in Philadelphia. Tanner was the first academically trained artist to paint African-American genre scenes. Tanner's "The Thankful Poor" (photo 8), which is currently in the collection of Dr. and Mrs. William H. Cosby, Jr., and "The Banjo Lesson" (photo 9), which is owned by Hampton University, are two outstanding examples of this. However, Tanner is primarily remembered as a painter of religious subjects and themes. In 1892 Tanner left the United States, returning only for brief visits and to sell his paintings. "The Banjo Lesson" has become one of the most recognized paintings by an African-American, and is one of the few paintings in world art history to portray the tender guidance of an older man to a younger one. This tender, inviting, and humanistic depiction is contrasted with the popular and unflattering caricatures of toothy, grinning, banjo-playing blacks such as those depicted in "Strummin' On The Ole Banjo" (photo 10), "Playin' The Banjo" (photo 11), and "Smiling Sambo" (photo 12). Perhaps Tanner's "The Banjo Lesson" was inspired by his reaction to these demeaning caricatures. Unfortunately those caricatures, with their distortions and rejection of real Black physiognomy, were the images of

Photo 4   Mary Edmonia Lewis
            "Hagar," 1875.
            carved marble
            National Museum of American Art, Smithsonian Institution
            Washington, D.C.
            Gift of Delta Sigma Theta Sorority, Inc.

Photo 5 Mary Edmonia Lewis
"The Old Arrow Maker," ca. 1872.
marble
National Museum of American Art, Smithsonian Institution
Washington, D.C.
Gift of Mr. Joseph Sinclair

Photo 6   Currier and Ives
The Darktown Series
"A Dude Swell," 1883.
chromolithograph
Collection of The Amistad Foundation
Wadsworth Atheneum, Hartford, CT

A DUDE BELLE.

Photo 7 Currier and Ives
The Darktown Series
"A Dude Belle," 1883.
chromolithograph
Collection of The Amistad Foundation
Wadsworth Atheneum, Hartford, CT

Photo 8 Henry O. Tanner
"The Thankful Poor," 1894.
oil on canvas
Collection of Dr. and Mrs. William H. Cosby, Jr.
Greenfield, Massachusetts
Photograph courtesy of Ms. Barbara A. Hudson

Blacks which most Americans of that time saw. By all accounts, images such as "The Banjo Lesson" were seen by a relatively small number of people. Almost every medium imaginable was employed to convey the message of Black inferiority. Black images, most often depicted in service roles, were used in advertisements to sell soap, clothing, and everything else, from grits to gin.

However, against overwhelming odds, Blacks created a full range of images that portrayed themselves as whole individuals. "The Awakening of Ethiopia" (photo 13), by the classically trained sculptor, Meta Warrick Fuller (1877–1968), is a statement about the cultural and artistic awakening of Africa and Black Americans. This sculpture incorporates stylistic elements of Egyptian aesthetics as it emerges from swaddling, expressing rebirth. Sculpted in 1914, "The Awakening of Ethiopia" was produced prior to the Harlem Renaissance, and represents one of the first pieces of American art reflecting an African aesthetic.

Photo 9 Henry O. Tanner
"The Banjo Lesson," 1893.
oil on canvas
Hampton University Museum
Hampton, Virginia

Photo 10 Anonymous
"Strummin' On The Ole Banjo," circa 1890.
ceramic
Collection of The Amistad Foundation
Wadsworth Atheneum, Hartford, CT

Photo 11 Anonymous
"Playin' The Banjo," circa 1890.
painting
Collection of The Amistad Foundation
Wadsworth Atheneum, Hartford, CT

Photo 12   Anonymous
            "Smiling Sambo," early 19th century.
            tambourine
            Collection of The Amistad Foundation
            Wadsworth Atheneum, Hartford, CT

Works such as "The Thankful Poor," "The Banjo Lesson," and "The Awakening of Ethiopia," portraying Blacks with dignity and pride, were certainly in stark contrast to the popular and widely distributed Currier and Ives *Darktown Series*.[5] These trivial stereotypes created in 1883 ridiculed "free" Black citizens. "A Dude Swell" (photo 6) and "A Dude Belle" (photo 7) are chromolithographs which ridiculed Black participation in refined activities, and although the clothing is no longer tattered and torn as in earlier depictions, the stereotype is still the same. Although "A Dude Belle" is dressed in fine clothing as she strolls down the street with her parasol, she is depicted demeanin-

Photo 13 Meta Warrick Fuller
"The Awakening of Ethiopia," ca. 1914.
cast stone and plaster
Schomberg Center for Research in Black Culture
Art and Artifacts Division
New York Public Library (Astor, Lenox, and Tilden Foundations)
New York, New York

gly. Her corsage is an oversized bouquet of wildflowers, and rather than walking her dog she carries it. Even her dog has exaggerated facial features, which creates the impression that the two look alike. Likewise, "A Dude Swell" has grossly exaggerated facial features, which ultimately serve to dehumanize him. The entire series attempted to undermine the strivings for equality of "free" Blacks.

Harlem Renaissance sculptor, Sargent Claude Johnson (1887–1967), perhaps weary of seeing images of Black women depicted as mammys and Aunt Jemimas in ceramic cookie jars and salt and pepper shakers, such as "I'm Telling You" (photo 15), created the monumental and stately "Forever Free" (photo 14). "Forever Free," the figure of a mother made of lacquered cloth over wood, presents a majestic woman looking proudly ahead with communal strength as she protects her obviously content and playful children. Johnson believed in the human uniqueness of each living being, even with the threat of conformity and assimilation.

Artist Aaron Douglas (1898–1979) was one of the foremost artists of the Harlem Renaissance. Douglas was one of the first Black artists to heed social philosopher Alain Locke's call for Black artists to look to their heritage for artistic inspiration. A masterful painter and illustrator, Douglas is perhaps best remembered for the murals he painted for the Countee Cullen branch of the New York Public Library. Painted in a sweeping, rhythmic, geometric style, "Aspects of Negro Life" visually tells the story of Blacks in America from slavery to freedom. "Building More Stately Mansions" (photo 16) is a bold depiction of Blacks at work, perhaps building a new identity and a new civilization rooted in their own cultural traditions and heritage. Douglas's paintings helped to pave the way for the acceptance of Blacks as subject matter. In his art Douglas consistently depicted Blacks as a proud and majestic people.

Young Black children were frequently depicted as "sambos," "coons," and "pickanninies," as in the twin images on this earlier but lasting box of "Gold Dust" (photo 20) washing powder. Against this backdrop Laura Wheeler Waring, a Hartford, Connecticut-born artist, painted the images of Black children. Her painting, "Frankie" (photo 17), is painted with great warmth and sensitivity. "Jennie" (photo 18) by Lois Mailou Jones (1905–   ) and "Negro Boy" (photo 19) by Hale Woodruff (1900–1980) also depicted children with affection, sensitivity, and clarity.

Other artists such as Allan Rohan Crite (1910–   ), who describes himself as a visual recorder, attempted to record the everyday world

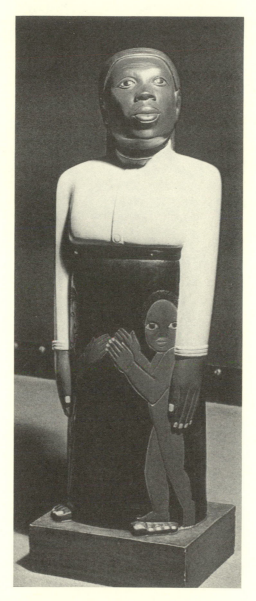

Photo 14   Sargent Johnson
"Forever Free," 1933.
lacquered cloth over wood
The San Francisco Museum of Modern Art
Gift of Mrs. E.D. Lederman
Photograph courtesy of Ms. E.J. Montgomery

Photo 15 Anonymous
"I'm Telling You," circa 1890.
ceramic
Collection of The Amistad Foundation
Wadsworth Atheneum, Hartford, CT

Photo 16 Aaron Douglas
"Building More Stately Mansions," 1944.
oil on canvas
Collection of Department of Art, Fisk University

Photo 17   Laura Wheeler Waring
              "Frankie," 1938.
              oil on canvas
              Private Collection
              Photograph courtesy of Ms. Barbara A. Hudson

Photo 18   Lois Mailou Jones
"Jennie," 1943.
oil on canvas
Collection of The Gallery of Art
Howard University, Washington, D.C.

Photo 19 Hale Woodruff
"Negro Boy," 1937.
oil on masonite
The Museum of African American Art
The Barnett-Aden Collection
Tampa, Florida

Photo 20 Lever Brothers, New York
"Gold Dust," circa 1910.
cardboard
Collection of The Amistad Foundation
Wadsworth Atheneum, Hartford, CT

Photo 21 Allan Rohan Crite
"A Bit Of Romance On Hubert Street," 1937.
oil on canvasboard
Collection of The Wadsworth Atheneum
Hartford, CT
The Ella Catlin Sumner and Mary Catlin Sumner Collection Fund

of Black people as they went about their daily lives. Crite's painting,
"A Bit Of Romance On Hubert Street" (photo 21), is a 1930s scene
in Crite's home town of Boston. This natural scene conveys the zeal
that Black folks had for life even in the midst of poverty. Realistic
scenes such as this were rarely seen by the public. Likewise, social
commentary paintings, such as "Mob Victim" (photo 22), painted by
Lois Mailou Jones in the 1940s, were not widely viewed. "Mob Victim"
protested the everyday occurrence of lynching of Black people during
the first half of the twentieth century. Dignity, compassion, and emotion are evoked as this man stands alert, with shoulders upright and
eyes open, as he looks at the perpetrators. Lois Mailou Jones taught
at Howard University in Washington, D.C. and, like Aaron Douglas,
heeded Locke's call for Black artists to embrace their heritage. She
continues to incorporate a range of Black subjects in her paintings.
Most Americans will recognize the image of this black "Jockey"
(photo 24) as an icon of Americana used to decorate front lawns, but

Photo 22 Lois Mailou Jones
"Mob Victim (Meditation)," 1944.
oil on canvas
First Honorable Mention for Oil Painting
Le Salon des Artistés Français, Paris, 1966
Collection of Dr. Lois Mailou Jones

Photo 23   Frederick Flemister
"Self-Portrait," 1941.
oil on canvas
Museum of African American Art
The Barnett-Aden Collection
Tampa, Florida

few would recognize this 1941 self-portrait of Frederick Flemister (1916–   ) (photo 23). This painting, in the style of Flemish art, with the figure in the foreground and the landscape receding into the background, was inspired by "Mona Lisa," and shows the subject looking boldly and timelessly at the viewer. This strong portrait of a Black man was not only unusual for its time but also a rare portrait of a Black man of any time.

In 1944 John Farrar (1927–1972) painted the stately "Mrs. Mitchell" (photo 28), a homage to older African-Americans. Similarly, Archibald Motley (1891–1980), in his 1924 "Mending Socks" (photo 27), a narrative painting, paid homage to the African-American elderly, and within this work conveys a great deal about the subject's life and lifestyle. The crucifix on the wall provides evidence of the importance of this woman's spirituality and religion. Books lying on the table convey her literacy and interest in knowledge. One can see that she likes the finer things in life, as evidenced by the lace tablecloth, the figurine, and the wall portrait. "Rain" (photo 25) painted by Jacob Lawrence (1917–   ) is also a narrative painting depicting life inside a Harlem tenement building. This painting, like many of Lawrence's paintings, captures the dignity with which Blacks lived their lives. His use of bold colors, which can not be appreciated in this black-and-white photograph, indicates optimism, and one can readily appreciate that, despite their present misery, the tenants will cope, repair, and persevere.

Sculptor Richmond Barthe (1902–1989) sought to capture the strength and dignity of a whole race when he fashioned this bronze sculpture, "The Negro Looks Ahead" (photo 26). Amidst the high hopes of the New Deal and excitement of pending change and better times for Blacks, Barthe captures the hopes and aspirations embedded in Black people's faith.

Black maternity has always been a rich subject for artist and sculptor Elizabeth Catlett (1915–   ). In "Mother and Child" (photo 29) carved in 1972, she depicts the strength of Black women. This figure sits proudly, shoulders erect, head upright, eyes looking forward, and firmly holding her offspring. The child appears to twist and turn in her lap, perhaps eager to experience the world outside the protective grip of the mother.

Finally, more than any other group, African-American artists have had to be visionaries, seeing African-Americans as a whole people and attempting to convey that to others who would not. Despite the flood of stereotypical images that continue today, and in spite of the distorted

Photo 24 Anonymous
"Jockey," circa 1870.
Collection of The Amistad Foundation
Wadsworth Atheneum, Hartford, CT

Photo 25   Jacob Lawrence
"Rain," 1937.
gouache on paper
Collection of The Wadsworth Atheneum
Hartford, CT
The Ella Gallup Sumner and Mary Catlin Sumner Collection Fund

Photo 26   Richmond Barthe
"The Negro Looks Ahead," ca. 1940.
bronze
Collection of The Wadsworth Atheneum
Hartford, CT
Gift of Vernon K. Kreible Foundation

Photo 27   Archibald Motley, Jr.
                 "Mending Socks," 1924.
                 oil on canvas
                 The Ackland Museum
                 The University of North Carolina at Chapel Hill
                 Burton Emmett Collection
                 Chapel Hill, North Carolina

Photo 28 John Farrar
"Mrs. Mitchell," 1944.
oil on canvas
Museum of African American Art
The Barnett-Aden Collection
Tampa, Florida

Plate 75

Elizabeth Catlett
Mother and Child

Photo: M. Yampolsky
Courtesy the Artist

Photo 29 Elizabeth Catlett
"Mother and Child," 1972.
wood
Collection of the artist
Photograph courtesy of Ms. Barbara A. Hudson

Photo 30 Phillip Lindsay Mason
"Family Scape," n.d.
acrylic on canvas
Collection of the Oakland Museum
Museum Donor's Acquisition Fund
Oakland, California
Photograph courtesy of Ms. E.J. Montgomery

depictions presented by the mass media about Black families, Black artists have continued to celebrate Black family life, whether it is nuclear or extended. Phillip L. Mason's (1939–   ) "Family Scape" (photo 30), painted in the 1970s, offers a portrait of hope and optimism. The placement of the bright sun in the background speaks to the hope that the Black family—in spite of the Middle Passage and enslavement, sociopolitical oppression, and distortion of image—will survive.

Even in the context of marginalization and racist critique of their work, African-American artists have produced a rich and diverse body of work. In addition to capturing the essence of what it means to be an American in black skin, they have also captured the essence of what it means to be an American. Their art has served to help construe a proud and noble African-American identity which confronted and still confronts popular, stereotypic imagery of African-Americans as inferior beings. It has indeed been and continues to be a great challenge for artists of color to find recognition and validation in a society which persistently devalues them and continues to conjure up images to represent Blacks in ways which reenforce White racist notions of White superiority.

Notes

1. Sowo is the Sande Society mask, the dancing spirit, whose visible persona consists of a sculpted helmet head and a costume of cloth and fibers, all in stark black.

2. There is limited information on early eighteenth-century Black artists. Samella Lewis and David Driskell discuss these artists in their publications (see References for those publications).

3. Mary Edmonia Lewis was the first artist of color to receive recognition for her sculptures, many reflecting her Native American and African heritage.

4. Tanner's father was the Reverend Benjamin Tucker Tanner, a minister and later bishop of the African Methodist Episcopal Church. A graduate-school-educated professional, Reverend Tanner was one of the most eminent Black men of his day—a clergyman, educator, journalist, and a leader in the fight for emancipation and freedom. Tanner's mother, also well-educated, operated a school and likewise participated in ongoing political and social struggles.

5. The Amistad Foundation's African-American collection at the Wadworth Atheneum contains the "Darktown Series." My appreciation to intern Kenya Washington for researching this series.

References

Anacostia Neighborhood Museum in cooperation with Barnett-Aden Gallery. The Barnett-Aden Collection. Washington, D.C.: Smithsonian Institution Press, 1974.

Boone, S. A. 1986. *Radiance From the Waters: Ideals of Feminine Beauty in Mende Art.* New Haven: Yale University Press.

Campbell, M. S. 1987. "Introduction," *Harlem Renaissance Art of Black America.* New York: Harry N. Abrams Inc. Publishers, pp. 11–56.

Driskell, D. C. 1976. *Two Centuries of Black American Art.* New York: Los Angeles County Museum of Art. Alfred A. Knopf.

———. 1985. *Hidden Heritage: Afro-American Art 1800–1950.* San Francisco: The Art Museum Association of America.

Hudson, B. A. 1993. *Facing the Rising Sun.* Hartford: Wadsworth Atheneum.

Lewis, S. S. 1978. *Art: African American.* New York: Harcourt Brace Jovanovich, Inc.

———. 1984. *The Art of Elizabeth Catlett.* Los Angeles: Hancraft Studios.

Locke, A. 1929. *The Negro in Art.* New York: Associates in Negro Folk Education, Hacker Art Books.

———. 1936. *Negro Art: Past and Present.* Washington, D.C.: Associates in Negro Folk Education.

McElroy, G. C. 1990. *Facing History: The Black Image in American Art 1710–1940.* Washington, D.C.: Corcoran Gallery of Art.

Nzegwu, N. 1992. "The Creation . . . of the African Canadian Odyssey." *The International Journal of African American Art,* 10 (1):16–37.

Porter, J. A. 1943. *Modern Negro Art.* New York: Dryden Press.

The Studio Museum in Harlem: 1987. *Harlem Renaissance: Art of Black America.* New York: Harry N. Abrams Inc., Publishers.

Thompson, J. F. 1984. *Flash of the Spirit.* New York: First Vintage Books Edition.

West, C. 1993a. "Horace Pippin's Challenge to Art Criticism," in *Keeping Faith: Philosophy and Race in America.* New York: Routledge, pp. 55–66.

———. 1993b. "The New Cultural Politics of Difference," in *Keeping Faith.* pp. 3–32.

8

National Nightmares: The Liberal Bourgeoisie and Racial Anxiety

Hazel V. Carby

This is an age of the world when nations are trembling and convulsed. A mighty influence is abroad, surging and heaving the world, as with an earthquake. And is America safe? Every nation that carries in its bosom great and unredressed injustice has in it the elements of this last convulsion. . . . Not by combining together, to protect injustice and cruelty, and making a common capital of sin, is this Union to be saved,—but by repentence, justice and mercy; for, not surer is the eternal law by which the millstone sinks in the ocean, than that stronger law, by which injustice and cruelty shall bring on nations the wrath of Almighty God!

Harriet Beecher Stowe

We live in chaos. . . . Everyone is trying to control their fear.

"Davies" in Grand Canyon

. . . the destruction of the racist complex presupposes not only the revolt of its victims, but the transformation of the racists themselves and, consequently, *the internal decomposition of the community created by racism.*

Etienne Balibar[1]

For a hundred and thirty years, Harriet Beecher Stowe's novel, *Uncle Tom's Cabin,* has been closely associated in the North American cultural and political imagination with the Civil War that followed on the heels of the book's publication in 1852. Indeed the association is now so close that Stowe's words appear prophetic of the bloody conflagration that was to come. In the same way, Lawrence Kasdan's film, *Grand Canyon*, has become haunted by the specter of the rebellion in the streets of Los Angeles that began on the night of April 29th, 1992.

My general concern is with the role of narrative in the production of what Etienne Balibar has called, "geneologies" of race and nation, what Toni Morrison has referred to as the inscription of national issues on Black bodies, and what Michael Rogin has described as "the surplus symbolic value of blacks, the power to make African Americans stand for something beside themselves."[2] My particular examples are narratives that both evoke and provoke a number of apparently contradictory racialized and gendered anxieties, fears, and desires. These narrative geneologies, in their production of symbolic power, have significant political resonance when they are produced in response to a perceived crisis in the social formation of a society. I believe that the process of inscribing national issues on all Black bodies accomplishes the ideological work which is necessary for the everyday maintenance of systems of racial injustice and inequality, but in this essay I wish to focus attention on and raise questions about the surplus symbolic power of Black male bodies.

I am particularly drawn to popular narratives that exhibit an explicit and self-conscious didacticism in their production, reproduction, or reconstruction of the meanings of race in order to create new geneologies, new surplus symbolic value, and new inscriptions of national concerns specific to a particular historical moment. Harriet Beecher Stowe's *Uncle Tom's Cabin* and Lawrence Kasdan's *Grand Canyon* are texts that self-consciously address the historical moment of their production and are explicitly didactic. But, of course, these texts are each specific to their time: Stowe invents her geneology of race and nation within a crisis of modernity, while Kasdan is reimagining relations between race and nation in ways that are symptomatic of a crisis in what is now frequently referred to as our postmodern moment.

A basic assumption of *Grand Canyon* is that we are living through a national crisis, a moment in history when the nation, as Harriet Beecher Stowe described it in 1852, "is trembling and convulsed" with its people on the brink of civil war. Indeed, the possibility of an imminent descent into chaos is a consistent visual and verbal motif of the film. Juxtaposing Stowe's description of the national tensions of the 1850s to Kasdan's filmic response to the social and political conditions of the 1990s is not a superficial gesture. The relation between these two cultural producers, even though they are separated by history and by ideological belief, is deeper than their shared premonitions of national disaster. Both *Grand Canyon* and *Uncle Tom's Cabin* are cultural texts that fear for the continued secure existence of the White and middle-class America to which they and their authors belong. Kasdan and Stowe each construct a racially defined and class-specific worldview, a worldview which is also, and not incidentially, the same class-specific and racially specific context that enables and secures the cultural production of their text; both are motivated by a desire to expose injustice and inequality; and each actively tries to construct a radical, political, and interventionist narrative of protest.

Grand Canyon and *Uncle Tom's Cabin* are texts which display a Dickensian urge to modify the existing social order through moral and ethical exortation. Both appeal to the hearts and minds of the privileged to intervene in the lives of those less fortunate than themselves. However, what appear to be appeals to undertake acts of selfless charity must also be identified as *selfish* acts: acts motivated by a desire to preserve both individual and class privilege. While stark inequalities of wealth, power, and privilege are identified in each text as being a threat to the continued existence of the social fabric, neither Stowe nor Kasdan calls for a dramatic change in the social organization of power and powerlessness, nor do they argue for a redistribution of wealth to end economic injustice. Neither text imagines the "destruction of the racist complex" which, Balibar, asserts, "presupposes not only the revolt of its victims, but the transformation of the racists themselves and, consequently, *the internal decomposition of the community created by racism.*"[3] While the narrative structures of both *Grand Canyon* and *Uncle Tom's Cabin* are haunted by the fear that the victims of injustice will rebel, they are blind to the necessity for social and economic transformation. Rather, both texts seek to preserve the powers and privileges of the White middle class by attempting to demonstrate why it is in the self-interest of that class to become the patrons of the underprivileged. Acts of patronage, far from transforming or destroying institutionalized inequality, actually reinforce such inequality, because the power of the patron is secured at the same moment that those subjected to patronage are confirmed in their powerlessness. Further, Stowe and Kasdan each construct the terms and conditions of a national crisis in their texts, so that the representation of the acts of White individuals, acts which are enacted upon Black bodies, serve not only the self-interest of the White middle class, but are simultaneously interpreted as acts that serve the national interest. In the face of imminent chaos, then, Stowe and Kasdan construct racialized and gendered geneologies that attempt to secure and confirm racialized national identities and, in so doing, attempt to bring narrative coherence and cohesion to the incoherence and fragmentation of their own historical time. Before turning to Kasdan's *Grand Canyon* I want to consider, briefly, the general terms of Stowe's creation of a narrative geneology, an inscription of national concerns onto Black bodies, in *Uncle Tom's Cabin*.

Planter paternalism was founded through the doctrines and practices of Anglicanism in the British mainland colonies, and by the Antebellum period was the dominant ideology that both justified and resolved the social contradictions that arose from the enslavement of African peoples in North America. Harriet Beecher Stowe directly confronted and, indeed, utilized the glaring contradictions between a doctrinal emphasis on sentiment, charity, and love within the Christian ethical system and the simultaneous blindness of Christians to the everyday acts of violence which were perpetrated upon Black bodies.[4]

Stowe became an Anglican as an adult. In 1851 she said that, while she was taking communion, she had a vision of "a saintly black man being mercilessly flogged and praying for his torturers as he died."[5] This vision and the novel which subsequently grew from it speak to the heart of one of the major contradictions in the ideology of planter paternalism. Stowe mobilized sentiment, charity, and love explicitly against two forms of social violence: against the violence of the slave system and against the potential violence of concerted acts of African rebellion. To enable her fictional act of dissent from the discourse of the dominant ideology of planter paternalism, Stowe actually had to reinscribe major portions of it: paternalism is not so much undermined in her text, as revised and reinforced. The creation of the character of Uncle Tom, the figure who can pray for his torturers while they torture him, is crucial to this process of revision.

Tom is consciously constructed as a de-Africanized figure; he is an embodiment of what Jon Butler describes as an African spiritual holocaust accomplished through the process of Christianization.[6] The surplus symbolic value of the figure of Uncle Tom consists of a fictive ethnicity which has the power to dislodge Blackness from its association with perpetual disobedience and rebelliousness. At the same time, Tom's restraint, his refusal to take revenge on those who abuse him, epitomizes absolute obedience to the Christian ethical system and subordination to the will of his persecutors. In other words, the figure of Tom is granted moral authority and occupies the ground of moral superiority only because he complies with the central doctrine of absolute obedience. The mechanism of his submission is Christianity which, while it separates Tom from those despised traits of African degeneracy, confirms the existence of African degeneracy in the un-Christian-ized. In this geneology of race and nation, Tom has an ideal existence in the category of humanity. The resolution of Stowe's grand narrative simultaneously asserts the necessity for the Christianization of Africans and the necessity to exclude them from the national entity, and this reinforces the insurmountable racial difference of their social existence. At the end of the novel, George, his family, and Topsy are re-Africanized outside the boundaries of America, and returned to Africa as Christian zealots and African patriots—a fictive ethnicity which denies the possibility that they could be imagined as American patriots.[7]

In the face of the institutional crisis and antagonistic social relations of the Antebellum period, Stowe's narrative accomplishes the ideological work necessary for a realignment of the national hegemonic structures of her time.[8] *Uncle Tom's Cabin* reconstructs a past, an alternative narrative of the meaning of slavery, in order to imagine an alternative national future: a future in which a paternalistic racial formation can be maintained under the hegemonic control of the White, Northern, middle class. This reimagining of the past, this new geneology, is produced in conjunction with the production of fear: a fear of supernatural retribution and a fear of the chaos that would inevitably result from the dissolution of the social order. It is this fear of what will happen in the present as a consequence of the slavery of the past that provides the motivation for action. Fear is Stowe's tool of persuasion, it inspires the White middle class to act in the interest of their own class security and, for Stowe, these class interests are synonymous with the national interest.

As Kasdan's film, *Grand Canyon,* opens a blank screen is all that can be seen. Within the darkness the audience can gradually hear the unmistakable pulsating sound of chopper blades. My mind, like so many others of my generation, is conditioned to make an immediate connection between this sound and a particular social and geographic space. For more than twenty years the noise made by a low-flying helicopter was used by film and television studios to signify the presence of Americans in the war zones of Southeast Asia, but I am unable to remember exactly when, in the last few years, I stopped associating the rhythmic sweep of these blades with Vietnam or Korea, and started, instead, to link the sound to Los Angeles.[9] Thus, although I knew nothing about the subject of the film, *Grand Canyon,* when I started to watch it I knew, because of this sound, that the blank screen would be replaced by the symbolic landscape of a Black urban neighborhood.

For Hollywood filmmakers, the Black neighborhoods of Los Angeles are important sites not just for the representation of death and destruction but for the enactment of social and political confrontations that constitute a threat to national stability. These neighborhoods are as fascinating in their exoticism, potential danger, and commercial marketability as Vietnam. In the United States, until quite recently, Southeast Asia has been culturally produced as the primary site of a national nightmare: a landscape through which North Americans moved under constant surveillance by a subhuman population of menacing "gooks." The "enemy" masqueraded as ordinary men, women, and children but, within the heart of the nightmare, these people were never ordinary and never innocent. This haunting vision has been supplanted in the popular cultural and political imagination by images of Black inner-city neighborhoods: neighborhoods that are spaces in which to enact the current national nightmares of the White, suburban, middle class; nightmares which are inscribed upon the bodies of young, urban, Black males and patrolled by the "Bloods" and the "Cripps."

Lawrence Kasdan's film, *Grand Canyon,* exemplifies the fascination of Hollywood with the Black inner city as the symbolic space of suburban anxiety. The film conceals its role in the actual production of White fear of Black aggression under the guise of merely confirming the already existing material reality of the threat which underlies the nation's anxieties. As the promotional material describes this process, "*Grand Canyon* is director Lawrence Kasdan's powerful and uplifting film about real life and real miracles . . . and about how, after the millions of choices we make in life, one chance encounter can change it all."[10]

At the begining of the film, Mack, an immigration lawyer played by Kevin Kline, searches for way of avoiding the heavy traffic leaving the Forum after a Lakers' game. He strays into a Black neighborhood that is so alien to him that he will later categorically assure his family, "You have never been where I broke down." What happens to Mack is evocative of the modernist journey into the "heart of darkness," a journey originally conceived in the context of European imperialism in Joseph Conrad's novel of that name, and recreated by Hollywood in Francis Ford Coppola's postmodern fantasy of war in Southeast Asia, *Apocalypse Now.* As Mack peers anxiously out of his windscreen at the unfamiliar and, to him, menacing aspect of a Black residential neighborhood, Warren Zevon's music plays in his car.

Music is very significant for Kasdan, and he selects the Warren Zevon sound track, "Lawyers, Guns, and Money," to establish a geneology for his protagonist. Clearly, the plea to "send lawyers, guns and money" strengthens the visual evidence that Mack is in physical danger, but the song also acts to situate Mack in history. Zevon's music is a product of seventies, White, yuppie, Southern California culture. Mack's familiarity with the words and apparent nostalgia for the song locate him within this culture and provide him with a history of who he is and where he comes from, a history that is otherwise absent from the film.[11] But Kasdan also uses music to signal the distance between the modernist conceptions of history and subjectivity at work in Conrad's novel and his own postmodern recognition of the fragmentation of social and political positionality. In Kasdan's editing room the Zevon sound track was dubbed to the film not only in order to register cultural and political conflict, but was intended to become the very ground of social and political contestation.

The words of "Lawyers, Guns, and Money" evokes, with a wry liberal irony, memories of the Cold War, of danger to Americans trespassing in exotic locales, and of covert U.S. intervention in other countries. The song establishes the liberal credentials of the protagonist, creates a mood of empathy for his mistake, and alerts the audience to the gravity of Mack's situation. As Mack's anxiety grows, Kasdan multiplies his visual and aural strategies for creating tension in the minds of the audience, who watch with an increasing sense of helplessness and panic if they identify with the plight of the protagonist. Mack switches off Warren Zevon in order to concentrate more effectively on finding his way home and, like a mouse in a laboratory maze, he turns his car around in a futile effort to escape. As Mack drives ever deeper toward the "horror" that awaits, he passes the shells of cars and the skeletons of abandoned buildings. As the landscape increasingly resembles a war zone, he begins to sing the words of the song himself in order to seek comfort in their familiarity and to raise the hope of summoning help. But as Mack mutters, "send lawyers, guns, and money," his words are overwhelmed by the taunting voice of Ice Cube, "ruthless, plenty of that and much more," emanating from what looks like a white BMW that slows down and drives beside him for a while. At this moment music becomes the prime vehicle for a cultural war which has encoded within it the political potential of a larger civil war. Ice Cube's band, NWA, is polarized against Warren Zevon in a symbolic confrontation which is central to the narrative geneology of race and nation that is about to pit a liberal, White, suburban male against Kasdan's creation of a "gang" of young, Black, urban males. The musical battle both produces and is the conduit for the wider class and racialized meanings of the scene; meanings which confirm ideological beliefs about what is currently characterized as the problem of the inner city and about what is imagined to be wrong with America.

However, the process of representing this war is structurally as well as ideologically unjust, and this is clear if we analyze the unequal editing of the musical battle. In contrast to the verbal and musical fragments of NWA's "Quiet on the Set," the audience is presented with coherent narrative selections from the Zevon lyrics. We are not played sequential sections of a verse or even complete sentences of the NWA lyrics, and, unlike "Lawyers, Guns, and Money," the narrative coherence of "Quiet on the Set," was abandoned to the cutting room floor. The voice of Ice Cube fades in and out in the cat-and-mouse game being played out on the screen, and the words that can be clearly distinguished, "ruthless, plenty of that and much more," are intended only to confirm the menacing intentions of the occupants of the BMW, five young, Black males who take careful note of the existence of an interloper in their territory. Mack responds to his surveillence by singing:

> I'm an innocent bystander . . .
> Send lawyers, guns and money
> The shit has hit the fan.

His car coughs, splutters, stalls, and finally breaks down, and Mack becomes a man under siege. He uses his car phone in an attempt to get help but on being asked for his location Mack suddenly hesitates: "I dunno . . . lets say . . . Inglewood," he decides, without conviction, as the car phone also crackles and then dies. Apparently having run to a convenience store to find a public telephone Mack continues to find it difficult, if not impossible to describe exactly where he is, or, to continue the military analogy, to give his coordinates: "Buckingham, yes," he pants, "but remember it's about half a mile west, I guess, of there." Mack is not only lost, he is in alien territory, and his very survival is at stake. On being told by roadside assistance that it will take forty-five minutes to get to him, Mack replies that he understands but states, "if it takes that long I might be like, ah, dead." He remains under surveillence and the NWA sound track changes to include fragments of "F—— tha Police," signifying, presumably, the imminence of the moment of confrontation. Mack returns to his car to wait for help, and the BMW pulls up behind him.

What follows is a filmic moment in which the entire gamut of language, sound, and image used up until this point to symbolize danger and to produce fear in the audience, coalesce into an intense evocation of an American soldier coming down in enemy territory. Mack vocalizes his own personal distress and simultaneously gives voice to the anxieties of a constituency of the White, suburban, middle class, whose greatest fear is being stranded in a Black urban neighborhood at night. The young Black men advance toward Mack's car framed through its rear windscreen. Mack's face is at the center of the screen; as his eyes flicker with recognition at the rearview mirror, his voice quietly but clearly calls to the audience: "Mayday, Mayday. We're coming down."

There is a great irony in what Kasdan excludes from his audience in this scene that only those who know the lyrics of "Quiet on the Set," and "F—— tha Police" would perceive. In fact, I would argue that Kasdan depends upon the ignorance of his target audience for this film. Those who know the album *Straight Outta Compton* would be aware that "Quiet on the Set" is actually about the power of performance and, specifically, about the potential power that a successful rap artist can gain over an audience. Power is, quite explicitly, the power of words over the body. For example, "ruthless, plenty of that and much more" is about controlling the movements of people on a dance floor and about the power to create "a look that keeps you staring and wondering why I'm invincible." But the invicibility is entirely the result of being able to persuade with words, "when you hear my rhyme its convinceable." Kasdan, however, disrupts NWA's intended narrative structure, and lines like "I'm a walking threat," and "I wanna earn respect" are transformed into a filmic representation of the contemporary figure of the disobedient and dangerous Black male who believes that respect is only gained through the possession of a gun. Perhaps the greatest irony of all is that the NWA song, in fact, predicts the misuse of their words. Near the end of the rap an interesting dialogue occurs between Ice Cube and an unidentified voice that mimics the supposedly dispassionate, analytic tone of the sociologist or ethnographer. Ice Cube asserts that he can create "lyrics to make everybody say," and the voice responds: "They can be cold and ruthless, there's no doubt about that but, sometimes, its more complicated." And Ice Cube concludes: "You think I'm committing a crime, instead of making a rhyme."

A tow truck driver, Simon, played by Danny Glover, comes to Mack's rescue at the height of his confrontation with the "gang."

Mack has been forced out of the safety of his car when a blaze of oncoming headlights announce his imminent rescue. However, the camera tantalizes the audience as it hesitates to reveal the identity of the man who climbs out of the truck. The camera swings from the truck to Mack flanked by the gang and then back again to the tow truck driver's boots, and then slowly pans upwards. What Kasdan does here is to reproduce the same low-angled shot that he used moments before to stress the menacing nature of the Black male faces that lean toward Mack in his car. The rescuer is revealed to be Black and to be armed with an enormous steel crowbar, the size of which is exaggerated by the camera angle, but before we can completely see his face, the tow truck driver bends into the cab to reach for a cap. This second of uncertainty about his identity is a cinematically produced hesitancy about the possible allegiance of the tow truck driver: is he a rescuer, as implied by the change to music evocative of the cavalry coming over the hill, or is he an additional figure of menace, as implied by the filming of his body? However, the hesitation is only momentary. Once the face is revealed to be that of Danny Glover, his filmic persona as LAPD's heroic cop, Sergeant Murtaugh, from a series of three Lethal Weapons so well established in our popular cultural imagination, assures the audience that he is Mack's savior.

The ideology that Kasdan reproduces in his geneology of race and nation works in a structurally similar way to the ideology that was reasserted by Harriet Beecher Stowe, in which the imagining of the good Black is dependent upon a rejection of an alien Black presence. Though Africa no longer functions, as it did for Stowe, as a possible metaphoric and material place for disposing of the alien element that threatens to disrupt the formation of national unity, I would argue that prisons function in our political imaginations as an equivalent site. Kasdan produces a visual narrative of what happens when disobedient, disaffected, and aggressive Black males are pitted against a lone, liberal, and well-meaning White male who made an innocent, if foolish, mistake.

For Kasdan, the figure of Simon is an important mechanism for solving the dilemma at the center of his visual reconstruction of our contemporary racial national narrative, a dilemma captured in the cinematic hesitation I have already described: how, exactly, can the White middle class distinguish between the good and the bad Black male? It is precisely at the moment of Mack's rescue that it is possible to speculate about the significance of Kasdan's manipulation of a specific performance of Black masculinity in his selection of the actor, Danny Glover, to play Simon.[12]

In *Lethal Weapon III* there is one particular scene, which I will discuss in a moment, that acts as a climax to the relationship between two LAPD homicide detectives, Martin Riggs, played by Mel Gibson, and Roger Murtaugh: a relationship which has gradually matured throughout the two previous films in the series. Considered together, the three films document the development of a close and increasingly intimate partnership between an older Black and a younger White male. It is interesting that it is not the history of the movement to gain civil rights that is the means for imagining a relationship of equality between Riggs and Murtaugh, but an evocation of the history of the desegregation of the United States Armed Forces in the "policing" of Southeast Asia that enables us, in the terms of the film, to imagine the possibility and conditions of their partnership. This filmic selection of history is important, as it establishes the possibility of their friendship as external, not internal, to the continental United States. What Riggs and Murtaugh share is not an internal political or historical condition, but the experience of Vietnam. This experience is the ground of their apparent equality and the basis for their mutual respect.

Lethal Weapon, the first in the series, forges Riggs and Murtaugh into an unbeatable fighting team as they defeat a rogue group of Special Forces mercenaries against a Los Angeles landscape that increasingly resembles Vietnam as the film progresses. In *Lethal Weapon II*, the national significance of their partnership is established in the narrative of a battle to save the nation from a drug cartel run by South African diplomats. Riggs's and Murtaugh's partnership and friendship also advance in this film when Riggs's antiracist credentials are secured, and he is declared by the diplomats to be a "Kaffir-lover." In *Lethal Weapon III*, Los Angeles and Vietnam are again fused in the landscape as they wage war against a homegrown enemy who has declared war on the entire Los Angeles Police Department, a police force which, at this stage of the series, has become a national entity.

The relationship between Riggs and Murtaugh also has an explicit homoerotic character which Richard Donner, the director, plays for laughs. Homoeroticism appears gradually, from a single question in the first film—"What are you, a fag?" shouts Riggs, in response to Murtaugh jumping on top of him in an attempt to extinguish the flames that threaten to consume his body—to a series of running jokes in the second film that stems from Riggs jumping with Murtaugh into a bath as he rescues him from a toilet wired to a bomb. In *Lethal*

Weapon III the homoeroticism is somewhat more mature and less directly inspired by anal humor.

In the scene which provides a climax to the terms and conditions of the friendship between Riggs and Murtaugh, Donner attempts to rewrite the mythical dimensions of the relationship between Huck and Jim on the raft through his two cops.[13] Riggs and Murtaugh face a crisis as partners and as friends, a crisis as serious as that faced by Huck and Jim when they missed the entry into the Ohio river and sailed ever deeper into the slave states of the South. In Mark Twain's novel, *The Adventures of Huckleberry Finn,* this mistake secured the historical terms and conditions of Jim's existence and his dependence on Huck Finn: as a Black male, in order to survive he had to "belong" to someone. In *Lethal Weapon III,* in a similar fashion, Donner reworks the contemporary terms and conditions of the relationship between his White male and Black male protagonists. The crisis has been precipitated by two events: Murtaugh is agonizing over the fact that, in an armed confrontation, he shot and killed a fifteen-year-old Black male, whom he discovered to be his son's best friend. Riggs is distraught because their partnership is about to be dissolved when Murtaugh retires from the force in just three days.

This long, eight-minute segment explores the complex and contradictory possibilities for expressing interracial male intimacy, and while the scene is, at times, intensely homoerotic, it simultaneously effects a series of closures, both visual and verbal, on the possibility that this intimacy could encompass a homosexual relation. As Huck and Jim's navigational error determined the public nature of their relation to each other, Donner likewise opens this scene in a way that determines the possibilities for interpreting what follows.

Riggs goes to find Murtaugh, who is hiding out on his boat, drinking whiskey. He finds Murtagh drunk and apparently out of control. Murtaugh holds a gun to Riggs's head and, in clichéd terms, threatens to harm the best friend he ever had. What has to be explored, therefore, is not the basis for their equality but the issue of how, in a relationship of partners, Murtaugh could possibly betray his friend, his "brother," who has clearly demonstrated his loyalty to him. The moment is fraught with the tension arising from the political anxiety evident in Riggs's agony and accusation of betrayal that Murtaugh's imminent retirement precipitates. This tension creates and reproduces on the screen a contemporary political anxiety, a commonsense understanding, that Black America, having demanded and gained equality, has somehow betrayed the White and middle-class America that graciously acceded to these demands. The political effect is such that when Riggs shouts at Murtaugh, "You selfish bastard," a large segment of White male America makes the same accusation.

The accusation of the betrayal of White America by an aggressive Black America informs and shapes the work of a number of contemporary liberal political analysts. Andrew Hacker, in *Two Nations: Black and White, Separate, Hostile, Unequal,* addresses this anxiety, and argues that the processes of racialization and nationalization imagined to be inherent in the social consensus to grant civil rights was, indeed, only imaginary. He concludes that such a consensus no longer exists, and that America must be regarded as two separate nations confronting each other. Hacker situates his discussion of the liberal anxiety evident in this political crisis in the context of the Black urban rebellions of the late 1960s. He states:

> After those disturbances, race relations never returned to their former plane. Whites ceased to identify black protests with a civil rights movement led by students and ministers. Rather, they saw a resentful and rebellious multitude, intent on imposing its presence on the rest of society. Blacks were seen as trying to force themselves into places and positions where they were not wanted or for which they lacked the competence. As the 1970s started, so came a rise in crimes, all too many of them with black perpetrators. By that point, many white Americans felt they had been betrayed. Worsening relations between the races were seen as largely due to the behavior of blacks, who had abused the invitations to equal citizenship white America had been tendering.[14]

Hacker's belief that White Americans have lost all sympathy for Black Americans shapes his political agenda. This political belief in this apparent lack of sympathy also influences Donner's decision to imagine the source for Black male and White male mutual respect as being in Southeast Asia rather than in the history of the struggle for civil rights. Hacker's genealogy of race and nation attempts to regain this lost sympathy through an extrordinary performance of intellectual blackface. In a chapter called "Being Black in America," in which Hacker provides an account of what he imagines it would be like to be Black, he reveals an intense masculine anxiety about Black male bodies.

Hacker is only one of many political critics who are busily constructing genealogies of race and nation that are centrally concerned with White male anxiety, particularly liberal anxiety, about relationships with Black men. For example, Hacker's argument that White men feel betrayed by actually or potentially rebellious Black men is echoed in Thomas Edsall's very influential book, *Chain Reaction: The Impact of Race, Rights, and Taxes on American Politics,* in which such betrayal is used by Edsall as an explanation for what he describes as the alienation of White, Democratic [male] voters from the special interest politics of racial injustice.[15] In the popular cultural imagination, this political anxiety is most frequently being reproduced against a nightmarish landscape of urban crisis.

What *Grand Canyon,* the *Lethal Weapon* series, and a number of other contemporary Hollywood films have in common is that they attempt to resolve what is presented as a national, racialized crisis through an intimate male partnership. What Danny Glover can bring to directors like Kasdan is his close association with a filmic performance of Black manhood which has money, is the law, and which embodies all the ethical codes of middle-class White America. In other words, what Kasdan can incorporate into *Grand Canyon* from the *Lethal Weapon* series is the national embodiment of the perfect Black male, a sensitive Black father and relentless seeker of justice. Danny Glover's persona is the lethal weapon that is used to eliminate representations of other Black men that Hollywood creates as dangerous. The cultural construction of such a figure is a direct political response to the national bourgeois dilemma: how to distinguish the good from the bad Black men.

Kasdan grants Simon the moral authority to exclude the five young men who constitute his rebellious "gang" from all acceptable definitions of what it means to be human. This moral authority is aquired gradually and in a number of ways. First, Simon manages to extract Mack and himself from the clutches of the young men without resorting to violence. He establishes who made the call and then continues to talk to Mack about the problem with the car as if the others are not there. This behavior is quickly identified by the young men as a sign of disrespect. Next, Simon tries to persuade them that he is just doing his job. As the young men are unresponsive to the terms of the work ethic, Simon tries another tactic, he identifies the young man he supposes is the leader and takes him aside. He explains that he is responsible for the truck, Mack's car, and Mack himself and asks a favor, to be allowed to go on his way. This exchange is a very important moment, because it establishes the ground upon which Simon's role as a mouthpiece for the philosophy of the film will be built. The young man asks:

"Are you askin' me a favor as a sign of respect, or are you askin me a favor 'cos I got the gun?" Simon pauses and then replies:

> Man, the world ain't supposed to work like this, maybe you don't know that but this ain't the way it's supposed to be. I'm supposed to be able to do my job without asking you if I can. That dude is supposed to be able to wait with his car without you ripping him off. Everything is supposed to be different than what it is.

The young man is clearly puzzled by this response, and says, "So, what's your answer?" To which Simon states, "You don't have the gun, we ain't having this conversation," which gets the response, "That's what I thought, no gun, no respect. That's why I always carry the gun."

Having confirmed that Simon can vocalize the moral codes and ethics of the middle class and can, simultaneously, be streetwise, Simon is also used to dehumanize the young men. In a conversation with Mack that takes place back at the service station while waiting for the car to be fixed, Simon adopts a folksy persona, a persona from which many Americans seem to draw comfort, and compares the young men to predatory sharks. Simon explains to Mack that what happened to him was a matter of chance, that:

> one day, just one particular day you bump into the big shark. Now the big shark don't hate you, he has no feelings for you at all, you look like food to him. . . . Those boys back there, they got nothing to lose. If you just happen to be swimming along and bump into them, well. . . . It might not be worth worrying about; it's like being in a plane crash.

Having dismissed these boys from the realm of humanity, they can be conveniently forgotten. They do not appear again in the film, and presumably they can disappear into jail, say, or be absorbed into statistical evidence of urban homicides, for do we really care or even think about what happens to sharks as long as they are contained and prevented from preying upon us? What is to be feared has been identified, given a body, but no name. The young Black men presented as "gang" have served their purpose, the conversation of Mack and Simon can shift to a more general level and establish the wider concerns of the film. For the confrontation of Mack and the five young Black men are a coda, a means to address what ails this nation.

However, Kasdan deliberately distances his male characters from the homoeroticism that permeates the *Lethal Weapon* series. When the noise of the helicopter which opens the film fades, a basketball net appears, surrounded by Black hands reaching upward. In a black-and-white opening sequence on an urban basketball court, the camera strays over sections of the bodies of the Black players, torsos, legs, hands, and feet. There is a clear visual analogy with the second half of the credit sequence, which takes place in the forum and is filmed in color. However, the force of the analogy is not established in the Black-White communality of the basketball court, a site which is reserved for the safe portrayal of intimacy between men; rather, the analogy works through the similarities between the straying gaze of the camera over Black male bodies in the first sequence, and the sexually desiring gaze of Mack across the court at the women who walk by. In this part of the credit sequence, again the camera lingers over sections of bodies, particularly torsos and breasts of the walking women.

Certainly the blatantly sexual and somewhat predatory stare of Mack at these passing female bodies is intended to lock him into heterosexuality, and to act as an early closure on the possibility of interpreting his later desire for Simon as homosexual. But these opening sequences, and the scene of Black-White urban confrontation that follows, and that I have already discussed, do establish the cultural spaces designated by the film as safe. Safe spaces are sites in which Whites can be in close proximity to, intimate perhaps, and gaze at Black bodies. Both opening sequences prefigure the establishment of a close relationship between Simon and Mack; a friendship that comes to a cinematic climax when they play basketball with each other in Mack's driveway.

What we are witnessing in the creation of these intimate Black and White male partnerships is a performance of Black masculinity that meets the desires of the White male liberal imagination for a perfect partner and partnership. Together, we are promised, these men can annihilate what ails this nation and resolve our contemporary crisis of race, of nation, and of manhood. In the face of the institutional crisis of the last decade of the twentieth century, these popular narratives accomplish the ideological work necessary for the realignment of the national hegemonic structures of our time. All we need to do is relax and place our faith in the LAPD.

Notes

An earlier version of the first part of this essay appeared as "Encoding White Resentment: *Grand Canyon*—A Narrative for Our Times," in Cameron McCarthy and Warren

Crichlow, eds. *Race, Identity and Representation in Education,* New York: Routledge 1993, pp. 236–247.

1. Harriet Beecher Stowe, *Uncle Tom's Cabin, Or, Life Among the Lowly,* (1852), New York: Penguin, 1981, p. 629. *Grand Canyon,* written, produced, and directed by Lawrence Kasdan, Twentieth Century Fox, 1991. Etienne Balibar and Immanuel Wallerstein, *Race, Nation, Class: Ambiguous Identities,* London: Verso, 1991, p. 18.

2. See Balibar, "The Nation Form" in Balibar and Wallerstein, *Race, Nation, Class,* pp. 86–106; Toni Morrison's introductory essay to *Race-ing, Justice, Engendering Power: Essays on Anita Hill, Clarence Thomas and the Construction of Social Reality,* New York: Pantheon, 1992; and Michael Rogin, "Blackface, WhiteNoise: The Jewish Jazz Singer Finds His Voice," in *Critical Inquiry,* 1991, 18, 3:417–44.

3. Balibar and Wallerstein, p. 18.

4. In an historical account of the process of the "Christianizing of the American People," Jon Butler dramatically describes how, in the eighteenth century, Christianity directly shaped the system of slaveholding, and led to what he calls an African spiritual holocaust in North America: "a spiritual holocaust that effectively destroyed traditional African religious *systems,* [if] not all particular or religious practices." An "emerging Anglican understanding of slavery" Butler argues, "fitted with uncanny precision the elaboration of slave codes and social behavior that increasingly specified the degraded condition of captive Africans after 1680 . . . the law that guaranteed liberty to English men and women became the seal of slavery for Africans." It was Anglican concepts of authority that "shaped a paternalistic ethic among planters," an ethic:

   > that not only coalesced with the doctrine of absolute obedience but made it all the more palatable and attractive. . . . [Anglican] clergymen helped planters explain slave "misbehavior" in ways that solidified the masters' prejudices about slave degradation. . . . [and] transformed planter views about laziness, lust, and lying among slaves into powerfully detailed pictures of African depravity.

   This paternalistic ethic, continues Butler, rooted as it was in the doctrine of absolute obedience;

   > reinforced the growing violence of eighteenth century slaveholding. It encouraged owners to excuse nearly all discrete instances of violence toward slaves. Ironically, paternalism loaded owners with obligations that were difficult to fulfill in a competitive, erratic economy where there were few effective restraints on the owner's treatment of their labor. Even "ethical" owners mistreated slaves. Worse, both "ethical" and unethical owners could readily agree that slaves disobeyed. A rigid doctrine fostered rigid responses. The stress on absolute obedience turned minor infractions of planter authority into major confrontations, and the result brought forth the first fixing of an indelible image in American race relations—the perpetually disobedient black . . . the meanings of blackness and disobedience had already begun to converge. . . .
   >   The emergence of absolutist, paternalistic, and violent slavery gave Christianity as thoroughly a different cast as Christianity had given to slaveholding. Christianity's interpretation of social behavior and religious ethics produced a distended

emphasis on sentiment, charity, and love utterly uncharacteristic of the society in which it was propounded.

See Jon Butler, *Awash in a Sea of Faith: Christianizing the American People,* Cambridge, MA: Harvard University Press, 1990, pp. 153, 144, 146, 147.

5. Ann Douglass, "Introduction: The Art of Controversy," Stowe, *Uncle Tom's Cabin,* p. 8.

6. Butler, *op. cit.*

7. The concepts of "fictive ethnicity" and geneologies of race and nation are drawn from Etienne Balibar and Immanuel Wallerstein, *op. cit.*

8. See Wallerstein, "Construction of Peoplehood: Racism, Nationalism, Ethnicity," *ibid.,* p. 78. "Pastness is a mode by which persons are persuaded to act in the present in ways they might not otherwise act. Pastness is a tool persons use against each other."

9. It is clear that this association between the war zones of Southeast Asia and Los Angeles has been progressively established. Of particular importance to this process are the three *Lethal Weapon* films, which will be discussed toward the end of this essay and which, like *Grand Canyon,* starred Danny Glover. *Lethal Weapon III* is a culmination of the themes of the previous two: policing is indistinguishable from military intervention, and the burning of a housing complex is visually evocative of the burning of villages in Vietnam. Our reading of this scene of fire is, of course, directly influenced by *Apocalypse Now,* which reinforces my sense that Hollywood has and continues to mediate and inform this process of transition in the political imagination of the culture industry.

10. Promotional description, *Grand Canyon,* FoxVideo, 1992.

11. This superficial way of locating Mack is of course a postmodern substitute for history. See Fredrick Jameson, *Postmodernism and the Cultural Logic of Late Capitalism,* Durham: Duke University Press, pp. 6, 67–68.

12. Perhaps it is crass to point to the biblical resonance of the choice of Simon as a name for Mack's rescuer, but it gains significance through the consistent references to the religious in the film, particularly the concern with spiritual and miraculous transformation. Kasdan's "gang" take pleasure not only in threatening physical harm but in taunting and mocking Mack:

And they spit upon him, and took the reed, and smote him on the head.
And after that they had mocked him, they took the robe off from him, and put his own raiment on him, and led him away to crucify him.
And as they came out they found a man of Cyrene, Simon by name: him they compelled to bear his cross. (Matthew 27, 30–32)

As Gary Wills has recently argued Even if it works only at a subliminal level, it is important to recognise that Mack (and the White middle class) are being rescued from a possible crucifixion, a metaphor which has political and ideological meanings. Mack (and the White middle class) are only innocent victims in such a scenario, and the subjects, therefore of unjust persecution.

13. I am grateful to Michael Denning for pointing out this literary parallel.

14. Andrew Hacker, *Two Nations: Black and White, Separate, Hostile, Unequal,* New York: Macmillan, 1992, p. 19.

15. Thomas Byrne Edsall, with Masry D. Edsall, *Chain Reaction: The Impact of Race, Rights, and Taxes on American Politics,* New York: Norton, 1992.

9

Puerto Ricans and the Politics of Racial Identity

Angelo Falcón

Everyone here seems quite content with the phrase "people of color." You said the minorities were not minorities any more. Of course, the women actually are in the majority anyway. But I was raised in the South and it was the white folks and the black folks. I work at City Hall a lot. I don't know, (Councilman) Israel Ruiz has red hair and blue eyes, and the Del Toros could be Italian or Jewish. And look at Adam Clayton Powell VI, look at young Adam. I knew his father. I say that a lot as I get older. I knew his father, and his father was absolutely white.

The whole business of "people of color" seems to be we're against the people who are not of color. I think "people of color" is pretty phony when you look at all the people who are not different, who could be white, and many of them list themselves as white in the Census in the Hispanic category. But, I don't know, apparently, everyone here is happy with the phrase "we people of color" and I'm not so sure that I'm happy about it because I was brought up where there were the people of color and there were the whites in the South. But I guess it's done, apparently.

Andy Logan (March 10, 1993)

Introduction

The demographic changes that made New York City in the mid-1980s a "majority minority" city for the first time in its history have national significance in the manner they have put serious conceptual strains on once widely understood terms like "race," "ethnicity," and "minority" (Falcón, 1988). With African-Americans, West Indian

Blacks, Latinos, and Asians together now in the majority, New York appeared to be in for a new racial-ethnic dynamic that, in a rather direct way, was expressed in the election of the city's first African-American Mayor in 1989. However, as the opening quote by a respected White journalist, made at a recent discussion on redistricting in New York City, illustrates, the meaning of these dramatic changes still eludes even the most astute observers of local politics (Falcón and Santiago, 1993).

The role of racial identity in determining relations between non-White groups is a critical one. Yet, when looking at the experience of non-African-American groups, it is not widely understood how they view themselves racially in an American context. Politically, this becomes increasingly important as the largest part of the demographic trends that are making the country's major urban centers "majority minority" has been the dramatic growth in the populations of Latinos, Asians, and West Indian Blacks at a time where the African-American population has largely stabilized in size. How this new mixture of groups will interact politically will determine whether these demographic changes will translate into anything distinctive politically that could in any way usher in something approaching a second civil rights revolution, or simply result in greater intergroup competition for limited resources.

New York City is at once unique and an important laboratory for observing the political and social implications of these changes for the country's urban centers. One of the last major American cities to retain a White population majority, New York was found by the 1990 Census to have a total population of 7,322,564 that was twenty-five percent Black, twenty-four percent Latino, seven percent Asian, and forty-three percent White. Among the Latinos, fifty percent were Puerto Rican, nineteen percent Dominican, five percent Colombian, four percent Ecuadorean, less than four percent Mexican, with fourteen other Latino groups making up the remaining eighteen percent (Department of City Planning, 1994). New York City houses the largest concentration of Puerto Ricans in the United States, numbering 896,763 in 1990, or thirty-three percent of the 2.7 million Puerto Ricans living in the United States (excluding Puerto Rico).

Of all the Latino groups, Puerto Ricans have the longest and most extensive experience with local New York City politics and in their contact with the city's African-American community (Falcón, 1984). Puerto Ricans also share with African-Americans the experience of migrating to urban centers in the North like New York while already possessing U.S. citizenship, in contrast to other Latino and West Indian groups. However, Puerto Ricans share with other Latinos stronger language and cultural traits, as well as a multiracial heritage. With a poverty rate of thirty-eight percent in 1989, Puerto Ricans are the poorest community in the city, making their socioeconomic status close to that of African-Americans.

The Puerto Rican experience, therefore, offers an interesting window from which to view contemporary Black-Latino relations in U.S. urban centers. In many ways, Puerto Ricans may represent the future of the other Latino groups in this country, rather than the exception that some argue (Chavez, 1991). By focusing on the role of race in how Puerto Ricans view themselves as a group and how they view a number of public policy issues, this paper will attempt to better contruct questions about relations between Latinos and African-Americans. This will be done by using previously unpublished data on Puerto Ricans from a national survey that also includes Mexicans and Cubans (de la Garza, *et al.*, 1992). The focus on Puerto Ricans will bring us both at the beginning and the end of this essay to New York City as the stage upon which to view these issues.

Race and Ethnicity in New York City

At the center of this dilemma is how these "minorities" or "people of color" view themselves within American society: as distinctive racial-ethnic identities marginalized from a common American experience, or as "meltable" ethnics or immigrant groups? "To our minds," wrote Glazer and Moynihan in their 1970 preface to their classic 1961 book, *Beyond the Melting Pot,* "whether blacks in the end see themselves as ethnic within the American context, or as only black—a distinct race defined only by color, bearing a unique burden through American history—will determine whether race relations in this country is an unending tragedy or in some measure—to the limited measure that anything human can be—moderately successful" (Glazer and Moynihan, 1970). In contrast, the other large non-European group at the time, Puerto Ricans, they found, "still see themselves in the immigrant-ethnic model; that is, they see their poor economic and political position as reflecting recency of arrival and evil circumstances that can still be overcome" (*ibid.*).

Discussing the city's newer immigrants in 1988, Glazer was led to a newer dilemma, namely, why were newer groups of West Indians,

Dominicans, Colombians, Koreans, and others apparently doing better than the older Black and Puerto Rican minorities? "Indeed," Glazer finds, "sheer hard work and the avoidance of the destructive mechanisms that ensure failure seem sufficient for socioeconomic mobility even in a changed New York." He closes his essay with a concern:

> We have to ponder this contrast, and try to understand it. But we also have to worry about what it will mean for the city as the native black and Puerto Rican population sees new immigrants—Hispanic, black, and Asian—passing them, and establishing the stable life and the platform for future advancement that still eludes them. (Glazer, 1988)

Glazer's verdict, if one may take the liberty of linking his writings over this time span, is that, in fact, Blacks and Puerto Ricans have come to accept a self-destructive and dependent identity as "colonized," to use his 1970 terminology. This "choice," Glazer solemnly points out, has its consequences. He (and Moynihan), after all, had warned us about this many years ago. Joining him today in raising this concern about Latinos in general are conservatives like Chavez (1991) and neoliberals like Skerry (1993).

The images of confusion and division that emerge about these dramatic demographic changes dominate the discourse on race and ethnicity in New York City and the United States as a whole today. Whether it is government reports (Department of City Planning, 1992), studies on race relations (Hacker, 1992), or other writings on immigration and the new ethnic groups (for example, Kasinitz, 1992, Grasmuck and Pessar, 1991, Foner, 1987, Paquin, 1983, Maldonado and Moore, 1985, and Fuchs, 1990), the picture is more of a hyperdiversity (or hyperplurality) that is beyond anyone's ability to understand adequately. The political significance of overarching notions like "majority minority," as well as "people of color," "Third World minority," "racial minority," and so on is reasonably open to question within such a context.

Ringer and others (Ringer, 1983; Ringer and Lawless, 1989; Nakano Glenn, 1985; Omi and Winant, 1986) have attempted to construct general theories about racial and ethnic identity in the United States by building on the earlier work of theorists like Blauner (1972). Ringer's "duality thesis" is based on granting race priority in the common experiences of domination of non-Whites by White European and American political, legal, and economic forces and traditions. It is an attempt to bring "together into a common conceptual framework a variety of historical experiences which share a similar motif. All have been directly or indirectly products of the dual processes of colonization and colonialization generated by the expansion of white Europeans over a span of five centuries" (Ringer and Lawless, 1989).

However, these ambitious attempts at theory-building have been rather marginal to the dominant discourses on race and ethnicity in this country. While some students of ethnicity have sought to find a middle ground, such as Yinger's (1986) proposal for an "ethnic continuum," prevailing theories and notions of race and ethnicity in the United States remain, at the very least, preparadigmatic and, at worst, trivialized by civic myth. As global demographic and other forces increasingly question our understanding of these issues in ways that call into question the dominant bipolar definitions of race in the United States (Root, 1992), they not only result in well-founded anxieties by African-Americans as the largest non-White minority group in the country (Cruse, 1987; Jennings, 1992, pp. 45ff), but also leave us on constantly shifting terrain that renders the very language used to attempt to describe this reality inadequate and ultimately unsatisfying (see Sniderman and Piazza, 1993, for a useful analysis of the difficulties in interpreting the role of race in determining public policy issues today).

Puerto Ricans, Race, and Ethnicity

The dimension of race within Latino communities has been a controversial and little-understood one. An important work on Chicano identity, for example, does not discuss race at all in its more than two hundred pages (Keefe and Padilla, 1987) nor does another important work on researching Hispanics (Marin and VanOss Marin, 1991). This appears to be a general pattern, as revealed in a more recent overview of group identity formation (Ponterotto and Pederson, 1993).

Rodriguez (1989) framed this dilemma for Puerto Ricans in particular as follows:

> Puerto Ricans presented an enigma to Americans because (from a North American perspective) Puerto Ricans were both an ethnic group and more than one racial group. Within the U.S. perspective, Puerto Ricans, racially speaking, belonged to both groups; however, ethnically, they belonged to neither. Thus placed, Puerto Ricans soon

found themselves caught between two polarities and dialectically at a distance from both. Puerto Ricans were White and Black; Puerto Ricans were neither White nor Black. From the Puerto Rican perspective, Puerto Ricans were more than White and Black. This apparent contradiction can best be understood through an examination of the contrasting racial ambiences and histories of the United States and Puerto Rico at the time of the "great migration."

She finds that the Puerto Rican experience with race (and one can extend it to that of other Latinos) has created a situation where "we are witnessing the strongest challenge ever to the U.S. bifurcation of race."

Building on her earlier pioneering work on Puerto Ricans in this area (1974), Rodriguez and her collegues (1991) extended it to look more broadly at Latinos. Based on the study of a small, nonrandom sample, she found that the experiences of Latinos "challenge the way in which race and racial identity are generally concieved of in the U.S. where phenotype and genotype are primary" (1991, p. 47). She tentatively concluded that "a Latino's racial identity is not (just) genetically determined but that it depends on many variables, including phenotype, social class, language, phenotypic variation within their family, and neighborhood socialization" (ibid.). Her work further suggested that "racial identity can vary over time and from situation to situation. In essence, . . . for Latinos, race is to a large degree socially constructed" (ibid.).

As Rodriguez has understood, an important starting point for arriving at a new understanding of the issues involved in a much-needed reexamination of race and ethnicity in contemporary American society should be the views of those most affected. All too often, such theorizing occurs in isolation without grounding in the realities of the everyday lives of African-Americans, Latinos, and Asians. Part of the reason for this has been the unavailability of adequate, large-scale, survey data that look at these issues seriously.

In 1989 to 1990, the Latino National Political Survey (LNPS), the largest privately funded social survey to date of the political attitudes and behavior of Mexicans, Puerto Ricans, and Cubans in the United States, was conducted in forty metropolitan areas throughout the continental United States (de la Garza, et al., 1992). It was developed to, among other things, allow for some analysis of the political significance (if any) of panethnicity among the various Latino subgroups that together make up about nine percent of the country and twenty-four percent of New York City's population. In addition, the survey also looked at the issue of race, and how Latinos placed themselves within a Black-White classification system. These questions are important to issues of community mobilization and definition within the American political system.

The manner in which race is defined in the United States is, of course, not universal (van den Berghe 1988, pp. 62–63). Racial stratification in the U.S. is dichotomous—one is characterized as either Black or White based on a genetic concept of what has come to be known as the "One Drop Rule." Puerto Ricans and other Latinos, on the other hand, come from societies in which the classification is more complex and based more on phenotype. The result is a more subtle racial continuum from Black and White, with any number of intermediate classifications, including mulatto, *moreno, trigeño,* and others. But, as Nieves Falcón is quick to point out when discussing this practice in Puerto Rico, "It should be made clear that the subtlety of racism's adaptation in Puerto Rico make it no less dehumanizing" (1992, p. 18).

An examination of these survey data will allow us to begin to explore a number of questions relevant to the issue of racial identity among Puerto Ricans. First, we will look at how Puerto Ricans identify racially. Second, we will examine evidence of whether Puerto Ricans view themselves, individually and as a group, as victims of discrimination. Third, we will look at how Puerto Ricans relate to African-Americans. Finally, we will see how racial classifications within the Puerto Rican community affect their view on public policy issues, such as welfare spending by government.

Two methods were utilized in the Latino National Political Survey to categorize Puerto Ricans racially. The standard Census Bureau racial self-identification was used to tap the respondents' subjective description of themselves as "Black, White, or Something Else." The "Something Else" response was refined by taking those who defined this category in ethnic terms, such as referring to their national origin, and calling these "Latino referents." Large numbers of Latinos (around forty percent) consistently reject the formally presented racial categories presented by the Census Bureau on their forms and check off the "Other" category.

The other method used relied on the judgment of the interviewers about the skin color of the respondents. The interviewers were asked to rate the respondents on a five-point scale that included "very light," "light," "medium," "dark," and "very dark" as the categories. They were asked to concentrate on skin color and not other physical features.

Table 1 Racial Self-Identification by Skin-Color Rating by Interviewers of
Puerto Rican Respondents (N = 561)

	Skin-Color Rating by Interviewers				
Racial Self-Identification	Very Light	Light	Medium	Dark	Very Dark
White	70.4%	70.6%	55.2%	30.6%	33.4%
Latino Referent	29.6	28.8	41.2	59	29.2
Black	—	0.6	3.6	10.4	37.4
Number of Cases	(78)	(175)	(218)	(71)	(19)

Source: Latino National Political Survey

This was our attempt to arrive at a more objective way to racially
categorize the respondents.

The majority of Puerto Ricans (fifty-eight percent) identified themselves as being White racially, with thirty-eight percent indicating "Latino referent" terms, and only four percent seeing themselves as Black.
In terms of their skin color, the interviewers rated the Puerto Rican
respondents as follows: fourteen percent very light, thirty-one percent
light, thirty-nine percent medium, thirteen percent dark and three
percent very dark. These two measures begin to reveal some inconsistencies. A larger percentage of Puerto Ricans were viewed by the
interviewers as dark-skinned (sixteen percent) while only four percent
of that sample self-identify as Black.

Cross-tabulating these two variables reveals only a moderate relationship between the two (Spearman Correlation = .27, significant at
.00 level) (see Table 1). Even among those rated by the interviewers
as being "very dark"-skinned, only thirty-seven percent see themselves
as being Black, with thirty-three percent seeing themselves as White
and twenty-nine percent using Latino referent terms. Among those at
the other extreme, those rated as being "very light"-skinned, while
none viewed themselves as being Black, thirty percent rejected the
White category for a Latino referent racial term.

Puerto Rican racial self-identity is, therefore, not defined exclusively
by skin color, and is further complicated by the rejection by many of
the bipolar Black-White categories that dominate racial discourse in
the United States. It could also be argued that those Puerto Ricans who
selected the Black or White categories may not see these as important
identities in relation to national origin, further weakening the significance of these racial identifications among them.

Table 2 Degree of Group Discrimination by Personal Discrimination Experience of Puerto Rican Respondents (N = 584)

	Discriminated Against?	
Degree of Perceived Group Discrimination	No	Yes
A Lot	26.2%	54.4%
Some	42.6	31.6
A Little	20.4	10.1
None	10.8	3.9
Number of Cases	(408)	(176)

Source: Latino National Political Survey

A critical factor in group self-identity is how the society at large views that group. For racial minorities, the defining experience has been that of discrimination by Whites. The Puerto Rican respondents were asked about their experience with discrimination from two perspectives: whether they had personally experienced discrimination, and how much discrimination they felt Puerto Ricans as a group experience.

Close to a third (thirty percent) of the Puerto Rican respondents indicated they had personally been the victims of discrimination based on their national origin. On the other hand, seventy-four percent felt that Puerto Ricans as a group experienced "some" to "a lot" of discrimination (see Table 2). When we run these two variables together, we find that more than three-fourths (seventy-eight percent) of the Puerto Rican respondents felt that they personally and/or their group experienced discrimination. This could, therefore, be seen as the basis for a strong feeling among Puerto Ricans that they are a racial-ethnic minority. Those who do not attribute any discrimination either toward them personally or toward their group accounted for only twenty-two percent of the total, a segment that would be more open to seeing themselves as an immigrant group that will soon be assimilating into U.S. society. Such a minority-versus-immigrant dichotomy can, however, only be suggestive, since in reality what probably exists is more of a continuum of attitudes between these two alternatives.

If the large majority of Puerto Ricans have a tendency to see themselves as a racial minority, how do they relate to Blacks as a group? Using a "feeling thermometer," the respondents were asked to indicate how warmly they felt toward a number of groups on a scale from 0° to 100°. Of four selected groups, Puerto Ricans felt most warmly

Table 3 Warmth Toward Selected Racial-Ethnic Groups by Puerto Rican Respondents

Degrees on Feeling Thermometer	Selected Racial-Ethnic Groups			
	Anglos	Blacks	Jews	Asians
0°–24°	5.2%	8.7%	15.9%	12.7%
25°–49°	5.5	10.4	18	21.6
50°	26.6	25.7	29.1	27.4
51°–74°	21.6	23.6	19	21.4
75°–100°	41.1	31.6	18	16.9
Number of Cases	(551)	(548)	(517)	(528)

Source: Latino National Political Survey

toward Anglos and Blacks, least warmly toward Jews and Asians (see Table 3). However, only thirty-two percent felt very warmly (indicating 75° or higher on the scale) toward Blacks, while forty-one percent felt very warmly toward Anglos.

Asked how much discrimination they felt African-Americans experienced as a group, eighty-six percent of the Puerto Rican respondents indicated "some" or "a lot." This is higher than the seventy-four percent feeling that Puerto Ricans as a group experience "some" or "a lot" of discrimination. There is, therefore, a recognition of the special plight Blacks find themselves in, even in comparison to Puerto Ricans. Not surprisingly, there was a large percentage (sixty-seven percent) of Puerto Ricans who felt that government spending on Black issues should be increased. On none of these measures—perceptions of discrimination against Blacks, warmth toward Blacks, or increasing government spending on Black issues—was there any significant variation related to either racial self-identification or the skin color of the Puerto Rican respondents.

Finally, there are a number of public policy issues that have high support among Blacks, while it is not clear what level of Puerto Rican support for them exists. One such issue is support for increased spending for welfare. Among Puerto Ricans, who suffer from higher poverty rates than Blacks, half (fifty percent) support increased spending, while twenty-three percent believe welfare spending should remain the same, and only eighteen percent believe that it should be decreased. According to the 1990 General Social Survey (GSS), forty-six percent of Blacks felt that there was too little spending on welfare, compared to twenty

Table 4 Percent of Puerto Rican Respondents
Agreeing That There are Too Many
Immigrants Coming into the U.S.
(N = 523)

Strongly Agree	18.5%
Agree	60.9
Disagree	19.3
Strongly Disagree	1.4

Source: Latino National Political Survey

percent of Whites (Davis and Smith, 1990). Therefore, there is greater similarity in levels of support for increased welfare spending between Puerto Ricans and Blacks than with Whites.

As already reported above, sixty-seven percent of Puerto Ricans supported increased government spending on Black issues. According to the 1990 GSS, eighty-six percent of Blacks felt there was too little government spending to improve the conditions of Blacks, compared to only thirty-three percent of Whites. This is another area where Blacks and Puerto Ricans are in much closer agreement than they are with Whites.

Another issue that is gaining much prominence today concerns immigration. The growing anxieties in African-American communities about the economic and political impact of the dramatically increased immigration of Latinos and Asians is becoming well known. However, this is a concern for Puerto Ricans and other Latinos themselves. Asked if there are too many immigrants coming into the United States, eighty-nine percent of the Puerto Rican respondents said they "agree" or "strongly agree" that there are too many immigrants (see Table 4). This is, therefore, another issue where Blacks and Puerto Ricans are in high agreement, along with Whites. However, there are differences on the leadership level in how immigration issues are being articulated (Schuck, 1993).

Conclusion

Do these data on Puerto Ricans, the literature we have reviewed, and the instances of the political expression of race and ethnicity in New York City that we have discussed provide us with any useful insights into the issue of racial-ethnic identity and its political expression? In broad terms, they indicate that we find ourselves in a very fluid state of affairs when it comes to these questions. This is the case both for the subjective definition of these issues and for their structural contexts. This is a situation that offers opportunities as well as dangers in the defining of racial and ethnic identities (or identity) of non-Whites in this society. Do we succumb to a bewildering and possibly immobilizing hyperpluralism that does not grant priority to the realities of race, or do we make race a central concept in the reconstruction and transformation of a new racial-ethnic theory or theories?

These issues have been put to a number of practical tests in New York City in the last few years. Efforts to develop a Black-Latino-labor coalition to unseat then Mayor Ed Koch in 1985, following the experience of the 1984 Jesse Jackson campaign for President, clearly indicated that Blacks and Latinos would not form coalitions without much effort. While Jackson received the Black vote and Koch lost the Black vote, the reverse was the case with Latinos. By Jackson's 1988 campaign the lesson had been learned that such an electoral coalition was only possible by throwing out past assumptions of a natural unity and realizing that each community required its own specific strategies and resources for mobilization. This momentum continued into the 1989 election of the city's first African-American mayor, David N. Dinkins, and again in 1993 when this electoral coalition held, although Dinkins was not reelected for a second term.

Currently, the newly elected Republican Mayor, Rudolph Giuliani, may be pursuing a strategy of courting the Latino vote while not being as responsive to the Black vote, the strategy that had been used so effectively by Mayor Koch throughout most of the 1980s. This is a strategy that returns us to a theme discussed at the beginning of this chapter which posed the alternatives for Latinos of identifying as either a racial minority or an immigrant group.

As Puerto Rican attitudes toward their own racial identity (or, rather, identities) reveals, the traditional way of conceptualizing racial-ethnic issues and strategies along a Black-White dichotomy will not be effective in mobilizing Puerto Rican and other Latino constituencies. While Puerto Ricans do not respond neatly to this bipolar racial classification, the notion of being a non-White grouping is a strong one and, on this basis, there appear to be many areas of public policy consensus between large majorities of Puerto Ricans and Blacks. As a more established African-American political leadership in New York City begins to see that failure to respond to this new and increasingly important reality can jeopardize their own strategies for empowerment, they will no doubt respond in creative ways. For Puerto Ricans and other Latinos, the challenge is how to come to terms with the new realities of race and racial politics in the United States.

If the Puerto Rican experience is any guide, Glazer and Moynihan's warnings against throwing their lot with that of African-Americans has gone largely unheeded. There are, however, indications that a small, but significant sector of the Puerto Rican population in the United States (about a fifth) does not see racial-ethnic discrimination as a problem (nor, therefore, as a group-defining experience). This only serves to underline the fact that how Puerto Ricans and other Latinos politically situate themselves racially is a process that is far from resolved. But it is perhaps through the very recognition of this dilemma that its resolution (if there is one) will be possible. In an early exmple of attempts to look at the commonality of Black and Puerto Rican experiences, more than twenty years ago William Cross nd Manuel del Valle y Colon (1972) collaborated on a proposal to explore, in a deliberate way, the problem of Puerto Rican identity development. Their conclusion was that: ". . . (A)n awareness of what the process of becoming conscious of one's Puerto Ricanness may allow the Puerto Rican to program Puerto Rican identity, resulting in that positive self-image which is the prerequisite for Puerto Rican pride and self-determination." (Cross and del Valle y Colon, 1972). This represents, perhaps, a reckless optimism that may have been lost, but needs urgently to be rediscovered today in the Puerto Rican community.

References

Blauner, R. 1972. *Racial Oppression in America*. New York: Harper and Row.

Chavez, L. 1991. *Out of the Barrio: Toward a New Politics of Hispanic Assimilation*. New York: Basic Books.

Cross, W. E. 1991. *Shades of Black: Diversity in African-American Identity*. Philadelphia: Temple University Press.

Cross, W. E. and del Valle y Colón, M. 1972. "William E. Cross, Jr. Research Model on Black Awareness as Applied to the Puerto Rican" (unpublished paper, Yale University)

Cruse, H. 1987. *Plural but Equal: Blacks and Minorities in America's Plural Society*. New York: Quill/William Morrow.

Davis, J. A. and Smith, T. W. 1990. *General Social Survey*. (Machine-readable data file). Principal investigators, James A. Davis and Tom W. Smith. Produced by the National Opinion Research Center, Chicago. Tape distributed by the Roper Public Opinion Research Center, Storrs, CT. Micro diskette and codebook prepared and distributed by MicroCase Corporation, West Lafayette, Indiana.

de la Garza, R. O., DeSipio, L. F., Garcia, C., Garcia, J., and Falcón, A. 1992. *Latino Voices: Mexican, Puerto Rican, and Cuban Perspectives on American Politics.* Boulder: Westview Press.

Department of City Planning, City of New York. 1992. *The Newest New Yorkers: An Analysis of Immigration into New York City During the 1980s.* New York.

Department of City Planning, City of New York. 1994. *Puerto Rican New Yorkers in 1990.* New York.

Falcón, A. 1984. "A History of Puerto Rican Politics in New York City: 1860s to 1945," in *Puerto Rican Politics in Urban America*, eds. Jennings, J. and Rivera, M. Wesport: Greenwood Press.

———. 1988. "Black and Latino Politics in New York City: Race and Ethnicity in a Changing Urban Context," in *Latinos and the Political System*, ed. Garcia, F. C. Notre Dame: Notre Dame Press.

———. and Santiago, J., eds. 1993. "Race, Ethnicity and Redistricting in New York City: The Gartner Report and Its Critics." *IPR Policy Forums Proceedings.* New York: Institute for Puerto Rican Policy, August.

Falcón, N. 1992. "La Ruta del Legado Colonial," La Tercera Raiz: Presencia Africana, in *Puerto Rico* (Catálogo acompañando la exposición), ed. the Centro de Estudios de la Realidad Puertorriqueña and the Instituto de Cultura Puertorriqueña. San Juan, Puerto Rico: Comisión Puertorriqueña para la Celebración del Descubrimiento de América y Puerto Rico.

Foner, N. 1987. *New Immigrants in New York.* New York: Columbia University Press.

Fuchs, L. H. 1990. *The American Kaleidoscope: Race, Ethnicity and the Civic Culture.* Hanover: Wesleyan University Press.

Glazer, N., ed. 1988. "The New New Yorkers," in *New York Unbound: The City and the Politics of the Future*, ed. Salins, P. D. New York: Basil Blackwell.

———. and Moynihan, D. P. 1970. *Beyond the Melting Pot: The Negroes, Puerto Ricans, Jews, Italians, and Irish of New York City.* Cambridge, MA: The MIT Press.

Grasmuck, S. and Pessar, P. R. 1991. *Between Two Islands: Dominican International Migration.* Berkeley: University of California Press.

Hacker, A. 1992. *Two Nations: Blank and White, Separate, Hostile, Unequal.* New York: Charles Scribner's Sons.

Hartstock, N. 1987. "Rethinking Modernism: Minority vs. Majority Theories." *Cultural Critique*, 7: 1.

Jennings, J. 1992. *The Politics of Black Empowerment: The Transformation of Black Activism in Urban America.* Detroit: Wayne State University Press.

Kasinitz, P. 1992. *Caribbean New York: Black Immigrants and the Politics of Race.* Ithaca: Cornell University Press.

Keefe, S. E. and Padilla, A. M. 1987. *Chicano Ethnicity.* Albuquerque: University of New Mexico Press.

Maldonado, L. and Moore, J. 1985. *Urban Ethnicity in the United States: New Immigrants and Old Minorities.* Beverly Hills: Sage Publications.

Marín, G. and VanOss Marín, B. 1991. *Research with Hispanic Populations.* Newbury Park: Sage Publications.

Nakano, G. E. 1985. "Racial Ethnic Women's Labor: The Intersection of Race, Gender and Class Oppression." *Review of Radical Political Economics*, 17: 3.

Omi, M. and Winant, H. 1986. *Racial Formation in the United States: From the 1960s to the 1980s.* New York: Routledge.

Padilla, F. M. 1985. *Latino Ethnic Consciousness: The Case of Mexican-Americans and Puerto Ricans in Chicago.* Notre Dame: Notre Dame Press.

Paquin, L. 1983. *The Haitians: Class and Color Politics.* Brooklyn: Multi-Type.

Ponterotto, J. G. and Pederson, P. D. 1993. *Preventing Prejudice: A Guide for Counselors and Educators.* Newbury Park: Sage Publications.

Ringer, B. 1983. *"We The People" and Others: Duality and America's Treatment of its Racial Minorities.* New York: Tavistock Publications.

———. and Lawless, E. R. 1989. *Race-Ethnicity and Society.* New York: Routledge.

Rodriguez, C. E. 1974. "Puerto Ricans: Between Black and White." *New York Affairs,* 1: 92–101.

———. 1989. *Puerto Ricans: Born in the U.S.A.* Boston: Unwin Hyman.

———., Castro, A., Garcia, O., and Torres, A. 1991. "Latino Racial Identity: In the Eye of the Beholder?" *Latino Studies Journal,* 2: 33–48.

Root, M. P. P. 1992. *Racially Mixed People in America.* Newbury Park, CA: Sage.

Schuck, P. H. 1993. "The New Immigration and the Old Civil Rights." *The American Prospect,* 15: 102–111.

Skerry, P. 1993. *Mexican Americans: The Ambivalent Minority.* New York: The Free Press.

Sniderman, P. M. and Piazza, T. 1993. *The Scar of Race.* Cambridge, MA: Belknap Press.

van den Berghe, P. L. 1988. "Colour Line," *Dictionary of Race and Ethnic Relations,* ed. Cashmore, E. E. London: Routledge.

Yinger, J. 1986. "Intersecting Strands in the Theorisation of Race and Ethnic Relations," in *Theories of Race and Ethnic Relations,* Eds. Rex, J. and Mason, D. New York: Cambridge University Press.

10

Black Religion and Racial Identity
C. Eric Lincoln

Three hundred fifty years and more
Three Thousand Miles from the shore
A new law
American!
A new language
American!
A new god
American!
A new name
American!
American!
American!
American . . . ?
But my face is black.[1]

Or, as T.S. Eliot has put it:

Between the idea and the reality . . . Falls the shadow.[2]

A Name to Go By

The conventional understanding of identity is not a fixed and unambiguous consensus. Who you are in the conventional mind may be determined in part by your place of origin, your principal associates, your ethnic or tribal name, your personal or family name, your intimate or nickname, your principal employment, your religion, your residence, your color, your speech patterns, some, or all of these, and more. "Who" is often a mosaic of bits of "what," and when that mosaic becomes too complex or too cumbersome, then the conventional shorthand settles on what seems to be the most prominent or compelling feature presented, and perceptive identity may be affixed to that. A name is not an identity, of course, but it may be and often is intended as an index to identity. Hence, in the rural South where I grew up, nicknames were common and usually reliable introductory appellations of constructs of personality, description, or behavior aimed at identification. Some were colorful: "Big Walking' Man," "Snout," "Ug," "Do Funny," "Tootie Fruity," "Shab," "Mallet Foot," "Guts." Some were practical means of sorting out and giving personal identity to related or closely associated individuals in the extended families which were the norm in that time and place: "Big Lucy," "Little Lucy," "Mama Lucy," "Big Daddy," "Big Mama," "Old Tom," "Son Tom." Some were less than complimentary: "Jackleg," "Low-Life," "Snake," "Bubble Head," and so on.

Names also function to relate identity to causes, movements, religions, and other matters which may be considered of critical import to the individual or the group with which he or she is commonly identified. In unusual cases they may represent an inverse or confused relationship to a pejorative identity. For example, almost a hundred years after the Civil War, one of the most popular names for Black males was "Robert Lee." And for every Black Ulysses Grant drafted in World War II, there was probably a score of Black Robert Lees to fight beside him.

Names are symbols of convenience and not paradigms of substance; but they do refer to real entities, and because they do they may take on consociational significance which in itself becomes a constitutive element in the construct of identity. In the conventional mind, for example, if "Nigger," or "Peckerwood," or "Dago" are words repeatedly linked with identifiable human types, the initial awareness that distinguishes the appellation from its object is likely to diminish with repetitive experience, and in time the two may become so interlinked as to require a considerable conscious effort to realize that they are not identical. This is a syndrome so commonly experienced by African-Americans as to produce a continuing anxiety regarding corporate identity, or "a name to go by." The long and painful odyssey from African to Negro—to Persons of Color—to Colored—to Black—to Afro-American—to African-American is well known, as are the less formal and more deliberately pejorative appellations of Nigger, Darkie, Coon, and the like. But formal or informal, the suspicion that the perception of significant others is diseased by the names by which they are identified has at times produced in the African-American a near-paranoia which itself has become a constituent of his perceived identity. How did it all come about? What is the genesis of the Black identity crisis? Why has it persisted so long, and what have been the principal internal efforts at resolution? That, it would seem, are the principle issues to which this volume is addressed, and while perspective requires some general comment on the larger issues, my personal effort is limited to a discussion of the part played by religion in the historic struggle for relief and normalization.

It is variously estimated that, during the centuries-long era of African slavery in the New World, somewhere between twelve and sixty million Africans were forcibly torn from the routine of settled life in their African towns and villages and involuntarily resettled as chattels in America. No one will ever know the exact number, of course, because the business of human bondage did not run to strict accounting for the silent percentages which, for one reason or another, were lost to the enterprise of slavery between capture and delivery of the human commodities of the trade. However, a reasonable estimate based on the numbers finally delivered to the slave markets in the New World suggests that the involuntary West African diaspora fed into the funnel of capture, chattelization, transport, and redistribution must have been sufficiently massive to leave its survivors struggling in the trauma of demoralization and cultural shock for centuries.

The depersonalization of the African that was to reach its perfection in America began in West Africa. The repugnance and indignity of the public slave coffles, the humiliation and the status-stripping of the undifferentiated herding of hostile strangers and cultural antagonists in the factories or barracoons, and the abject dehumanization of the Middle Passage were all preparatory to the terrible finale to be played out in Charleston, or Baltimore, or Savannah. There, on the auction block, the last claims on human respectability would be denied, and at the fall of the gavel, identity, personal and corporate, would be forever consigned to the oblivion of chattelry. Only spiritual identity remained, and on that slender filament the reconstruction of the African-American sense of self would ultimately depend.

As we must look to Africa to find the roots of the process which stripped the African-American of his identity, so must we also look to Africa for the primary sources of its restoration. Critical to this task is some understanding of the West African religious cosmos, out of which came the vast majority of the African forebears whose life and labor constitutes the primary cultural base of contemporary African-American existence. It is obvious that no detailed analysis is possible here, but the principles to be cited are commonly agreed upon by responsible scholarship. Traditional West African religion allows for one supreme or high God who is the creator of mankind. Man is not the end product of an evolutionary process, but came into existence through a deliberate act of his maker. At a minimum, man is body and spirit, which together constitute his humanity. The body is susceptible to destruction and decay, but the spirit, which is immortal, may be of divine essence, or may have certain critical offices or responsibilities in the divine cosmogony. A sustained or meaningful relationship with God would be patently impossible if human or spiritual identity, which is the principal index of human accountability, is confused or nonexistent. As a matter of fact, from the African understanding of religious priorities, the confusion of identity in the world of the living must of necessity reverberate in the world where the spirits of the departed continue their existence after death, for there is no disjunction between these two worlds, which represent different but interrelated aspects of reality.

The spirit world is an aspect of the physical world, and the spirits who inhabit it are in large part ancestral, which is to say that they are the abiding manifestations of the primogeniture to which the living owe their existence. More than that, they are ever-present, or they can be summoned by the living for advice and council, and other forms of support, in times of crisis, or in times of celebration. So long as the name of the departed ancestor is remembered or called, so long will his or her spirit be available to champion the interests of the individual, the family, the community, or the clan of which he or she was (and remains) a member.

But the ancestral spirits have an even more critical role. In traditional West African religion, while God cares about people as his superlative creation, the Western notion of God as immanent or ever-present is not a feature of the God-man relationship. African myths and cosmogonies abound which account for God's distancing himself from the human community, even though he cares about it. Here the ancestral spirits perform a crucial service as intermediaries between God, the lesser divinities, if any. Men or women, as individuals, or family, or community in distress, need only call upon the ever-present ancestral spirits to make the case for them before the High God who lives beyond their direct experience, but who is available to them through these ancestral emissaries.

It is at this point that identity takes on extra-ordinary significance. The world of spirits is not necessarily irenic, but rather the invisible counterpart of the more familiar world we know of human passions and behaviors. The ancestral spirits contend and compete with other spirits and with each other for power and influence and approbation. Individual spirits may be benign, evil, or indifferent, but the ancestral spirits are characteristically protective of their own living counterparts, and it is here that precise identity takes on compelling significance. The identity of the clan, the tribe, the family, the individual ward, or petitioner must be established beyond any doubt before the ancestral spirits may be successfully invoked. Hence tribal names, family names, personal names, and day names converge in an interlocking system of precise identification. (In tribal tradition, an infant could not be named until certain ritual procedures could be completed; hence the child was given an informal name, "day name," until formal naming could occur. Often these names translated into something like "one who was born on Saturday.")

The African individual is always more than merely an individual: he or she is always located within an expanding system of relationships which ultimately links him or her to God. If that system breaks down or is ruptured at any point, the African's sense of identity is lost and he or she belongs nowhere. A Malawan proverb puts it this way: "A man is a man because of others . . . life is when you are together, alone you are an animal."[3] It is these interlocking linkages between clan, tribe, and family, including the ancestral spirits, that pose such formidable cultural barriers between Africans in Africa and Africans of the diaspora. The sentiments for conciliation and common cause may all be present, but the problem of "identifying" the expatriate and relocating him or her in his or her proper niche in the African cosmos has at times been frustrating for all concerned. African life is never causal or arbitrary; and identity is the primary key to inclusion and participation in that life.

By the time the African slaves arrived in America, their identities had already been substantially blurred, and nothing in the experience ahead held any promise of relief. Woloff and Fulani, Yoruba and Fanti, Mandingo and Ibo, Whydah and Ashanti; Muslim, naturist, warrior, sorcerer, priestess, herdsman, chief, prince, diviner, sage, and woodcarver were all cast into the common cauldron or facelessness and rootlessness that American slavery required. History was suspended, and that part out of which all status and all relationships derive, and which constitutes the only sure reality in African cosmology, was summarily denied or washed away. American slavery offered "no place to be somebody," and no chance to know the difference.

Nevertheless, it took time for the slave syndrome to perfect itself, and the slave mentality it was designed to produce never did become absolute. This is not the time to reargue the celebrated debates about African retentions, or slave resistance, psychological or otherwise. Suffice it to say that the Africans who came to America still called themselves "African" long after "the system" had supposedly accomplished its goals of cultural *tabula rasa* for its chattels, and long after the *particularities* of African identity had been lost in the process of reduction and homogenization. There remained to haunt the involuntary expatriates a residual awareness, an afterimage of something that once had been, that, as it were, needs must be again. However, the religious modalities of West Africa, which had been so critical to the African's sense of style and place, could not be replicated in America. The evolving policies of efficient slave management required the dispersal of slaves from the same tribe or speaking the same language, as a precaution against insurrection. Furthermore, slave gatherings for purposes of religious worship were routinely forbidden as paganistic or as time stolen from the slavemaster. The drum, the essential instrument in African worship, was forbidden; and slaves caught participating in African religious rituals of any kind were flogged, branded, or sold. No substantive efforts to include the African slaves in the religious life of America occurred unil 1701, when The Society for the Propagation of the Gospel in Foreign Parts (SPG—the missionary arm of the Anglican Church), petitioned the planters to permit them to exhort selected slaves gathered on the "Big House" commons. This was almost a hundred years after the first American interface of Englishmen and Africans at Jamestown, Virginia in 1619. In the meantime, slave identity was a secondary derivative of ownership: "Mr Whitley's Jim," or "Miss Tillie's Zenia." Racial identity was no longer a question to be addressed, for the "peculiar institution" had long since become a Black institution: every African was presumed to be a slave, and every slave was presumed to be of African derivation. Thus the Africans had an identity thrust upon them. The enslavement of Indians, and the indenture of Europeans was relegated to a past America felt no need to remember, and "slave" and "African" became synonymous categories. Still the Africans clung to the only identity that made sense to them despite the slow erosion of the values it once represented. In the evolving culture of the plantation, the "lying Africans," "thieving Africans," "malingering Africans" perceived from the perspective of the "Big House" gradually found counterpart expression in "ol' Africans," "ugly Africans," and "Black Africans" perceived from the perspective of the slave quarters themselves. The implied justification of the chattel-ization of the African had seeped into the psychological infrastructure of its victims. And as the external slave trade gradually diminished and the introduction of freshly caught Africans abated, the once proud Africans were increasingly defined and frequently defined themselves by other appellations. Their personal names were usually determined by the master, or by his policy or decree, and the only corporate identity to be recognized was that of "darkies," "negroes," "colored," or other pejorative designations designed to identify the African sight unseen.

The simplistic rendering of identity would be modified somewhat, at least internally, by the eventual development of Black religion as the primary institutionalization of the corporate schedule of values peculiar to African interests in America. After a protracted resistance to the protestations of the SPG that its missionaries be granted access to the heathen souls of the benighted Africans on the plantations, the planters finally relented. They succumbed to the arguments that "conversion would in no case work manumission" (causing them to forfeit their property to Christ), and that a Christianized slave was a safer, more reliable, and less troublesome slave than the "raw hea-thens" fresh out of the African bush. In due course the missionaries and other exhorters were permitted on the plantations, carefully watched by the planters, and preaching mostly to the "Big House" retainers gathered under the magnolias on an occasional Sunday after-noon. The spiritual message of this "magnolia mission" was not one calculated to stir any feelings of discontent with the life of bondage, or any longing for an identity that used to be. Rather, the existing confusion of identity was reenforced by having the slaves understand that, cursed by God, they and their descendents were forever destined to be "hewers of wood and drawers of water" under the gratuitous oversight of the White Christians God himself had appointed to be their wardens.

In time the most intimate retainers of the "Big House" compound—the nannies, the body servants, grooms, dressmakers, and so on—would be permitted to attend the White man's church with their masters and mistresses. Dressed in the discarded finery of the "Big House," they were assigned segregated benches placed for their use along walls or in the rear of the church. When their numbers increased beyond this convenience, some churches built galleries for their Negro members up under the rafters of the sanctuary. Inevitably, these ethereal areas came to be known colloquially as "nigger heavens," and are so known to us today.

Perhaps this was progress of a sort; from the magnolia missions on the "Big House" compound to the cathedral heights of the master's church; but in the eyes of the world he knew most intimately the African in America was still a Negro, a darkie, *a nigger*—without so much as a name of his own to anchor him to any reality he cared about or understood.

It is clear from the Black experience in the White church that identity is not a fixed value to be arbitrarily conferred or inferred from principles of reason or rationality. In classical Islam, for example, religious values transcend all others and unite all believers in one universal umma, or brotherhood, transcending race, class, and nationality. In the West, and more particularly in the United States, it is racial rather than religious identity that represents superlative human value, thus fixing forever the conditions of individual acceptance, or participation in the ongoing human cavalcade. In consequence, the African-American struggle for identity has always been in the face of established convention, which precluded *a priori* any investiture of commonality in religion; or to put it another way, in America, "Christianity" has never been sufficient identification to open any doors of consequence. The established criteria for an acceptable identity requires that one be Christian *and* White. To be Christian is not enough, yet, as we shall see, it was precisely on religion that African-American identity ultimately staked its claim for recognition.

In the meantime, all of the laws, customs, conventions, and taboos which functioned together to preclude a negotiable identity for any person of any degree of African descent whatever flew in the face of logic, even as they now scramble before the uncompromising revelation of modern genetic investigation.

There probably has not been a "pure" African born in America for a hundred years, for the universal tendency of the human species to mix and mingle, despite all disclaimers, has left America with a numerous and historic progeny, which, if law and convention count for truth, is altogether imaginary. Imagination needs no identity, but people are not people without one.

Despite all the arguments pro and con, the African-American's struggle for identity has never been a struggle to be White, but rather to find parity and equivalence, by whatever designation, in being human. While tens of thousands of African-Americans have found it expedient to "pass" (for White) in pursuit of common values precluded by identity, or lack of it, the success of their daring would seem to be the best evidence that they were "passing" for what they were.

Nevertheless, in the search for identity, "passing" is almost always an expedience and seldom a priority. The critical question for Americans of African descent is how to fashion a "new" identity out of a new experience in a new environment.

Scholar/philosopher W.E.B. Du Bois grappled with this problem in his famous soliloquy on double consciousness ". . . two souls, two thoughts, two unreconciled strivings, two warring ideals in one dark body. . . ."[4]

But Du Bois's inner turmoil was essentially intellectual—a clash of the rational refinements produced by the most prominent citadels of reason available to him with the abject suppression of that same reason beyond the narrow parameters of the mind. Hence the Du Boisan dubiety was a confusion of reason and experience, a contradiction that was to haunt Du Bois at every level of engagement throughout his long life.

But W.E.B. Du Bois was not Black Everyman, and his peculiar set of personal circumstances did not equip him as the archetypical expression of the Black experience. Born free of mixed parentage in Massachusetts, and educated at Fisk, Harvard, and Heidelburg, while W.E.B. Du Bois was certainly, by virtue of prevailing American sentiments, a "Negro," with all that term implied, he was also, by virtue of his unique set of personal circumstances, unconfined by the implications of the definition, and unaccommodated to the role he is so frequently called upon to dramatize for all other African-Americans. If Du Bois's search for identity was essentially a personal intellectual enterprise in self-clarification, the struggle of the Black masses to achieve identity was a gut struggle in the pursuit of corporate recognition and parity. When it became clear that the White man's Christianity could not or would not afford the inclusive cover human parity required, some other *modus vivendi* would have to be discovered or invented. But slavery provided no institutional bases, other than the church, accommodated in any way to Black interest, and the traditional church was a White institution primarily accommodated to Black debasement.

But there was an alternative church, an "underground church," an "invisible institution."[5] It was a *Black* church, developed outside and independently of the White man's church, which would ultimately give definition to the individual Black person, and would become a powerful force in the reclamation of racial identity. The invisible Black church was totally African, and it met clandestinely in the deep woods and thickets, as far removed from the White man's sight and his sense of the proper scheme of things as could be accomplished. The invisible Black church was the outdoor church of the field hands who could not be accommodated with the favored "Big House" retainers in the nigger heavens of the White church, although they often depended upon Black preachers who had learned something of the Bible in the White churches. But in the outdoor tabernacles of the swamps, the sandhills, and the backwoods, the ambience was different; the music, the prayers, and the testimonials were rooted in the day-to-day experiences of plantation life, and the prevailaing message was not, "obey yours masters," which was the constant theme from the White man's pulpit, but rather: "*God wants you . . . Free!*"

Despite the general policy of suppression, by the last quarter of the eighteenth century, a number of small, Black, Baptist churches had been allowed to develop along the Eastern seaboard, particularly in Virginia, South Carolina, and Georgia. These "independent" Black churches were always under the oversight of White men, for religious gatherings were prohibited by law except in the presence of Whites. Nevertheless, these Black congregations represented the only institutional nexus available to Blacks, and they immediately became the popular reference of identification. While the Big House slaves in their masters' churches had also called themselves Methodist, Baptist, or occasionally Presbyterian, as the case indicated, not until the coming of the independent Black churches did "church identity" take on the substance of reality. Evidence suggests that denominational or "church identity" was in some cases considered a critical index of human evaluation. Among the slaves, for example, White Methodists, Baptists, and Quakers were widely considered to be less hostile to Blacks. Nat Turner, in planning his sanguine assault on slavery in 1831, is said to have given explicit instructions that "the people called Methodist" were not to be harmed.

Even to this day, in parts of the rural South, some settlements or communities are still identified as "Baptist" or "Methodist" by long time residents who remember when such terminology functioned as primary identification.

For the African diaspora, church identity was the perfect complement for their larger identity in Christ. The first Black denomination was chartered in 1815, and the Black churches began a rapid and truly independent development following the Civil War. The fact that Africans were featured prominently in the Bible, and were therefore in some demonstrated sense "People of God," weighed heavily against the pursuit of a new identity when the true African identity was so prominently established. The African sojourn in slavery, like that of the Jews in Egypt, was a transitory thing, but Africa of the biblical experience was there from the beginning of things and would be there in the end. Hence, the commitment to African identity was a prominent feature of the earliest Black churches—the First African Baptist in Savannah (1788); the Abyssynian Baptist in New York (1808); the First African Episcopal Church of St. Thomas, and Bethel African Methodist Episcopal Church, both founded in Philadelphia in 1794, and both were the progeny of the Free African Society, the first self-consciously Black organization in America. The first two Black denominations, the African Methodist Episcopal church (1815), and the African Methodist Episcopal Zion Church (1820) were both "African" communions.[6] The spiritual challenge of the evangelists and exhorters, both Methodist and Baptist, who followed the union armies into the South on their mission of liberation, was "come out from the devil's den of segregation, and join onto your own! Be African!" And out they came indeed, by the tens of thousands, for the African churches had already become the cultural womb of the Black experience, and "African" was this chosen identity.

Religion is not race, but it is often made to function as if it were. In the African-American experience, where every critical index of racial and cultural identity had been forbidden, supressed, or denied, religion became the closest approximation of African corporate identity—not because all African beliefs were the same, but because belief and practice was sufficiently common to the African-American minicultures to provide a framework of reference from which a common identity could reasonably be inferred. Significantly, it was *not* a reference sufficiently common to Black and White Christians to transcend the race-rooted schedule of values and behaviors which still alienate Blacks in white churches to this day. The Black church became African-Americans' chief index of identification because in every critical sense it was theirs, a projection of themselves that found less resistance from the significant others whose consensus could make that identity negotiable.

Nevertheless, the metaphysics of racial identity are not quite as simple as all that. And though African-Americans may have had an intuitive understanding of their African heritage, rooted as it was in a world of ancestral African spirits, or of the African presence proclaimed in the sacred book for all to witness, though their faithfulness to the African motherland was attested in the naming of their earliest societies, churches, and communions; though their celebrated African style in ritual and worship had all worked together to mandate and to reaffirm their African identity, that was not the end of it. "Between the idea and the reality . . . Falls the shadow."

Identity may be intensely personal, but in the final analysis it is a social rather than a personal determination, and therein lies the answer to the persistent problem of African-American identity, whether individual or corporate. "A name to go by" is the symbol by which identity is revealed or projected, but the symbol is useless unless it is consensual or negotiable. Self-perception is ever the grist of social refraction, and identity is in limbo until there is some level of agreement between how the self perceives itself and how it is perceived by significant others. In situations where power is the determining factor, an identity of sorts—Negro, nigger, darkie, master, and so on—may be created by social flat, of course. But to the degree that the power behind that fiat is compromised for whatever reason, personal perception will struggle to redress the balance with a consensus nearer to the heart's desire.

The issues may appear ever trivial at times. For example, there is strong resistance in the print media to spelling "black" with an upper case "B" when it is used as a proper noun to signify racial identity. But there is no such resistance in the case of "White Russian," or "South Dakotan," or "West Virginian," "Blackfoot Indians," "Green Berets," or other proper nouns which may also function as common nouns. Such inconsistent reactions to names as symbols of identity suggests that, deep in the human psyche, names may still be confused with identity, and identity with power. A name *is* more than the sum of letters; it is a statement about identity, and identity is the mystique of personal or corporate essence. Hence, identity in the conventional mind may indeed be a repository of power, the expression of which must be carefully negotiated lest it disturb the prevailing social equilibrium. In the early days of World War II, the state of North Carolina refused to grant a birth certificate to a child christened "Tojo Hitler." The African-American dilemma is still about how to assert the full power of a self-perceived identity in a way that is not peremptorily rejected by significant others. The musical chairs represented by "Negro," "Colored," "Black," "Afro-American," and all the rest are no more than the constant probing and testing of the parameters of negotiability. Under the aegis of Black religion, we have come full circle to the point of departure. We are Africans . . . by descent, and African-Americans by heritage . . . still searching for the consensus "American" seems to require.

Notes

1   "The Derelick." C. Eric Lincoln, *This Road Since Freedom*. Durham: Carolina Wren Press, 1990, p. 3.

2   "We are the Hollow Men," in *Collected Poems of T.S. Eliot from 1909–62*. New York: Harcourt, Brace, and Jovanich, 1963, p. 79.

3   Traditional.

4   W.E.B. Du Bois, *The Souls of Black Folk*. Greenwich; Fawcett Publications, 1961, p. 17.

5   E. Franklin Frazier, *The Negro Church in America*. New York; Schocken Press, 1974, p. 23.

6   C. Eric Lincoln and Lawrence H. Mamiya, *The Black Church in the African American Experience*. Durham; Duke University Press, 1990, pp. 47ff.

11

Conclusion: The Pageantry of Difference: The Psychological Development and Creative Expression of Racial and Ethnic Identity

Howard C. Blue

It is not possible to view the life of man apart from culture; for there is no man whose life has not been shaped from birth to death by its cultural matrix.

Wheelis, 1958

Our world is full of the creative pageantry borne of our differences in perception and experience. This pageantry can enrich our lives and broaden our understanding of each other. What would world civilization be without the exquisite poetry of Keats or Derek Walcott? The storytelling of Melville or the brilliant lyricism of Toni Morrison? The riveting jazz of Louis Armstrong or the quiet passion of Ravel? The startling impressionism of Van Gogh or the vibrant and potently noble art of Jacob Lawrence? The classical marble sculptures of Rodin or the bronzes of Meta Warrick Fuller? When we look upon thought provoking images, or drink in a writer's words and visions, or sway to the beat of music, do we not wonder about the source? Do we not ask where the inspiration comes from, or what message is being imparted and from what experience? Attempts to answer those questions take us onto the terrain and into the nature of creativity wherein one tries to capture the essence of feeling and being and to make those essences consciously available.

The forces which give meaning and definition to culture also give meaning and definition to the self, and in turn influence creative impulses. Identity, encompassing both conscious and unconscious elements, is a psychic organization developed from successive phases throughout life and is a coherent sense of a self which gives an individual a sense of wholeness, of integration, of knowing what is right and wrong and of being able to choose (Erikson, 1956). The development of identity takes place within a psychosocial matrix, and is influenced by a variety of intrinsic and extrinsic factors, including race and ethnicity.

The psychological forces which shape identity do impact on the process of creative expression. In the psychoanalytic literature, creativity is viewed as having multiple purposes involving a wide range of psychological structures and drives (Kohut, 1986). Indeed, creative expression can be understood as one of the means through which the individual attempts to resolve certain psychic conflicts and to objectify affective responses to those conflicts. This objectification is not limited to the construction of visual displays, such as in painting, nor the use of patterned sounds to make music, nor the development of texts, as in literature, nor carefully choreographed movements, as in dance. Creativity may also manifest itself in the ways the individual or a group tries to modify, shape, define, and adapt to the realities of existence. In this regard, political action and religious faith may be simultaneously a way of identifying oneself, a way to express that identity, and a way to modify and adapt to the consequences of that identity.

Although many disciplines have attempted to understand the subjective psychological experience of race and ethnicity, few have ever explored the impact it has on the creative process. Moreover, contemporary discourses on race and ethnicity have often emphasized problems associated with minority status in America. These discourses have often been rooted, explicitly and implicitly, in theories of minority people's self-hatred, which has putatively devolved from the shame associated with diminished self-esteem caused by repeated devaluations by the society's majority culture. Such self-hatred theses have been used to variously explain escalating violence, epidemic drug abuse, and the deterioration of social institutions within some minority communities. This book has deviated from the prevailing trends which debate the self-hatred thesis. We have attempted to expand the discourse on race and ethnicity by examining the interface between the psychological processes involved in the development of racial and ethnic identity and aspects of creativity. Little has been written about ways in which racial and ethnic minorities respond adaptively to the universal conflicts they experience as human beings as well as to the particular conflicts they experience as members of a specific minority group. In this book we have tried to inform you about the nature of the experience of being and feeling as an ethnic or racial minority, and we have further tried to convey how that feeling and being become manifest in concrete, creative ways.

Essentially, three topics were covered in this book. We examined developmental aspects of racial and ethnic identity, which encompassed the ways in which society interacts with the individual in shaping identity. Secondly, we examined sociopolitical dimensions of the development of an identity. Finally, we examined how ethnic and racial identity shape creative processes, and how those identities influence the ways symbols and images are construed, how political action and religion can form the core of identification and identity, and the ways in which certain critical, social issues come to be inscribed on and attributed to racially and ethnically different people.

Dr. Harris introduced the book with a thorough conceptual overview of race, ethnicity, and identity. His introduction set the stage for a multidisciplinary approach to understanding the topic and connecting it to aspects of creativity.

In Chapter One, Paul Gilroy examined some of the sociopolitical processes which shape identity. Holding the position that racial identity is not fixed and invariant, and is more than the simple repetition of a racialized culture, he explored the syncretic (blending) dynamics of identity, and situated the discussion of Black identity within the context of the "globalization of culture" (p. 15). Gilroy argued quite forcefully that, in order to understand Black *identities,* one must understand that these identities everywhere have been shaped under the impact of hemispheric global relations (p. 29). Furthermore, he cautioned that identity cannot be understood within a political and historical vacuum.

In Chapter Two, Dr. Spencer examined identity processes in at-risk, vulnerable, African-American, male adolescents. Dr. Spencer's previous research, which showed conclusively that there was no significant linearity between race dissonance and negative self-concept, has helped lead to a reconsideration and a recontextualization of earlier findings of race dissonance in African-American children. Under careful scrutiny, race dissonance is a normative stage in the development of racial and ethnic identity, and may be more reflective of the African-American children's social learning, which attributes negative characteristics to Black people and things, than of how children feel about themselves. In this chapter, Dr. Spencer examined African-American adolescents in their own context and provided new data on the ways identity helps these young men cope with adverse, at-risk circumstances. The research findings have significant policy implications, and invite a reconceptualization of many of our interventions to combat the adolescents' academic difficulties and violence.

In Chapter Three, William Cross undertook an examination of African-American identity change in adulthood. He, like Dr. Spencer, accentuated the importance of conceptualizing identity as a longitudinal and dynamic process. Dr. Cross described various stages of Nigrescence (process of becoming Black) and within his discussion underscored the interlocking internal and external processes which may fuel changes in one's conception of what being Black entails. Whereas identity development in childhood and adolescence is in the service of developing effective, competent, psychologically healthy individuals, it is clear from Dr. Cross's conceptualizations that Black adult identity has certain defensive functions. By this, neither he nor I mean that Black identity is somehow a defensive reaction to perceptions and projections of the White majority; some defined reaction against the "other." These defensive functions refer to the ways in which any group in diaspora constructs a sense of safety and solidarity in who they are. Among the functions of Black identity in adulthood are self-protection, social anchorage, and bridging. These three functional components help African-Americans to negotiate a potentially racist society and to develop means through which they can interface with the larger White society without feeling threats to their own identity or being consumed by rage.

In Chapter Four, Elaine Pinderhughes examined identity formation in biracial children. Professor Pinderhughes described some of the psychological issues which often confront biracial children and adults who live in a society which is not necessarily tolerant of diversity and ambiguity about race and ethnicity. Biracial children must "overcome powerful forces which have prevented the recognition of dual ethnic heritages, and have denigrated the minority status to which these children are assigned traditionally" (p. 75). The psychological tasks for biracial children involves developing an integrated, whole self in face of parentages which have origins in groups which are often seem as complementary polars. In order to accomplish these tasks, the child must find ways to "separate the evaluation of others, including various pejorative and grandiose labels and mislabels" (p. 79) from his self-conception. These children must find ways to transcend the continuing denigration of minority status as well as the lack of a readily available reference group.

In Chapter Five, Dr. Griffith and Ms. Silverman confronted the politically charged issue of transracial adoptions. In light of our knowledge about the development of racial and ethnic identity and the resiliency of children exposed to racism, there is nothing prohibitive about such adoptions. The forceful objections to transracial adoptions seem to be rooted in the assumptions that transracially adopted children will be psychologically damaged by placement in an environment which may lack cultural relativity or encourage Eurocentric attitudes and preferences. However it is quite clear from research, including Dr. Spencer's, that Black children can develop positive self-concepts and positive self-esteem as members of their defined racial group even if they exhibit Eurocentric attitudes and preferences. The key to this has less to do with the racial phenotypes of the parents, and more to do with the parents' attitudes about race, and their ability to expose the child to the culture of his or her reference group. Perhaps some of the furor over transracial adoptions emerges from the kind of "racial narcissism" and "ethnic absolutism" to which Paul Gilroy refers. Additionally, Dr. Griffith and Ms. Silverman examined this issue in the context of current law, including the Equal Protection Clause in the Fourteenth Amendment and *Palmore vs. Sidoti*. In challenging the efforts of the National Association of Black Social Workers (NABSW), which has fervently resisted the placement of Black children in White households, and the action of adoption agencies which persistently use race to determine placements, they pointed to the equal protection clause in the Fourteenth Amendment of the U.S. Constitution which prohibits, among other things, racial discrimination.

In Chapter Six, Ian Canino described the Art Program at the Museo del Barrio. The program is located in a large urban setting, and primarily serves African-American and Latino children, although there are some biracial children. This program's specific goal is in helping children develop effective coping mechanisms by developing a sense of individual and ethnic empowerment through art. Through artistic endeavors children are able explore the stresses of their everyday lives, examine their own ethnicity, and see the common relationship among people of different cultures in their use of art to express universal human needs and feelings. The program's major aim is the prevention of disease by helping these children assemble an arsenal of problem-solving skills, including artistic expression, to reduce stress.

In Chapter Seven, Barbara A. Hudson surveyed images created by African-American artists to combat "White racist art". Hudson described the artistic creations of African-Americans in their quest to depict Black life more realistically and perhaps to counter the widely consumed White racist art which made caricatures of and debased African-Americans. The creations of African-American artists often captured themes important to African-American identity, such as the transcendence over adversity while also attempting to display the sheer humanity of Blacks. Racist critique and denigration of their work and limitation of exposure of their art made it difficult for African-American artists to counter the images manufactured in white racist art and artifacts. Although arguments for such are difficult to make, it seems likely that these artists indeed attempted to dampen the impact of White racist art which perpetuated the images of Blacks as sources of servitude and limited humanness.

In Chapter Eight, Hazel Carby examined the role of narrative in evoking and provoking "a number of apparently contradictory racialized and gendered anxieties, fears, and desires" (p. 174) which "in their production of symbolic power, have significant political resonance when they are produced in response to a perceived crisis in the social formation of a society" (p. 174). She used the narrative structures of Harriet Beecher Stowe's novel, *Uncle Tom's Cabin,* and Lawrence Kasdan's film, *Grand Canyon,* to explore the symbolic power of Black male bodies within their construction of "a racially defined and class-specific worldview" (p. 175). Professor Carby argued that both Stowe and Kasdan, although separated by time and ideology, produced texts in which there is fear for the continued secure existence of the White and middle class in America. Impinging on this security is possible rebellion by the underprivileged and unjustly treated. Both texts examine the state of race relations at a particular moment in time and are instructive in their uses of narrative to construe both Black and White identity. In *Grand Canyon,* for example, sounds, images, and language are woven into a fabric that evokes class and cultural identities, which are then placed in a "cultural war" (p. 179) with each other. Black male bodies become the landscape onto which racialized anxieties and crises are projected and White angst explored. America's present preoccupation with crime and violence, and the frequent uses of Black males in print and visual media to represent clear and present dangers, are emblematic of the processes which Professor Carby addressed. There is a striking propensity for racializing these concerns and developing simplistic interventionist strategies, rather than examining how to bring about "dramatic change in the social organization of power and powerlessness" and the redistribution of "wealth to end economic injustice" (p. 175). Beyond the use of Blacks as a context for situating contemporary concerns, the African-American presence in America, as Toni Morrison argues, has had an immense impact on our literature and on our definition of Americanness. In the following paragraph from *Playing in the Dark: Whiteness and the Literary Imagination,* Morrison presents her thesis:

> For some time now I have been thinking about the validity or vulnerability of a certain set of assumptions conventionally accepted among literary historians and critics and circulated as "knowledge." This knowledge holds that traditional, canonical American literature is free of, uninformed, and unshaped by the four-hundred-year-old presence of, first Africans and then African-Americans in the United States. It assumes that this presence—which shaped the body politic, the Constitution, and the entire history of the culture—has had no significant place or consequence in the origin and development of that culture's literature. Moreover, such knowledge assumes that the characteristics of our national literature emanates from a particular "Americanness" that is separate from and unaccountable to this presence. There seems to be more or less tacit agreement among literary scholars that, because American literature has been clearly the preserve of white male views, genius, and power, those views, genius, and power are without relationship to and removed from the overwhelming presence of black people in the United States. This agreement is made about a population that preceded every American writer of renown and was, I have come to believe, one of the most furtively radical impinging forces on the country's literature. The contemplation of this black presence is central to any understanding of our national literature and should not be permitted to hover at the margins of the literary imagination....

Both Carby's and Morrison's arguments invite us to contemplate the ways in which particular cultural productions embody conceptions of race, ethnicity, and nation and how those conceptions serve the producer and consumer in their understanding of those of a different hue or experience.

In Chapter Nine, Angelo Falcón examined politics as a medium for expressing racial and ethnic identity. He used the political environment of New York City to examine this issue. He evoked several questions which ultimately hinge on our conceptions about race, ethnicity, and minority status, particularly in the context of ongoing immigration and changing demographics. An essential issue is the question of the particular terrain of struggle which links divergent minority populations. These issues have serious implications for coalition-building as well as intergroup competition for power. Falcón's concerns reflect Gilroy's earlier point that the understanding of identity is "reconfigured at different times" for political aims.

In Chapter Ten, C. Eric Lincoln explored religion as an expression and source of African-American identity. He examined the issue of African-American identity within the context of a historical understanding of the vicious, involuntary settlement of Africans in America. This history included the removal of the African from the cultural base which gave him identity, and further fragmentation of this identity through systematic attempts at status-stripping and chattelization. Dr. Lincoln argued that the identity crisis resulting from displacement from their cultural base and the succeeding systematic humiliations of the Africans left only spiritual identity intact. He then reasoned that this "spiritual identity was the slender filament upon which the reconstruction of the African-American sense of self would ultimately depend" (p. 211).

This book has attempted to examine the psychological processes associated with the development of racial and ethnic identity, and to explore how these processes manifest themselves in creative expression. The reader will, it is hoped, understand that the processes of racial and ethnic identity development are quite complex and under the sway of biogenetic, sociopolitical, economic, and historical forces. Equally complex are the ways identity-related issues become manifest in creativity. In reading this text, it is hoped that you have appreciated these complexities. Moreover, it is hoped that this work will help many of you reconceptualize your ideas about race and ethnicity and fully comprehend the longitudinality of its development and the variability of its expression. During the process of identity integration, members of a racial and ethnic minority group may feel marginalized, alienated, and devalued, but they may also have feelings of pride, belonging, and achievement. Such emotional processes can be seen as universal experiences when anyone who perceives themselves as different is confronted with a more homogeneous majority. However some differences are encoded with meanings specific to a certain social and political order, and can evoke intense reactions both from the bearer of that difference and from those with whom he or she interacts. Hence this book has relevance far beyond the narrow framework of racial and ethnic identity.

This book was not intended to answer every question about the psychological nature of ethnic and racial identity and creativity. It was written in an attempt to open up the discourse on racial and ethnic identity, and to challenge its readers to explore their easily essentialized notions of the social and political constructions of such identity. Furthermore, it is hoped that such discourse can expand our understanding about the ways in which identity shapes perceptions of reality and experience and how they, in turn, influence creative expression.

References

Erikson, E. 1956. "The Problem of Ego Identity." *Journal of the American Psychoanalytic Association,* 4:56–121.

Kohut, H. 1986. "Forms and Transformations of Narcissism," in *Essential Papers on Narcissism,* ed. Morrison, A. P. New York: New York University Press.

Morrison, T. 1992. *Playing in the Dark: Whiteness and the Literary Imagination.* Cambridge, MA: Harvard University Press.

Wheelis, A. 1958. *The Quest for Identity.* New York: W. W. Norton & Company, Inc.

Index

Notes on the Contributors

Howard C. Blue, Assistant Clinical Professor, Yale University School of Medicine, New Haven, CT

Ian A. Canino, Associate Clinical Professor of Psychiatry, Columbia University College of Physicians and Surgeons, New York, NY

Hazel V. Carby, Professor, Department of African and African-American Studies, Yale University, New Haven, CT

William E. Cross, Jr., Associate Professor, African Studies Research Institute, Cornell University, Ithaca, NY

Angelo Falcón, President, Institute for Puerto Rican Policy, New York, NY

Paul Gilroy, Reader in Cultural History, Goldsmiths' College, University of London, London, UK

Ezra E. H. Griffith, Director of the Connecticut Mental Health Center; Professor of Psychiatry and of African and African-American Studies, Yale University School of Medicine, New Haven, CT

Herbert W. Harris, Senior Staff Fellow, National Institute on Aging, National Institutes of Health, Bethesda, MD

Barbara A. Hudson, Curator of African-American Collection, Wadsworth Atheneum, Hartford, CT

C. Eric Lincoln, Professor, Department of Religion, Duke University, Durham, NC

Elaine Pinderhughes, Professor, Graduate School of Social Work, Boston College, Boston, MA

Ina L. Silverman, Attorney and Research Assistant, Department of Psychiatry, Yale University School of Medicine, New Haven, CT

Margaret Beale Spencer, Professor of Psychology, University of Pennsylvania, Philadelphia, PA